Radical American Partisanship

Chicago Studies in American Politics

A SERIES EDITED BY SUSAN HERBST, LAWRENCE R. JACOBS, ADAM J. BERINSKY, AND FRANCES LEE; BENJAMIN I. PAGE, EDITOR EMERITUS

Also in the series:

Additional series titles follow index

Radical American Partisanship

Mapping Violent Hostility, Its Causes,
and the Consequences for Democracy

NATHAN P. KALMOE
AND LILLIANA MASON

THE UNIVERSITY OF CHICAGO PRESS   CHICAGO AND LONDON

The University of Chicago Press, Chicago 60637
The University of Chicago Press, Ltd., London
© 2022 by The University of Chicago
Published 2022
Printed in the United States of America

31 30 29 28 27 26 25 24 23 22   1 2 3 4 5

ISBN-13: 978-0-226-82026-2 (cloth)
ISBN-13: 978-0-226-82028-6 (paper)
ISBN-13: 978-0-226-82027-9 (e-book)
DOI: https://doi.org/10.7208/chicago/9780226820279.001.0001

Library of Congress Cataloging-in-Publication Data

Names: Kalmoe, Nathan P., author. | Mason, Lilliana, author.
Title: Radical American partisanship : mapping violent hostility, its causes,
    and the consequences for democracy / Nathan P. Kalmoe and Lilliana Mason.
Other titles: Chicago studies in American politics.
Description: Chicago ; London : The University of Chicago Press, 2022. |
    Series: Chicago studies in American politics | Includes bibliographical
    references and index.
Identifiers: LCCN 2021040663 | ISBN 9780226820262 (cloth) | ISBN 9780226820286
    (paperback) | ISBN 9780226820279 (ebook)
Subjects: LCSH: Party affiliation—United States. | Radicalism—United States. |
    Political violence—United States. | Political culture—United States. |
    United States—Politics and government—2017–2021.
Classification: LCC JK2271 .K35 2022 | DDC 320.973—dc23
LC record available at https://lccn.loc.gov/2021040663

♾ This paper meets the requirements of ANSI/NISO Z39.48–1992 (Permanence of Paper).

DEDICATED TO THE MEMORY OF
MARTIN JOHNSON
LEADER, HUMANITARIAN, SCHOLAR, MENTOR, FRIEND
AND
TO THE KALMOE AND MASON KIDS
WHO ARE BRINGING MORE GOOD INTO THE WORLD

Contents

CHAPTER ONE

Recognizing Partisan Extremes

The mob was fed lies. They were provoked by the president and other powerful people, and they tried to use fear and violence to stop a specific proceeding of the first branch of the federal government which they did not like. — Senate Minority Leader Mitch McConnell (R-KY), January 19, 2021

Hate just hides. It doesn't go away, and when you have somebody in power who breathes oxygen into the hate under the rocks, it comes out from under the rocks. — Presidential candidate Joe Biden, June 1, 2020[1]

Racism is real in America and it has always been. . . . Xenophobia is real in America and always has been. Sexism too. — Vice President Kamala Harris, March 19, 2021[2]

Democracy ultimately prevailed on January 20, 2021, when Joe Biden was sworn in as the forty-sixth president of the United States. That result was not a forgone conclusion.

Biden had won the national vote eleven weeks earlier, and the result was constitutionally affirmed by the Electoral College in December. But from election night onward, defeated president Donald Trump claimed fraud without evidence and fielded dozens of baseless lawsuits. His challenges were denied or dismissed by dozens of judges—some appointed by Trump himself. The results were verified, reverified, and reverified again by state and federal officials.

Trump never did concede to Biden. Instead, on January 6, 2021, the sitting president, with fourteen days left in office, encouraged a mob of his supporters to violently attack the US Capitol building while Congress met inside. The intent was to disrupt the formal tally of Electoral College votes that would constitutionally certify Joe Biden as the next president.

The mob injured 138 Capitol and DC police officers, and two officers died. Members of Congress and Vice President Mike Pence narrowly escaped rioters who intended to "capture and assassinate elected officials in the United States government," according to federal prosecutors.[3] A makeshift gallows was erected on the west side of the US Capitol grounds with a noose hung from the top. Some insurrectionists could be heard chanting "HANG MIKE PENCE!" Trump was publicly furious with his own vice president for refusing to use his ceremonial role to interfere with the Electoral College certification. As rioters broke through Capitol windows and doors, the president tweeted "Mike Pence didn't have the courage to do what should have been done to protect our Country."[4] Clearly, his followers were ready to mete out violence on Democrats *and* any Republicans who dared disobey their undisputed party leader. Congress finally certified the election results late that night as Republican congressmen continued to make seditious objections.

Why was it so easy to stoke an insurrection by thousands of Americans— many of whom carried their nation's flag as they desecrated its Capitol and hunted its elected leaders? How are self-professed patriots driven to violent sedition? Trump's incitement is the obvious, immediate answer, but that raises more questions. Part of the deeper answer is that the bases of each party are divided into nearly warring factions with radically opposed visions for America. After decades of realignment and consolidation, core groups in each party now pull forcefully in opposite directions.

Republicans increasingly pursue outsized power and benefits for dominant social groups while working to undercut government by the people. The party has been overtaken by those who long for the stricter racial hierarchies of the old white South, who envision a Christian theocracy, and who steer government benefits to the rich, all of which have had national constituencies since the founding. Not coincidentally, many of the Capitol insurrectionists displayed Confederate symbols and Christian iconography, and a surprising number were business owners or white-collar workers.

By contrast, Democrats today are a pluralistic multiracial party increasingly committed to advancing democracy through electoral representation and equal rights and liberties. They are reckoning with and attempting to overcome America's legacy of oppression by race, sex, religion, and class, among other categories. This is a battle over the future— and the past—of the United States. No wonder, then, that many Americans (though not most) engage in politics with a spirit of violence and not comity or compromise—today's parties pursue *fundamentally incompatible* visions for America's future.

Conflict between democratic movements and dominant groups is inherent and perpetual in American politics, but it rarely cleaves the parties so neatly. When it has, it has produced mass violence. The last time the parties were so divided, their positions were reversed. The Civil War–era Democratic Party was pulling backward to enshrine Black enslavement, white supremacy, and ever-diminishing democracy. The Republican Party pushed toward a more democratic future by opposing the expansion of Black enslavement, by violently suppressing an armed rebellion against the 1860 election, and by unabashedly ramming through constitutional amendments that nationalized Black Emancipation, voting rights, and equality—in law, but not fully in practice.[5]

Three years before the war, Republican senator William Seward described an "irrepressible conflict between opposing and enduring forces" dividing the parties over Black enslavement. That environment radicalized millions of ordinary Americans who came to see their partisan opponents as existential threats to their place in the nation—often correctly— and then killed each other on an enormous scale. Three-quarters of a million Americans died in the Civil War—a per capita equivalent of eight million dead today. In making this comparison, we certainly do not envision violence on the same scale, but it shows what is possible given the same basic divisions. Those are the stakes—for our politics, our lives, and our hopes for a full democracy.

How radical are American partisans today? In this book, we show for the first time how many ordinary partisans endorse violence, who they are, and how that radicalization happens. In contrast with most prior research on political violence, we focus on the public rather than profiling small extremist groups or individual attackers. Our studies track shifts in violent hostility in recent years, trace how violent views translate into aggressive political behaviors, and uncover the roles of political leaders and political contexts in enflaming and pacifying partisans. While we generally find *similar* levels of violent hostility in both parties, our results show it is driven by opposite forces in each party, consistent with macro-partisan trends. Those views among Republicans are found most among those who want to maintain the old social hierarchies, while among Democrats, radicals are most prevalent among the egalitarians who want to dismantle those biased systems.

We think of "radical partisanship" in a few ways. Our immediate attention is on support for partisan violence and vilification that enables violent acts—the empirical core of our book. But to tell that story, we also discuss radicalism involving election rejection and systemic change toward and away from democracy, defined by representative elections and equal rights. The radical forms are closely linked, but we set aside public attitudes on democracy for now. Others ably address those views in the meantime (e.g., Bartels 2020; Clayton et al. 2021; Bright Line Watch 2021; Davis, Goidel, and Gaddie, forthcoming).

The approach here is rigorous social science—our objective measures and tests are our main contribution—but our normative commitments are also clear. The promise of American democracy is at stake in today's partisan conflicts, and achieving that ideal is where we stand—a government in which every citizen has equal say in choosing our leaders, with rights upheld equally for all. Expressing value commitments in public-facing work is unusual for political scientists, especially when those values now indict one party more than the other. But there is no truthful way to write a book on partisan violence today that pretends both parties are equally culpable, that their actions are morally equivalent, or that they pose equal dangers to the democratic project.

We continue the chapter with a review of recent violence and an outline of the book to come.

What Is Happening?

The Capitol insurrection was not the first partisan violence observed in the 2020 election cycle, let alone during Trump's 2015–16 presidential campaign.[6]

In October 2020, the FBI foiled a domestic terrorist plot by eight men to kidnap and kill the Democratic governor of Michigan, Gretchen Whitmer. Trump supporters had been publicly protesting Whitmer's decision to enforce social distancing requirements meant to slow the spread of the global pandemic known as COVID-19—a move that protesters claimed was a threat to their rights. The plotters were part of a group that staged a series of armed protests at the state capitol building months earlier, carrying signs with violent threats as they took over the building.[7] Trump encouraged them. As the men were plotting, Trump tweeted "LIBERATE MICHIGAN!" in reaction to Whitmer's pandemic safety measures. The same group discussed retaking the state capitol building and executing state legislators on live television.[8] Governor Jay Inslee of Washington wrote, "The president is fomenting domestic rebellion and spreading lies."[9]

Four days before the election, a caravan of vehicles driven by Trump supporters surrounded a Biden campaign bus on a Texas highway in a clear attempt at intimidation.[10] While the FBI investigated the incident, Trump tweeted "I LOVE TEXAS" and called the group patriots.[11] Days later, Trump mused about knocking Biden down: "A slight slap. You don't even have to close your fist."[12]

In the first presidential debate of 2020, the moderator asked if Trump would condemn the violent white supremacist groups that had been publicly supporting him.[13] Trump initially demurred, falsely suggesting that all the political violence was coming from left-wing, not right-wing, organizations. When Trump's opponent, Joe Biden, urged him to "Say it. Do it. Say it," Trump again feigned ignorance, asking, "Who would you like me to condemn?" Biden responded, "Proud Boys"—a white supremacist and misogynist armed militia backing Trump. Trump's reply, asking the Proud Boys to "Stand back and stand by," was not exactly a condemnation, and the group took it as a rallying cry.[14] At subsequent events, the Proud Boys could be seen wearing custom T-shirts emblazoned with "Stand Back. Stand By,"[15] and many members participated in the Capitol attack.[16]

These stories are the most prominent examples of political violence in just the last six months of Trump's presidency. Other partisan attacks include the 2018 pipe bombs sent by a Trump supporter to more than a dozen national journalists and top Democratic leaders, and a Democrat's 2017 attack on the Republican congressional baseball practice. Meanwhile, federal and state lawmakers in both parties receive thousands of threats from citizens every year.

Other recent violence fused partisanship with hate crimes. During an August 25, 2020, protest against police violence in Kenosha, Wisconsin, a seventeen-year-old Trump supporter shot and killed two racial-justice protesters and wounded a third. Republicans publicly defended him. An internal memo from Trump's Department of Homeland Security encouraged federal law enforcement officials to make sympathetic public comments about the killer, implicitly endorsing his murder of political opponents.[17] Similar attacks include the 2019 El Paso shooting targeting Latinos that killed twenty-three people and the 2018 Pittsburgh synagogue shooting that killed eleven people, both motivated by bigoted conspiracy theories touted by Republican leaders and their news outlets. These examples are in addition to racially biased violence by police who hold Republicans as their staunchest defenders.

Our Project

As American partisan conflict deepens by the day, how far have ordinary partisans gone? And how far will they go? Our book helps make sense of the contentious present with a groundbreaking study of radicalism among ordinary American partisans. Our results show that mass partisanship is far more volatile than we realized; it may even be dangerous.

We start with a history of American political violence, cross-national comparisons, and partisan psychology. Each puts America's fractiousness in context, clarifies broad patterns of political and social change, and isolates the processes that lead individuals into group conflict. Those precedents help us judge where we stand today, and where we might be headed. These are not exact road maps to our future, but they force us to confront a broader range of possibilities than most political observers have been comfortable doing before.

To answer our main research questions, we fielded more than a dozen new nationally representative surveys that we collected between November 2017 and February 2021, with dozens of questions tapping different aspects of radical American partisanship. YouGov conducted our nationally representative surveys, including two election studies and panels interviewing the same people repeatedly to track individual and aggregate stability and change. We also take care to measure and consider a wide range of correlates and tests for whether partisans are being hyperbolic or serious in their responses.

Each of our surveys included embedded experiments to test the causal effects (not just correlations) of interventions that might shift radical partisan views, including messages from party leaders. By randomly assigning participants to one treatment or another, we use the power of large numbers to equalize all attributes across groups. Any differences we observe must then be due to the treatments we assign or occur by chance (the likelihood of which we can calculate).

Our main contributions show the breadth and nature of violent mass partisanship through opinion surveys, far beyond the bounds of standard public-opinion research. But in characterizing how large numbers of Americans think and act in relation to partisan violence, we cannot speak directly to the causes of extreme violence carried out by individuals or small groups—illegal threats, murders, assassinations, militia attacks, displays of force. Even so, we think of the substantial levels of violent partisanship in the public as a risk factor for violent acts by each citizen, both as part of a broader context that encourages other people to act and as plausible insight into the Americans who would be most likely mobilized into violence if conflict worsens.[18]

Plan of the Book

We begin with a deeper dive into the history and psychology of partisanship to understand why contemporary American partisanship goes to greater extremes than previously recognized. Chapter 2 briefly reviews the long history of partisan violence in the United States and party-organized violence in other countries. Chapter 3 considers psychological explanations for partisan radicalism in the US today, including the mechanisms that bind people to social groups, attach them to parties, and predispose some people to aggressive and violent behavior.

Chapter 4 presents survey evidence on the scope of radical partisanship, using our first survey from 2017 as a baseline for the rest of the book. Most Americans rejected partisan violence, but a substantial minority expressed support, as many as one in five. Providing some reassurance, however, only a fraction of those who endorse violence have lethal attacks in mind. Other extreme views, like dehumanizing partisan opponents, labeling them evil, and seeing them as a national threat, are much more widely held, sometimes by large majorities. The chapter also shows that there is just as much openness to threats toward leaders as toward ordinary citizens and that the measures are distinct from more standard metrics of partisan animosity. The chapter concludes with evidence boosting our confidence that people are serious in their responses. We aim to keep our statistical analysis easily intelligible for general readers, relegating more technical details to notes and an online appendix (nathankalmoe.com/radical-american-partisanship/), starting in chapter 4.

Chapter 5 traces trends in radical partisanship over the past several years, from that first 2017 data through February 2021. We find rising radicalism on most of our measures, with high points after the January 2021 attack on the Capitol, following the Biden inauguration, and amid Trump's second impeachment—a time of enormous partisan tension. By then, nearly three-quarters of partisans viewed opponents as a national threat and nearly 60 percent considered them to be "evil." Twenty percent of Republicans endorsed partisan violence "today," compared with one in eight Democrats. In contrast with our prior surveys in which we found few partisan differences, these final measures show Republicans unambiguously more radical than Democrats on all dimensions. We also find spikes in radicalism around Trump's first impeachment, suggesting that these attitudes do respond to political context (something we return to in chapters 8 and 9).

Chapter 6 profiles radical partisans on the basis of social, demographic, political, and psychological traits, as well as racial resentment and hostile sexism. We find radical partisans have stronger psychological attachments to their party, and they tend to have aggressive personality traits that guide their everyday behavior. Republicans and Democrats generally don't differ in these extremes for most of our surveys, and ideology has little effect. However, we find striking differences in the roots of radicalism for each party. For Republicans, hostility toward Black Americans and women strongly predicts partisan moral disengagement—in fact, those attitudes are the *most important* factors in shaping Republican radicalism. The reverse is true for Democrats, for whom those views cut against their party reputation rather than reinforcing it, though the relationships are more muted. These findings reinforce the centrality of group status at the core of partisan hostility today.

Chapter 7 identifies the *behavioral* consequences of violent partisan attitudes. We find large numbers of Americans report being insulted or threatened in politics, and a handful even report being physically assaulted over their political views. In short, politics for ordinary Americans are far more aggressive than most research has described. We find smaller numbers of partisans who report behaving aggressively themselves. Notably, those who have insulted, threatened, or physically assaulted other Americans because of politics are far more likely to endorse partisan violence, a fact that helps to show the behavioral correlates of radical partisan attitudes. We also directly observe physically aggressive political behavior with procedures from psychology—asking survey respondents to deliver a painful noise blast to opposing partisans. The degree of partisan bias in assigning painful noise to opponents closely resembles percentages in the self-reports. We conclude by discussing how the evidence gathered on perpetrators of the Capitol attack relate to our findings.

The last three empirical chapters investigate how political context shapes radical partisan views (or fails to do so). Chapter 8 examines views on historical episodes of political violence and political conditions that might justify violence. We find that the vast majority of Americans support political violence in some cases—the American Revolution, or when a government's leaders are corrupted by bribery, for example. Thus, rather than asking *whether* Americans support political violence, the better question is *when*. We also find that the public generally sees rights-based grievances as relatively more legitimizing for violence than threats to fair elections.

In chapter 9, several tests show that election losses increase support for partisan violence, including experiments anticipating election outcomes and directly observed changes after elections. Violence also begets more violence. Partisans are twice as likely to endorse violence if the opposing party is violent first. Likewise, our analysis of real-world partisan terrorism during the 2018 campaign shows sharply enflamed violent views in the immediate aftermath of the attacks, and reminders of past partisan violence have some radicalizing effects.

Chapter 10 tests the experimental effects of vitriolic and pacifying political messages on partisan radicalism. We start with the elephant in the room: there is no question Donald Trump's postelection rhetoric caused the January 2021 attack on the Capitol, as Mitch McConnell acknowledged in the epigraph. Our most important practical result in the book shows that antiviolence messages from Biden and Trump significantly reduced support for partisan violence in 2019 and 2020 tests, particularly for violence tied to election losses, with the greatest reduction among the strong partisans who are most inclined to support violence. We also tested a variety of one-shot inflammatory messages from Biden and Trump, which generally did not increase radical views in an already enflamed environment. Only Biden's accusation that Republicans try to steal elections by disenfranchising Black voters had a clear effect, which produced more support for partisan violence among Democrats with that truth-telling. Democrats should continue highlighting Republican threats to democracy while also disavowing violence (when other means are available), as Biden and other Democrats have done. We also find that partisan news media—particularly Fox News—are associated with significantly higher levels of radical partisan attitudes among consumers.

Chapter 11 concludes the book by reflecting on the future of radical American partisanship. We summarize our findings, identify upcoming flashpoints, and describe the contingency of outcomes yet to be determined: leaders and ordinary citizens ultimately have agency to determine which paths we go down. We also reassess the roles parties play in a democracy. Far from decrying parties, we recognize that they are essential for well-functioning democracies. Managing their excesses is the challenge. And contrary to convention, we argue for the democratic *necessity* of partisan polarization when one party aims to advance democracy and the other is violently opposed to it. The Democratic Party should not moderate or compromise for the sake of peace—though, to be clear, violence is not the answer unless all other means of defeating the threat are exhausted.

Half a century ago, Martin Luther King Jr. wrote about the same fundamental conflicts in his "Letter from a Birmingham Jail"—a letter to white moderates who worried the civil rights movement was pushing too much and too fast: "the present tension in the South is a necessary phase of the transition from an obnoxious negative peace, in which the Negro passively accepted his plight, to a substantive and positive peace, in which all men will respect the dignity and worth of human personality" (King 1964, 95). As the letter suggests, conflict is inevitable when advocates for democracy rightly confront governing institutions, parties, and parts of the public that preserve an undemocratic society. If advocating for democracy causes conflict, so be it. The alternative is worse.

In the face of antidemocratic perils today, the good news is that one party may be set to put its full might into realizing a true multiracial democracy in response to activists and movements pressuring them to belatedly join the cause. In our more optimistic moments, today's partisan radicalism may signal the bumpy part of the road on the way to real democracy. We hope the wheels stay on the car, but we can't turn around. Chapter 2 illustrates the costs of U-turns on democracy.

CHAPTER TWO

Radical Historical Roots

Here [in Saint Landry Parish, Louisiana] occurred one of the bloodiest riots on record, in which the Ku Klux killed and wounded over 200 [Black] Republicans, hunting and chasing them for two days and nights through fields and swamps. Thirteen captives were taken from the jail and shot. A pile of twenty five dead bodies was found half-buried in the woods. Having conquered the Republicans and killed and driven off the white leaders, the Ku Klux captured the masses, marked them with badges of red flannel, enrolled them in clubs, made them vote the Democratic ticket, and then gave them a certificate of the fact. — W. E. B. Du Bois, *Black Reconstruction in America: 1860–1880* (1935)

Many Americans are surprised by the recent rise in intense partisan hostility and the concurrent rise in disorder, political violence, and one party's moves against democracy. Perhaps they thought it couldn't happen here, but, as historians tell us, all of it has *already* happened here. Our unfamiliarity with American history makes violent threats harder to recognize before they strike, particularly when the perpetrators are white. Today's challenges urgently motivate us to find historical precedents that help diagnose the causes and illuminate what we can do about them.

The epigraph above describes one of many episodes of racial-partisan violence that few Americans know. The Reconstruction historian W. E. B. Du Bois ([1935] 1997) documented violence in the 1868 presidential election and long after, when white Southern Democrats—most of whom were rebel combatants in the 1860–65 rebellion—fought to reestablish white supremacy with attacks on Black Republicans and their few white allies in the South. Then, as in other eras and places, racial-partisan violence joined authoritarian legal tactics to undermine multiracial democracy. With the late twentieth-century racial-partisan realignment, white supremacist violence followed white Southerners into the Republican Party along with continuing efforts to disenfranchise Black voters.

We begin our investigation of radical American partisanship today by reviewing historical and cross-national perspectives that ground our expectations for the studies that follow. We dive into the violent history of US politics—focused on partisan conflicts over enduring social and political hierarchies—in which recurring fights took on greater significance in the ebb and flow of US democracy. Our sketch focuses especially on white supremacy as a defining cleavage in many of the largest, most persistent violent episodes. Race is a powerful lens for interpreting present political violence. That does not minimize the importance of violence against organized labor, religious groups, women's rights organizations, and others, including violent strike breaking, anti-Mormon violence, and antisuffrage violence (McArdle 2017; R. Smith 2003; D. Smith 2015). Indeed, class, religion, sex, and other hierarchies often intersect with racial and partisan violence, past and present.

Our violent past shows partisan violence was never just a theoretical concern. Ordinary citizens organized some of that violence, leaders and governments mobilized other episodes, and many violent periods like the Revolution, the Civil War, Reconstruction, and Jim Crow included combinations of elite and mass violence, with democratic and authoritarian aims. We argue these disparate cases have enough in common to warrant consideration together—their primary differences are in organizational capacity and resulting scope, not social and psychological motives.

Finally, we briefly review research on partisan violence around the world, finding more precedents to contextualize US conflicts. These historical and cross-national perspectives anticipate some degree of radical partisanship today, and they hint at factors that enflame or pacify it. Such insights are key to averting violence when possible, but history also shows the need, at times, to defend democracy with violence against its violent foes.

Early American Political Violence, 1607–1860

Any account of American political violence must begin in the seventeenth century at Jamestown and Point Comfort, Virginia, the start of over two centuries of colonial violence against Indigenous people and enslaved Black colonists before the US founding. That racist foundation—often mixed with crusading Christianity—provided impetus and structure for much of the violence that followed.

The American Revolution is our glorified national origin story. That violent insurrection divided American colonists into party-like factions. Historians estimate 40 to 45 percent of white colonists (roughly 800,000 of 1.8 million) supported American independence while 15 to 20 percent of whites were actively loyal to Britain (Calhoon 1973). The largest group stayed neutral. The vast majority of four hundred thousand Black colonists were enslaved by whites (Berlin 2003). Indigenous people generally sided with the British as the lesser of two evils compared with rapacious colonists.

The Revolution was partisan warfare. The colonial insurgents who launched the independence movement explicitly identified with the British Whig Party before the war, opposing the Conservative Party "Tories" who led Parliament before and during the American Revolution. It followed that Loyalists were called Tories. Like parties, the groups were political coalitions designed for collective political action, and like parties, they reflected social divisions such as religion, economic standing, and age (Calhoon 1980).

Roughly one in six colonial men (17 percent) fought for the Patriot cause, compared with about 2 percent fighting as Loyalist forces. Tens of thousands died, mostly from disease and exposure rather than combat. Thousands of Black men fought for the Patriots—freemen or those promised freedom through war service—while twice as many fought for the Loyalist cause in exchange for emancipation (Nash 2012). Others used the chaos of the war to escape enslavement without taking either side. With decisive help from France and Spain, the colonial revolutionaries managed to inflict sufficient human and financial costs on Britain over eight years to outlast the British will to continue the fight. After General Charles Cornwallis surrendered in Virginia in 1782, British parliamentary elections transferred power to the Whig Party, which promptly voted to end the war in the colonies.

Ever since, the American Revolution has provided the ideological and historical model for much of the US political violence (and threats of violence) that followed, including the 2021 attack against the US Capitol building that aimed to stop the peaceful transfer of power. The widespread cultural *approval* of that insurrectionist violence is what makes it a natural touchstone to justify subsequent American violence, including vague appeals to liberty. (In chapter 8, we find over three-quarters of Americans back the Revolution's violence in our surveys on historical political violence.)

The Revolution is the most remembered episode of American political violence, but more scrutiny brings other early American episodes into view. Shays' Rebellion against taxes in Massachusetts from 1786 to 1787 was a key factor behind George Washington, James Madison, Alexander Hamilton, and John Jay's successful effort to overthrow America's first constitution—the Articles of Confederation—and replace it with our current Constitution, including a stronger central government capable of suppressing rebellions (Ellis 2015). Rival politicians in the new American republic fought duels over personal and political affronts, even when forbidden by law. And partisan conflict in the 1800 presidential election produced a number of brawls and threats of more serious violence (Mettler and Lieberman 2020).

Slave uprisings and their suppression were another form of political violence in the early nineteenth century. Enslaved Black Americans took up arms against impossible odds to overthrow their oppressors in several dozen incidents, and they were slaughtered as a result (Gates 2013). The best known is Nat Turner's 1831 uprising, in which the insurgents killed over fifty white Virginians before they were subdued, at which point over fifty insurgents were executed. White militias massacred another 120 local Blacks, most of whom had no connection to the violence.

Twenty years earlier, inspired by the successful Haitian Revolution, over five hundred Black Louisianans rebelled and marched toward New Orleans with their sugarcane knives in hand, chanting "Freedom or Death!" and carrying copies of the French Declaration of the Rights of Man (Fessenden 2016). US troops fought them back, killing dozens. Local white leaders executed the captured leaders, dismembered their bodies, and put their heads on pikes along the Mississippi River to discourage more revolts. Likewise, pro-slavery white mobs nationwide ransacked antislavery newspapers and killed editors in the 1830s and 1840s (Grimsted 1998; Holzer 2014). These violent conflicts over the status of Black Americans split both major parties internally until party realignment in the 1850s. Consequently, both parties generally sought to suppress national contention over slavery (Potter 1976).

In another violent episode, white South Carolinians threatened rebellion against the federal government during the Nullification Crisis of 1832. Democrats claimed exemption from tariffs imposed by prior president John Quincy Adams, whose faction became the Whig Party. White Carolinians thought the tariffs hurt their agricultural economy, which depended on enslaving Black workers. However, Democratic president

Andrew Jackson ended the contention by threatening to suppress any rebellion with the US military, in a split with his vice president, John Calhoun.

Partisans frequently brawled at election time in the mid-nineteenth century, especially around polling places physically dominated by one party or the other (Grimsted 1998). They refused to let opposing partisans vote in those party strongholds. Both parties tolerated this behavior by the other so long as the suppression remained relatively equal. Occasionally, campaign and election violence got out of hand and resulted in several deaths. In those few cases, strong local party organizations tamped down violence by their members, keeping it regulated at a low level (Grimsted 1998).

As the United States forcibly took more western lands from Native Americans, the legality of enslaving people in those territories became a violent flashpoint among Americans. The Whig Party died after the 1852 presidential election, and it was replaced in Northern states by an anti-slavery Republican Party that added Free Soil (generally against slavery's expansion) activists to its Whig base (Earle 2004; Kalmoe 2020). Republicans opposed a Democratic Party divided between a Southern faction that aggressively sought to expand Black enslavement and a relatively less radical Northern pro-slavery faction. Republicans attracted the dominant Protestant group while Democrats attracted Catholic immigrants in a religious divide, including hostility between partisans in the North, but it was the racial-partisan realignment that fueled the violence that escalated into a massive civil war.[1]

The violent partisan conflict centered on the Kansas territory in the mid-1850s (Potter 1977). Dozens or perhaps hundreds of people were killed there in several years of fighting by Free Soil settlers opposing pro-slavery Kansans and their allies next door in slave-state Missouri. Pro-slavery Missourians crossed the border to illegally swing elections on the Kansas territorial constitution, leading to rival state capitals and constitutions, with each protected by armed troops. The federal government led by Democrats interceded, siding with the pro-slavery group.

Concurrent with "Bleeding Kansas," the historian Joanne Freeman (2018) found records of several dozen fights between Democratic and Republican congressmen, including politicians pulling knives and guns on one another, melees, and at least one member viciously beaten to within an inch of death. Then, in 1859, the evangelical abolitionist John Brown launched a failed antislavery assault on the federal arsenal at Harpers

Ferry with hopes of fomenting a violent abolition crusade throughout the South, with financial backing from several high-placed Republicans (Horwitz 2012). The state of Virginia executed him for treason, turning him into a martyr for fervent antislavery activists. In a fitting development that speaks to the parallels of race, partisanship, and violence across American centuries, Brown's gravesite in Elba, New York, was transformed into a Black Lives Matter shrine in 2020 with dozens of signs naming Black victims of white supremacy, present and past (Grondahl 2020).

From Civil War to Modern Violence

Racial-partisan violence in the 1850s foreshadowed the massive violence of the Civil War along the same lines. Few described their motives in partisan terms, but partisanship divided the elites and the public in their willingness to kill and to die. The war began after Southern Democrats refused to accept the result of the presidential election of 1860 (Kalmoe 2020). South Carolina began secession immediately after Abraham Lincoln's 1860 election as the first Republican president, and several other Deep South states followed soon after. In April 1861, the rebels fired on US troops at Fort Sumter, prompting Lincoln to call for militias to suppress the rebellion. Most enslaving states responded to that call by abandoning their professed neutrality and joining the rebellion. White Southerners were ultimately responsible for the killing of three-quarters of a million Americans (Hacker 2011), a portion of the population that would equal nearly eight million dead today.

The partisan mechanisms mobilizing Civil War violence become even clearer when we look at party conflict just within the North. Although most Northern Democrats supported the war early on against their party brethren, their support rapidly shifted to vicious opposition in the latter half of the war, especially as Emancipation became a war measure for achieving military victory. Republican voters and Republican voting places provided substantially larger portions of their military-age men to fight the war to sustain the newly elected Republican government against Southern Democrats in rebellion (Costa and Kahn 2008; Kalmoe 2020).

More pointedly, the war years saw substantial violence between Democrats and Republicans within the North, including partisan fights, murders, militia actions, governors' furloughing opposing legislatures, federal and state leaders' temporarily closing opposing newspapers, US troops' threatening to shut down hostile portions of state governments, partisan mobs' ransacking rival newspaper offices, and even plots by prominent Democrats to launch open rebellions in the North against Republican governance (e.g., Holzer 2014; Neely 2002; Weber 2006). Some Democrats collaborated with and took money from Confederates to fund their plots and acquire weapons: these Democrats' mistaken belief that they would win the 1864 presidential election was a key reason they gave up plans for insurrection. The author of the 1864 Democratic Party platform, Clement Vallandigham, was one of those plotters: these were high-level Democrats involved in violent sedition against Republican governance. After the war, Northern and Southern Democrats quickly reunited in opposition to the Republican Party, showing how minimal their 1860 split had been—and the eagerness in both factions to seek revenge against Republicans.

All this time, presidents from both parties continued to violently push Native Americans from their lands out west to make way for white settlers, and they continued to do so for the rest of the century.

Reconstruction Violence

Racial-partisan violence continued after the war during Reconstruction— the political and military effort to reintegrate rebelling states into the Union. On a small scale, white partisans in border states like Kentucky killed each other over wartime divides (Fisher 2001). On a much larger scale, white Democrats killed thousands of newly emancipated and enfranchised Black Southerners and their Republican allies over the next several decades.[2] That multidecade campaign was aimed at regaining white social, political, and economic power and reestablishing Black enslavement in all but name (Blackmon 2008; EJI 2017; Gates 2019; Klinkner and Smith 1999; Schermerhorn 2017).

White Democrats staged insurrections and coups against democratically elected state and local governments in Louisiana and North Carolina, acts they organized locally through the Ku Klux Klan, the White League, and other white supremacy groups (Gates 2019). Most members were Confederate veterans, who continued civil war violence long after their supposed surrender. A New Orleans monument memorializing an 1874 insurrection by the White League forthrightly carved "reestablishing white supremacy" as its principal goal in the monument's stone. The monument had to be removed in 2017 in the dead of the night owing to death threats from white Southerners who still celebrated the monument to violent white supremacy.

Two years after the monument was erected, in an effort to help a Confederate general win the governorship, white South Carolinians in "rifle clubs" killed six Black men and threatened to kill the incumbent Republican governor (Shafer 2020). Similar armed groups of whites blocked Black voters from polling places throughout the South in the 1876 presidential election. Decades later, US senator Benjamin Tillman bragged about his leading role in the Red Shirts' partisan violence: "We set up the Democratic Party with one plank only, that this is White man's country, and White men must govern it. Under that banner, we went to battle. It was then that we shot them. It was then that we killed them. It was then that 'we stuffed ballot boxes,' because this disease needed a strong remedy" (quoted in Shafer 2020).

Federal Reconstruction of the South required thousands of federal soldiers to uphold the Constitution and maintain law and order against the seething white population—in other words, the constant threat of federal violence was essential to maintaining democracy. White Democrats eventually succeeded in sapping the will of Northern voters and politicians, winning the withdrawal of federal troops, much like the British forfeiting the colonies in 1783. The result was the rise of Jim Crow in the late nineteenth century and the death of democracy in the South for more than a century.

Jim Crow Violence

With white supremacy restored, white Southerners systematically disenfranchised their states' Black voters through electoral rules, arbitrary imprisonment, and racial terrorism that killed thousands. That oppressive societal blueprint later became an aspirational policy model for Nazis in Germany (Ross 2018; Whitman 2017). As a result, Black voter registration plummeted from 80 percent to near zero for decades in Louisiana, to name one example (Keele, Cubbison, and White 2021). Beyond a racially corrupt legal system that effectively enslaved and killed Black Americans by the thousands, Blacks were also lynched by white mobs too impatient to wait for *legal* injustices (EJI 2017).

The Tulsa Massacre in 1921 was one of the largest mass killings of Black Americans by whites seeking to reinforce white supremacy. As was often the case, the spark for the violence emerged from rumors about a

Black man's interactions with a white woman, and white journalists fanned the flames (Tulsa Historical Society and Museum 2021). Ultimately, white Tulsans looted and burned thirty-five city blocks in a well-to-do part of town known as Black Wall Street, murdering dozens and possibly hundreds of Black Tulsans. This pattern was common: whites throughout the South targeted successful Black neighbors, whose social, economic, and political power put the lie to the hateful ideologies of spiteful whites. In this way, whites violently stole much of the wealth Black Americans had accumulated since the Civil War, in addition to stealing lives and democratic rights (Newkirk 2019). With millions economically, politically, and socially oppressed, large numbers of Black Southerners uprooted and moved north in the early twentieth century in hopes of escaping the worst of the racial violence and suppression they faced in the South. Their hopes were only partly realized.

The Great Migration changed the face of Northern party politics, propelling a major midcentury racial-partisan realignment (Grant 2020; Schickler 2016). The political change began in the 1930s when Northern Democrats and their union allies began appealing to Black city residents. That ultimately produced what amounted to a three-party system— Republicans, Northern Democrats, and Southern Democrats—in which the first two factions competed for the legislative votes of the third. It yielded what looked like substantial partisan depolarization in the mid-twentieth century, a situation that so many modern pundits pine for, but it was built on a foundation upholding white supremacy.

Modern Political Violence

The late nineteenth and early twentieth centuries saw substantial class-based violence as workers tried to unionize against industry titans. Prominent incidents include the 1894 Pullman railway strike, which killed dozens and was ended by National Guardsmen and US federal troops; the 1897 Lattimer massacre, which saw nineteen unarmed immigrant miners on strike in Pennsylvania murdered by a sheriff's posse; and the 1914 Ludlow massacre, in which an antiunion militia in Colorado attacked striking coal miners and their families, killing twenty-one of them. Democrats generally supported unionization efforts while Republicans remained allied with business against labor, but the violence against unions was less explicitly tied to partisanship and elections than the racial violence that was often partisan.

Some antiunion violence coincided with racial violence, including the 1887 Thibodaux massacre in Louisiana. There, the white state militia attacked striking Black sugarcane workers and their families, killing fifty people. It was part of broader efforts to consign Black workers to a kind of second slavery (Blackmon 2008). Similarly, in 1919, federal troops and local whites joined forces to kill 237 Black sharecroppers and their families in Arkansas who were attempting to unionize. Locals tried to blame the violence on Black residents, arrested and beat over one hundred of them, and sentenced several to death on false charges (Francis 2020). And, in the Pullman strike, Black workers served as strikebreakers, increasing tensions with white workers.

The twentieth century included several other violent episodes, though much of it was unaligned with party: anarchist bombings in the 1920s, dozens of urban race rebellions in the 1960s, thousands of radical left bombings in the 1970s, antiabortion murders in the 1980s and 1990s, and other right-wing attacks like the Oklahoma City bombing in 1995. Black leaders from the 1960s through the 1980s attempted to resist racial oppression with militant organizations like the Nation of Islam, Black Panthers, and MOVE, but many were killed, and their organizations dismantled through joint actions by federal, state, and local governments and citizen assassins.

Racial-Partisan Realignment and Federal Force

It wasn't until the Northern faction of the Democratic Party overcame Southern dominance in the Senate to embrace civil rights (alongside New England Republicans) that federal machinery lumbered into motion to enforce the Constitution in the South. That included sending in US troops and federal marshals to uphold the law with force. None of this would have happened without heavy pressure from the civil rights movement activists, who mobilized public opinion as they lobbied their overcautious allies in government (Klinkner and Smith 1999; Lee 2002).

As usual, white Southerners and their faction of the Democratic Party offered maximum resistance, including murderous mob violence and the deployment of armed state militias. But with the threat of federal violence—and sometimes the deployment of troops—ending de jure segregation and racial discrimination and enforcing Black voting rights began in earnest. It was ninety years after the federal government abandoned democracy in the South with the retreat of federal troops in the 1870s in the face of racial-partisan violence. Federal troops reintroduced democracy in the 1960s.

The national Democratic Party's embrace of civil rights was a decisive victory for its Northern faction, naturally prompting white Southerners to flee the party. First, they realigned their votes and then their partisan identities with a Republican Party that was more than willing to take up the mantle of white supremacy (Carmines and Stimson 1989; Kuziemko and Washington 2018; Valentino and Sears 2005). That racial-partisan sorting took decades, but it means the two parties are once again antagonists over the most violent cleavage in American history.

Angie Maxwell and Todd Shields (2019) write in *The Long Southern Strategy* that the Republican Party "nationalized southern white identity" when they "emphasized an 'us vs. them' America, preached policy absolutes, accused the media of liberal bias, prioritized identity over economy, insisted that the southern way of life was under attack, promised that southern white fears were right and southern white anger was justified, and championed a politics of vengeance" (336). Donald Trump's main political achievement was cementing the link between Republicans and the defenders of the traditional social hierarchy—not only overtly white supremacist and misogynist groups but also regular people who sustain systemic racism and sexism by refusing to admit they exist. Racial and gender violence become partisan violence when the two parties differ on the social worth of those who are not white, Christian men.

*   *   *

Can it happen here? It *has* happened here, and in many ways, it is still happening. The United States has a long history of political violence, much of it entangling partisanship with white supremacy. Some of it was carried out by citizens and groups, often with the assent of local, state, and national government officials, who pursued legal means to accomplish the same goals in parallel. One important facet to notice from history is that this kind of radicalism is not rare: it has often been supported by large numbers of Americans, even majorities in the enfranchised public.

Notably, partisan violence has sometimes served the cause of liberal democracy. Several US democratizing moments required political violence for their success: the Revolution, the Civil War, Reconstruction, and the 1960s federal reinstatement of the Constitution in the South. Each of these had partisan roots in one form or another. Likewise, the most substantial democratic backsliding occurred when the federal government signaled a loss of will for using state violence to ensure compliance with the Constitution.

The concepts of partisan identity, violence, repression, and democratization are not as separate as we might think. Much of this history is forgotten, but violent touchstones like the American Revolution are widely applauded. Other cases, like rebellions by enslaved people and violence against white supremacy, are roundly denounced by most white Americans. In other words, Americans seem to support political violence in some historical cases and under certain conditions. Race and party seem to play a big role in those determinations, beyond near-unanimous views of America's founding. The questions, then, are these: When is political violence widely accepted? When, if ever, do Americans resist and fight? And how many Americans believe those conditions exist today? We answer all these questions in the chapters that follow.

Cross-National Views of Partisan Violence

Political parties organize and mobilize mass political action, and, around the world, that action sometimes includes violence and repression. Partisan violence remains a rare subject in American politics research owing to our field's focus on the more peaceful party politics of the past century or so. In contrast, research outside the United States routinely tests the conditions that produce party-motivated and party-facilitated political violence.

Some of these studies focus on "greed and grievance" conditions for violence (e.g., Collier and Hoeffler 2004; Kalyvas 2006), which can include identity-based group conflicts. Ethnic and party identities and organizations often align in mutual reinforcement to propel conflict, with ethnic identity usually predominant even when parties organize that violence (e.g., Bar-Tal et al. 2009; Ginges et al. 2007; Halperin et al. 2011; Horowitz 1985; Posner 2004; Skocpol 1979; Urdal 2008; Varshney 2003; Wilkinson 2006).

Risks for political violence rise dramatically when several social identities align (Gubler and Selway 2012). For example, civil wars are over ten times more likely in places where ethnicity aligns with socioeconomic class, geographic region, or religion. The alignment of these identities makes conflict more intense as more social groups are involved in a single fight. For example, rather than pitting two ethnicities against each other, an alignment may match each ethnicity with a religion, deepening the divide and increasing the stakes of the competition.

On the flip side, shared social capital and social networks *across* groups—often called cross-cutting identities—help to prevent conflict in similar ways (Varshney 2003). Two ethnic groups might be in conflict, but if members of both groups share the same religion the likelihood of conflict is reduced. In the case of cross-cutting identities, ethnic group leaders find less receptive audiences for nationalism, they have less influence over their own groups, and their group communication networks are stymied (Gubler, Selway, and Varshney 2016).[3] These insights build on long-standing research on social-group alignments fueling or dampening political conflict (Dahl 1967; Lipset 1960). By all accounts, the collapse of cross-cutting social identities and interparty interactions before the US Civil War would be consistent with that theory (Potter 1976).

Parties sometimes encourage violence to gain strategic advantages in elections and governance, either to change immediate outcomes or to set the stage for future gains (Blattman 2009; Bratton 2008; Dunning 2011; Hafner-Burton, Hyde, and Jablonski 2014; Harish and Little 2017; Höglund 2009; LeBas 2006; Powell 1981; Snyder 2000; Wilkinson 2004; but see Collier and Vicente 2014 for signs of pacifying effects from elections). Related research shows that some parties encourage electoral participation and violence simultaneously (e.g., Kalyvas 2006). As Charles Tilly (2003) puts it, large-scale "collective violence and nonviolent politics intersect incessantly" (27). Similarly, public opinion surveys in some countries show that democratic values and violent attitudes among ordinary people are not mutually exclusive (Fair, Malhotra, and Shapiro 2014). We expect the same overlap of voting and violent views in the US.

Comparative politics scholars generally recognize the intergroup conflict that underlies many of the dangers of partisanship, far more than most American politics scholars. For example, Humphreys and Weinstein (2008) test individual-level ethnic and partisan correlates of civil war participation in Sierra Leone, including how these identities encouraged or discouraged participation and shaped susceptibility to elite mobilization. Chapter 6 will consider the role of social-group prejudices in driving radical partisanship, and chapters 8 and 9 will directly test some of the political conditions that spur more support for political violence.

What Shifts Groups from Peace to Collective Violence?

Peace and cooperation are more common for competing social and political groups than conflict and intransigence (Fearon and Laitin 2003).

Contemporary US politics are increasingly contentious, but our present is not nearly as violent as many of the historical cases we described above. So, what changes produce these eruptions of mass violence?

The public's general predispositions for group conflict probably don't change much over time—broad ethnocentrism (Kinder and Kam 2010) and aggressive personality—even as particular views of groups may shift with circumstances. Instead, conditions and contexts—including conflicts stoked by leaders—are key to determining when conflict is held in check and when it escalates into mass violence. We focus on several potential explanations: social-identity alignment, population changes, big changes in the electorate, and the influence of group leaders.

Some conflict-related conditions shift gradually over the long haul, leading to greater or lesser tensions. Correspondence between social and political identities changes over time, yielding more cross-cutting or cumulating identities that can reduce or increase conflict, as described above. Shifts in party coalitions and political structures can raise or lower the tensions. For example, Daniel Posner (2004) finds that ethnic tensions are relatively low between Chewas and Tumbukus in Zambia because both groups compose a small portion of the population, without hope of securing predominant political control for their group. In contrast, politics and the party system in Malawi centers on these two groups because the two are closely competitive for national power. That leads to substantial intergroup conflict in and out of politics in Malawi but not Zambia.

In the lead-up to the US Civil War, the partisan alignment of social groups shifted from dividing each party internally to defining the party divide (Potter 1976). As in Malawi, party realignment dramatically enabled the political expression and mass mobilization of that conflict. In modern times, we see this change with the role of Republican identification in increasing Christian identity and religious activity among white Americans (Margolis 2018), and the growing correspondence of white identity with Republican partisanship (Jardina 2019), opposed by a diverse multiracial and multireligious coalition of Democrats. Put simply, party realignments can change the mechanisms for expressing conflict in politics in the short term. Once hostile social groups distinguish the parties, party control of government has dire group consequences.

Some societies see political demographic change—sometimes rapid change—because of large-scale immigration, substantially different birth rates across groups, or unequally distributed deaths from violence or disease. The US had high immigration rates in the mid-nineteenth century, bringing in many Irish and German Catholics, to the chagrin of nativist

Protestants. Most recently, large-scale immigration from Central and South America, peaking around the year 2000, have raised the portion of foreign-born US residents to equal their highest historical levels. Meanwhile, native-born Americans are more diverse than ever, with white non-Hispanic Americans set to become a minority of the population in the next few decades. Most Americans of color are predominantly Democratic leaning when casting their ballots, though particular nationalities within umbrella categories are more Republican leaning, including Cuban Americans and Vietnamese Americans (APIA Vote 2020).

Proximate Provocations

What about the short-term emergence of political violence? Part of the story of mass violence is about its immediate origins. Conflict scholars speak of "sparks" that turn into "fires." In many cases, the conditions for mass violence are present for quite some time, but a particular event and the immediate responses to it by leaders and citizens serve as the "spark" that rapidly shifts conflicted societies from high-tension peace to mass violence in short order. Individual acts of violence and other minor outrages involving hostile groups can spread violence like wildfire. That makes the timing of violent outbreaks hard to forecast with precision, even when it is easy to identify the places most likely to see a mass outbreak. Nonetheless, some anticipated events like elections ratchet up the tension and make both sparks and fires more likely around these times.

The social-political landscape can also shift rapidly with the new enfranchisement or disenfranchisement of large social groups, like Black Americans during Reconstruction and Jim Crow. In other cases, major electorate changes do not substantially change the nature of party conflict, as with US women's enfranchisement (Corder and Wolbrecht 2016). Secession or incorporation of new territories can also shift the political balance of social groups—something Civil War Republicans took advantage of to pass nation-altering legislation once Southern Democrats abandoned their seats in Congress. Likewise, grievance-related conditions sometimes change suddenly, as in an impoverishing economic crash that raises the stakes.

Leaders and Group Norms

What role do leaders play in stoking or pacifying political violence? One version of this story is known as the "boiling pot" theory, articulated by the sociologist Charles Tilly, among others. In this view, the public in tense societies is like a heated pot always ready to boil over into violence. Group leaders hold the lid on to cause a violent boilover or remove the lid to let off steam. In other words, leaders mobilize violence or pacify their followers. Wilkinson (2004) argues that elections incentivize party leaders to stoke conflict when the result is likely to be close, and a recent history of violence makes additional violence more likely. He notes that government decisions to protect minorities from violence (or not) are key, as exemplified by federal intervention in the US South, among several other cases.

Other scholars, including Timothy Kuran and Sidney Tarrow, focus on the social importance of group norms. They describe political groups as "inward looking circles," with group members monitoring each other for cues on how to behave in public—including how to react to threats from other groups. When the taboo on violence is broken by some group members, others may take up violent tactics until a tipping point is reached and violence becomes the group norm. If group leaders and members engage in, encourage, or ignore violence—as large portions of the contemporary Republican Party have done with the 2021 Capitol attack—they grow increasingly likely to grow more violent as a group. Sometimes a violent act by a few group members can embolden other group members to join in the violence (Kuran 1989; Tarrow 1998).

Conclusions

America's past is full of political violence, but much of it remains unremembered. We sought to illuminate that history here. Most important, understanding the past helps us answer the question, why now? for our present racial, religious, and partisan contention. The answer that emerges from historical and cross-national comparisons points to the alignment of all three social identities. Those broad alignments supercharge conflict and make violence more likely, especially when the inordinate social-political power of white supremacy and Christian nationalism has been threatened. The racial alignment that drove mid-nineteenth century political violence faded in the early twentieth century as both parties abandoned the short-lived multiracial democracy for men during Reconstruction, though religion continued to divide the parties. Racial conflicts came roaring back with that partisan realignment in the mid-twentieth century, plus religious-partisan realignment starting in the 1980s. Republicans now represent historically dominant groups on race *and* religion—and these group members grow increasingly reactionary as the relative numbers and power of those dominant groups decline.

The American Revolution and the Civil War are the best-known cases of partisan and factional violence, but the prevalence of racial-partisan violence throughout the late nineteenth and early twentieth centuries shows enduring patterns and not just exceptional cases. Often, that violence emerged most when racial and religious conflict aligned with party politics in some fashion. Some of that violence was democratizing—advancing popular sovereignty and equal protection for all citizens against violent authoritarians—while much of it sought to undermine America's democratic project by corrupting elections and advancing the cause of white supremacy.

We see the same prevalence of ethno-partisan violence when we look beyond America's shores. There, too, social cleavages aligned in political coalitions caused more conflict than societies full of cross-cutting cleavages. Periods of high-risk contention are easier to anticipate than outbreaks of violence. In other words, the sparks that burst into mass conflagrations are hard to predict—though elections are often periods of great danger in contentious societies. Political leaders play important roles in fanning or suppressing those flames, but citizens also take cues from ordinary social-group members on whether violence is acceptable, essential, or beyond the pale.

Our broad historical and cross-national review shows that violent partisan hostility has plenty of precedent, which should help us see our intensifying ethno-partisan conflicts as a return or continuation of familiar patterns rather than a surprise. Scholars of race and ethnic politics and American political history have known all this and said as much, but those insights have been shunted aside too often. Much of the overconfidence about nonviolence in American politics and the broader resilience of American democracy is due to many elites and ordinary people overlooking the authoritarianism and violence that pervades America's distant and recent past (Weaver and Prowse 2020). Those blind spots leave us unprepared to effectively recognize and suppress the violent political threats we face.

In the next chapter, we shift our focus from macro to micro foundations. There, we sketch the individual social-psychological factors we expect to shape radical partisan views and behaviors in the public today, including the influence of political leaders and social contexts.

CHAPTER THREE

Radical Partisan Psychology

So strong is this propensity of mankind to fall into mutual animosities, that where no substantial occasion presents itself, the most frivolous and fanciful distinctions have been sufficient to kindle their unfriendly passions and excite their most violent conflicts. — James Madison, *Federalist No. 10* (1787)

America's founding leaders worried about the dangers of partisan violence, having just witnessed the violent factionalism of the American Revolution. The Constitution's primary author, James Madison, identified the social-psychological nature of the group-based threat in his most famous *Federalist Papers* essay, quoted in the epigraph above. In doing so, he unintentionally helped explain his own unrepentant enslavement of Black Americans—and that white supremacism fueled many partisan conflicts since.

Until recently, however, most pundits and scholars considered American partisanship to be a relatively benign, and sometimes helpful, way to organize politics and provide citizens with simplified choices. Here, we look at the contrast between the traditional political science view of partisanship and the concurrent social-psychological view of intergroup conflict—which was far more foreboding. We also consider more recent theories that may help explain partisan radicalism. All of this motivates and guides our individual-level investigations in the chapters ahead.

The foundational studies of partisanship took place in a strangely quiescent time. The conventional view of mild partisanship was developed by University of Michigan political scientists who inaugurated the systematic study of American voting behavior in the mid-twentieth century (often referred to as the Michigan School theory of partisanship). The legacy of their work profoundly informs our understanding of modern partisanship and voting behavior, but its limited scope may have inadvertently foreclosed research into more dangerous partisan expressions. As a result, most research on American political behavior has little to say on the broad questions about radical partisanship that we pose in this book. That scholarly view of partisanship as a mild force is also common among political elites. Failing to recognize radicalism in American partisanship has left us without good research to understand its gravest extremes.

We contrast that early American voting research with social psychology from the same time, which was motivated by the maximal violence of Nazi partisanship. The stark gap in focal human behaviors in these two fields—presidential voting versus participation in genocide—succinctly illustrates the chasm in conventional wisdom that we hope this book will begin to fill. Both poles capture what ordinary people sometimes do in politics, but we rarely recognize that both extremes can fit the same public. Learning how people move across that huge spectrum is essential, and this chapter outlines the psychological insights in between that help make those connections.

I Like Ike: A Mild View of American Partisanship

After World War II, the popular general Dwight "Ike" Eisenhower was courted by both parties, with offers of a presidential nomination in 1948 and again in 1952, something unimaginable in our current polarized era. He assumed office in 1953 as the first Republican president in two decades. More generally, the two parties seemed to be so lacking in policy differences that the American Political Science Association (1950) infamously called for *more* party polarization so that voters could better distinguish between the parties and then hold them to account, assuming (incorrectly) that voters cast ballots primarily with policy, performance, and principle in mind.

The moderation and mildness of Eisenhower-era national partisanship depended on a bipartisan truce ignoring white supremacy in the South and beyond. Beneath this anodyne veneer was the reality that white Southerners were systematically preventing millions of Black Southerners from voting through combinations of laws, police violence, mobs, and murders. The racial conflicts that neatly divided national parties in the Civil War and Reconstruction eras no longer divided the parties from each other. Instead, low national polarization between the parties hid huge divides *among* Democrats, whose odd coalition joined New Deal northerners with Southern white supremacists.[1]

In that context, four political scientists in Ann Arbor, Michigan, remade our knowledge of voting behavior in the United States. Angus
Campbell, Philip Converse, Warren Miller, and Donald Stokes (1960)
built on sociological studies in Midwestern towns (Lazarsfeld, Berelson,
and Gaudet 1944) by bringing new nationally representative surveys and
psychological theories to bear for a full portrait of American electoral behavior in *The American Voter*. They also shifted attention from long-term
voting patterns among social groups to short-term factors that explained
shifts from one election to the next. Undoubtedly, the authors' identities
as white men in the North influenced the bounds of their perspectives.[2]

The Michigan scholars combined an individual-level approach to
studying voting behavior with sensitivity to the social forces and institutions that oriented those attitudes and behaviors. Their biggest contribution conceptualized and tested partisanship as an enduring psychological
identity, which anchored loyal voting and shaped political views. They
were careful to theorize party identity's position in a "funnel of causal-
ity," flowing through time from broad historical-societal influences into
individual factors determining voting decisions right up to Election Day
(Campbell et al. 1960, 24).

They found that most people's views of the parties centered on how
prominent groups in society benefited or lost ground with the wins and
losses of each party. Party identity itself was largely a product of group
identities and attitudes, including race and religion. Parents were especially influential in imparting social and political identities, group prejudices, and other values to their children through socialization, especially
when parents were politically active. Partisanship also distorted perceptions of politics, which cut against democratic theories that assumed voters
were highly informed and economically rational in their decision-making.

Crucially, *The American Voter* narrowly aimed to explain the voting
decision, not to fully articulate the broad consequences of partisanship.
And while the work refers frequently to American political history and a
few cross-national comparisons, the authors mainly focused their explanations of voting behavior on the 1956 US presidential election. That sci-
entifically modest and efficient choice had long-term effects on the shape
of subsequent research about American mass partisanship, limiting our
understanding of its radical potential.

The mild partisanship of that era meant that their analysis of partisan animus began and ended with questions probing what voters liked
and disliked about the parties. The authors occasionally mentioned more

contentious moments in American history, including the Civil War, but they did so only to explain the regional persistence of party votes. The potential for a resurgence of partisan violence went unmentioned, and in fact they explicitly posed elections and violence as opposing alternatives.[3]

Social Psychology's Specter: Nazi Violence

As midcentury political scientists developed the study of American voting, the fresh horrors of Nazi violence haunted the psychologists who founded the field of social psychology—the study of how humans interact with each other. The genocidal Holocaust and the global cataclysm of World War II that killed at least seventy million people shaped their foundational works on the social and personal roots of evil actions and the nature of intergroup conflict. A figure like Hitler could conceivably be dismissed as an aberration, but violent behavior by the tens of millions of ordinary people who willingly participated begged for explanation.

The motivations for many top scholars, including Stanley Milgram, Theodor Adorno, and Henri Tajfel, were more than academic. Each was a European Jew who witnessed the rise of anti-Semitic fascism firsthand, or whose relatives were murdered in the subsequent Nazi genocide. In their efforts to explain humanity's worst behaviors, those midcentury psychologists discovered the theoretical underpinnings for a far darker set of attitudes and behaviors, which speak to the political extremes we pursue in this book and then far beyond.

How did it start? The Nazi Party rapidly gained power in Germany through the mundane mechanisms of multiparty democracy. Free elections and governing coalitions produced the most apocalyptic result imaginable. The leading conservative party needed support from the extreme right wing if it was to maintain its majority coalition, especially after Nazis became the top vote-getting party in the early 1930s with roughly a third of the votes. Conservative leaders could have chosen principles over power, but instead they made a fateful pact that elevated Adolf Hitler to national leadership despite full awareness of Nazi Party extremism and its history of violence.

Psychologists in the postwar era hoped to explain what motivated ordinary people to go along and carry out political and genocidal violence on an unfathomable scale, annihilating marginalized groups that had faced centuries of discrimination. They focused their studies on leadership effects, conformity pressures, authoritarian personality traits, and ethnocentrism.

The most famous psychologist among them was Stanley Milgram, who studied personal obedience to leaders. Milgram's parents emigrated from Europe, but his extended family was caught in the Holocaust. Milgram (1965) found that many people obeyed an investigator's orders to physically hurt strangers. Most participants were willing to apply ever-more-painful electric shocks to another person, unaware that there were no real shocks, and that their target was an actor who feigned pain and then non-responsiveness to simulate losing consciousness or death. People obeyed most when physically distant from their victim and least when they could see and touch the victim. Although critics questioned the ethics of his work and the extent and circumstances of obedience (e.g., Burger 2014; Reicher, Haslam, and Miller 2014), Milgram concluded that leaders can persuade large numbers of ordinary people to commit terrible abuses. The Nazi Holocaust organizer Adolf Eichmann famously claimed that he was "just following orders" at his trial in Jerusalem. Milgram's work suggested a wide prevalence for the "banality of evil" across societies that the political theorist Hannah Arendt (1963) identified in her contemporaneous book on Eichmann's trial. Arendt herself was a German Jew who was arrested by the Gestapo for her research in the 1930s and who narrowly escaped death in Nazi-occupied France in the early 1940s.

Theodor Adorno and his colleagues (Sanford et al. 1950) turned intergroup conflict studies toward individual differences to identify the nature of prejudice and to discover why some people were more inclined to support fascism and violence than others. Adorno fled Germany in the early 1930s when Nazis revoked his teaching rights and police raided his university office. While initially looking for roots of anti-Semitism, Adorno and colleagues found that authoritarian personality traits predisposed people toward prejudice and aggression against a wide range of minority groups.

The work of Henri Tajfel is most important for our purposes.[4] He was a Polish Jew who fought with the French army against the Nazis, was captured, and imprisoned. Nazis murdered his family in Poland while he was detained. He only survived because he pretended not to be a Polish Jew during his six years of imprisonment. The power of that simple lie about which group he belonged with inspired his future research. Together with John Turner (Tajfel and Turner 1979), he conceptualized social identities and showed how even the most inconsequential group distinctions could lead to discrimination, prejudice, and violence.

Tajfel and Turner found that even when researchers assigned participants to random and meaningless groups, the participants still exhibited high levels of in-group favoritism and out-group discrimination. These biases arose because people attached their own self-worth to the status of the groups to which they were assigned, however slight their identification with it. People receive psychological rewards for status gains even without material benefit for themselves; they feel group losses as personal blows. What's more, group members are willing to harm their own group's absolute interests if they can harm the other group more. In other words, they prefer their own group's *relative* advantage over other groups to the greater good of all groups, and they're willing to sacrifice their own well-being to maintain higher status, even on behalf of pretend groups.[5] Partisanship, race, and religion are all powerful and enduring social identities, and so their influence on behavior is vastly more potent than that of imaginary groups (Huddy 2001). The lengths people go to ensure a gain in status for *meaningful* and *central* group identities is much greater—and deadlier.

In short, while the Michigan scholars were finding mild and generally harmless effects of partisanship, the first social psychologists grappled with human behavior at its most violent and hate-filled extreme.[6] They generally concluded that, under certain conditions, Holocaust-type violence could potentially happen anywhere, let alone conflicts and violence on smaller scales. We argue that partisanship, like any other identity, is capable of driving the types of behavior that the psychologists feared and that partisanship researchers in political science have long overlooked.

Additional Influences on Radical Partisanship

Beyond the theories described above, political psychology—the combination of political science and psychological theory—has made additional discoveries that are also likely to feed radical partisanship. We briefly summarize them here.

Status Threat

Owing to the importance of group status in individual psychology, any threat to the status of a person's group is likely to draw attention to that identity. In politics, most partisans may not think much about other party members until election time, at which point they prioritize group victory and feel solidarity with other group members more than usual (Huddy, Mason, and Aarøe 2015). But elections aren't the only source of partisan status threats—the daily barrage of news framing partisan "wins" and "losses" in Congress and courts, taunting tweets, partisan media, and uncomfortable family phone calls can all elevate the salience of partisan identities, making them more habitually active (Dunaway 2008; Hitt and Searles 2018; Lawrence 2000).

National and Local Opinion Leadership

Of course, ordinary partisans aren't mobilized for political battle by individual identities alone—leaders are crucial. As we've already hinted, people are moved by the messaging of political leaders who share their partisanship. These effects range broadly across policy views, perceptions of political reality, group attitudes, and even mobilization into violence (Barber and Pope 2019; Bartels 2002; Berinsky 2009; Kalmoe 2020; Karpowitz, Monson, and Preece 2017; Lenz 2012; Zaller 1992). One mechanism for this influence is deference to trusted experts who help guide followers through the mass confusion of politics, including election leaders and partisan media personalities.

Another mechanism is group conformity. Group leaders help to set standards for attitudes and behaviors of good group members. These are not necessarily inspiring "good" behaviors. For example, in the aftermath of the January 6 insurrection, the Republican Party's leaders set behavioral norms denying that the attack occurred. This norm was on full display when Representative Liz Cheney, a Republican, insisted on telling the truth about the attack—and was summarily shunned and marginalized by the party. The few others who, like Cheney, have refused to parrot their party's violent lies are now facing primary challenges that threaten their chances of retaining elected office.

Local leaders matter too. In tests of partisan media effects, the political scientists Jamie Druckman, Matthew Levendusky, and Audrey McLain (2018) found relatively few Americans actually watch partisan news— somewhere around 10 to 15 percent. However, that group has strong, polarized opinions about politics, and they polarize their family and friends who don't watch.

Aggressive Psychology

We expect aggression in politics to come partly from people's predispositions for aggressive behavior in everyday life, because people tend to draw on their ordinary modes of thinking and action during the brief moments they engage in politics (e.g., Caprara et al. 2006; Gerber et al.

2010; Kalmoe 2013; McDermott 2016; Mondak and Halperin 2008). In fact, personality traits linked to aggressive behavior may be more strongly linked to hostile and violent political attitudes and behaviors than political orientations.

Some people tend to behave more aggressively than others generally, across a range of circumstances. But there are also some provocative circumstances that will make many kinds of people respond aggressively. The two interact, in that individuals with more aggressive personality traits are likelier to interpret ambiguous situations as provocations, and small provocations produce bigger reactions among generally aggressive people. As a result, exposure to aggressive cues usually causes more aggressive behavior among people predisposed to aggression in everyday life (Marshall and Brown 2006).

Symbolic provocations—toward valued political-cultural totems, like flags, statues, and group status—are especially relevant to partisan aggression, where harm is conceptualized on a society-wide scale, in place of interpersonal harms. These provocations could include party losses, which are potent triggers for anger (Huddy, Mason, and Aarøe 2015). They can also be violent cues. People can react aggressively when they experience violent events (in-person or mediated) or receive messages that explicitly promote aggressive behavior (Anderson and Bushman 2002; Kalmoe 2014).

Moral Disengagement

Finally, social norms generally forbid seriously harming people. Moral disengagement cushions the ego when people contemplate behaviors that hurt other people, both before the act and after as a post hoc rationalization (Bandura et al. 1996; Moore 2015). This set of rationalizing attitudes makes it easier for people to harm others in ways they otherwise wouldn't, either owing to social norms or because harming others poses a threat to one's self-image as a good person. Moral disengagement includes vilifying out-groups, hyping the morality of in-groups, minimizing harms done, shifting blame, and focusing on righteous ends that justify aggressive means. Among these, vilification is the most potent for producing aggressive behavior (Bandura et al. 1996). Caprara and colleagues (2009) expand moral disengagement to cover harms caused in the public sphere, beyond interpersonal aggression. That expansion is key to radical partisanship, when most of the political world is seen through mass communication, beyond our direct experience (Lippmann 1922), and when conflict centers on groups competing for power in the public sphere.

Conclusions and Expectations

This chapter outlined the psychological foundations for radical American partisanship today. We are especially interested in the influence of social identities, personality traits, and the effects of changes in the political environment. A few basic psychological mechanisms are surprisingly adept at explaining how people think in extreme contexts, as democratic politics grow more violent and authoritarian.

We began with the starkly diverging scholarly perspectives from mid-twentieth-century political scientists and social psychologists, who alternately sought to explain American vote choice in the Eisenhower era and the mass perpetration of Nazi atrocities. Connecting those polar human behaviors provides a new way of thinking about American partisanship and broader group conflicts in the United States, past and present. We then dove deeper into political and social psychology to understand status threats, leader rhetoric, aggressive behavior, and moral disengagement.

Now that we recognize the historical, cross-national, and social-psychological roots of radical mass partisanship, we need to learn its nature here and now. The questions are these: How many Americans embrace radical partisanship in the form of partisan moral disengagement, support for partisan violence, and aggressive political behaviors? What kinds of people are more likely to think and act in these ways? And what contextual factors enflame or douse the fire?

Our review produces several expectations, which we elaborate in subsequent chapters. We expect to find radical views in a sizable minority of American partisans, with support declining as the questions grow more extreme. Partisan radicalism may rise and fall—sometimes drastically—with changes in social-political context and leadership, but we don't think partisan radicalism ever disappears entirely. In the opposite direction, we expect most Americans would endorse political violence under some circumstances, and we anticipate finding that in reactions to historical violence.

Our impressionistic read of American politics is that partisan radicalism has gotten worse in the past few years, given changes in leader rhetoric and violent behaviors in the public. Election times are especially contentious, and that could produce more radicalism. Reactions to loss of political power may be especially potent, and violent responses to real political violence seem especially likely. That makes election time a grave risk for spirals of retaliatory violence.

We expect strong social identities and hierarchical views of social groups to play an important role, and we expect political aggression to have deep roots in interpersonal aggression. Morally disengaged partisan views should be more likely to support partisan violence and aggressive political behavior. Rightly and wrongly, Democrats and Republicans each have motives to endorse radical views, and we expect to find levels in each more similar than many readers may expect.

Above all, we think party leaders make a difference in regulating levels of partisan radicalism including violence, especially when party leaders are unified in their advocacy. Our ability to systematically test leadership effects is limited, but if we find pacifying and enflaming effects from one-off messages, it will suggest powerful potential for broader effects from repeated messages.

We begin in the next chapter by introducing our key measures, which reveal the prevalence of radical American partisanship in recent years. Subsequent chapters follow our expectations in examining trends over time, individual differences that distinguish radicals, and situational factors that change levels of radical partisanship in the public.

PART I

Identifying Radical Partisans

CHAPTER FOUR

The Scope of Radicalism

This is now our greatest fight since the Civil War, the Battle of righteousness versus Satan. Yes, Satan. Because these leftists are evil, corrupt, and they want to tear down this nation. — Jon Voight, actor and supporter of Donald Trump in a video uploaded to Twitter on November 10, 2020, claiming the election had been stolen from Trump.[1]

What is most concerning is that the number of domestic terror plots and attacks are at the highest they have been in decades," said Seth Jones, director of the database project at CSIS, a nonpartisan Washington-based nonprofit that specializes in national security issues. "It's so important for Americans to understand the gravity of the threat before it gets worse. — Quoted in the *Washington Post,* April 12, 2021.[2]

W hen we began this project, we weren't sure what to expect. How radical are American partisans? No one knew because no one was asking. How many Americans are open to harming their partisan opponents? And what other attitudes allow partisans to think this way?

Over the span of four years, we conducted several national surveys testing dozens of radicalism measures. After a long process testing relationships between items and looking for patterns, we condensed our findings into seven survey questions measuring two major concepts: partisan moral disengagement and partisan violence. This chapter begins our empirical investigation of radical partisanship by explaining these key concepts and their core questions. We begin by describing our new measures and then show their prevalence in the American public overall and within each party. Next, we compare how the two forms of radicalism relate, we contrast our items with standard partisan polarization measures, and we begin to make the case that these are mostly serious beliefs and not trolling or hyperbole.

Identifying Partisan Extremes

We focus on radical partisanship related to *physical harm*—in which ordinary partisans (1) hold views that rationalize harming opponents (moral disengagement) or (2) endorse physically threatening or harming opponents (violence). These concepts represent different levels of radicalism, with moral disengagement plausibly being psychologically easier to endorse than overt violence. Consistent with psychology research on aggressive behavior, we consider partisan moral disengagement to be a major risk factor for adopting violent attitudes—perhaps the most proximate and powerful.

Moral disengagement allows partisans to endorse harmful behaviors against opponents with less remorse or shame. By removing political opponents from a circle of empathetic care, disengagement gives partisans the moral leeway to harm others in ways they would not otherwise find acceptable. These attitudes are distinct from direct support for violence, but they constitute a key risk factor for developing violent attitudes (Bandura et al. 1996). To be clear, moral disengagement does *not* mean immoral—in some forms, it could be an objective evaluation or perhaps even a moral view. Moral disengagement merely describes the attitude's function.

Violent partisan attitudes are the most straightforward and the most extreme. We are interested in direct, explicit, unambiguous endorsement of intentional threats and violence against partisan opponents under present political circumstances rather than theoretical or historical examples of violence under extreme tyrannical conditions. We include threats against leaders and citizens that make them fear for their physical safety alongside overt support for violence, consistent with classifications for interpersonal aggression in psychology (Buss and Perry 1992) and definitions of terrorism in politics.

Having decided on this conceptual typology for radical partisanship, we collected survey data beginning in 2017 and regularly thereafter through the 2020 election and beyond. As our research progressed, we refined these measures. Below, we describe the survey items that most effectively measured these concepts. We pared down moral-disengagement items to focus on vilifying attitudes over other dimensions like displacing blame, minimizing harms, and viewing one's own group as morally righteous. Vilification is also the dimension that predicts interpersonal aggression best (Bandura et al. 1996). As an introduction, we present the results from our first nationally representative survey in November 2017, which was part of the Cooperative Congressional Election Study (CES— formerly CCES) overseen by the YouGov survey company.[3] We track subsequent trends in chapter 5.

Our Core Radical Partisanship Questions

Table 4.1 lists our core survey questions for partisan moral disengagement and violence. Most of the items use the respondent's individual partisan identity—recorded earlier in each survey and automatically inserted into the question—to fill in the spaces marked in brackets. For example, a Republican respondent would read item MD1 as "Would you say Democrats are a serious threat to the United States and its people, or wouldn't you go that far?" Those who initially identified as Independent but then reported that they tend to lean toward one party are treated as members of that party. In many surveys, we asked similar questions of Independents who

TABLE 4.1 **Radical partisanship questions**

	Moral disengagement
MD1	Would you say [Opposing partisans] are a serious threat to the United States and its people, or wouldn't you go that far? [1. They are a threat. 2. I wouldn't go that far.]
MD2	[Opposing partisans] are not just worse for politics—they are downright evil. [1. Strongly agree 2. Somewhat agree 3. Neither agree nor disagree 4. Somewhat disagree 5. Strongly disagree]
MD3	Many [Opposing partisans] lack the traits to be considered fully human—they behave like animals. [1. Strongly agree 2. Somewhat agree 3. Neither agree nor disagree 4. Somewhat disagree 5. Strongly disagree]

	Political violence
PV1	When, if ever, is it OK for [Own partisans] to send threatening and intimidating messages to [Opposing party] leaders? [1. Never 2. Occasionally 3. Frequently 4. Always]
PV2	When, if ever, is it OK for an ordinary [Own partisan] in the public to harass an ordinary [Opposing party] on the internet, in a way that makes the target feel frightened? [1. Never 2. Occasionally 3. Frequently 4. Always]
PV3	How much do you feel it is justified for [Own partisans] to use violence in advancing their political goals these days? [1. Not at all 2. A little 3. A moderate amount 4. A lot 5. A great deal]
PV4	What if [Opposing party] win the 2020 presidential election? How much do you feel violence would be justified then? [1. Not at all 2. A little 3. A moderate amount 4. A lot 5. A great deal]

Note: Inserted text: Democrat(s) or Republican(s). Early versions of PV2 replaced the word "frightened" with "unsafe." The 2017 results in this chapter used the term "unsafe," but we prefer "frightened," owing to political connotations now associated with the idea of "safe spaces."

do not feel close to either party (generally under 20 percent in our samples), but all our descriptions and tests in the book focus on the partisans.[4]

Statistical analysis confirms that the moral-disengagement and political violence items form two distinct factors. The moral-disengagement items are consistently correlated with each other as a scale ($\alpha=0.68$), as are the violence items ($\alpha=0.74$).[5] We take this to be sufficient evidence that these two "levels" of radical partisanship are both empirically and theoretically distinct.

How Radical Are We?

Our first empirical contribution of the book simply documents the depths of partisan animosity and openness to violence in ordinary American partisans for the first time. We begin with partisan moral disengagement. Figure 4.1 shows the percentage of partisans who placed themselves on the "morally disengaged" end of the scale for each item. Roughly four out of five respondents identified as partisans in this study ($N=785$).

In November 2017, just over 60 percent of partisans believed the opposing party was a "serious threat to the United States and its people." Forty percent described the opposing party as "evil." And nearly 20 percent agreed that people in the opposing party "lack the traits to

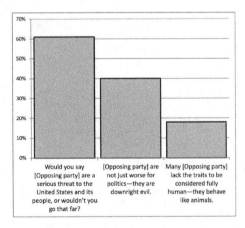

FIGURE 4.1. Prevalence of partisan moral disengagement. *Note*: Data from our 2017 election survey. The threat item is dichotomous. The other two bars represent the percentage of partisans who "somewhat" or "strongly" agreed with the item.

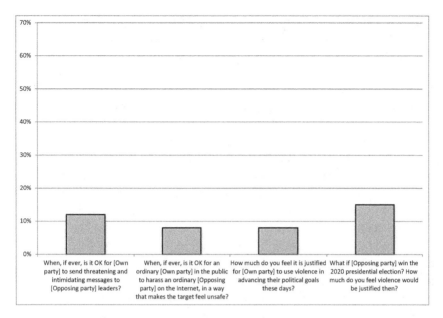

FIGURE 4.2. Prevalence of support for partisan violence. *Note*: Data from our 2017 election survey. Figure represents the percentage of respondents for each question who answered with a response other than "never."

be considered fully human—they behave like animals." These results are alarming compared to traditional measures of partisan animosity, in which the most hostile response is feeling "cold/unfavorable" toward opponents or feeling "very unhappy" if a family member married an opposing partisan. Even the lowest bound of partisan moral disengagement—dehumanization—provides cause for concern. Extrapolated to the public at large, tens of millions of partisans believe that their political opponents are not fully human. The findings for the "evil" and "threat" questions at over 40 and 60 percent respectively represent two to three times more Americans.

We show the levels of support for partisan violence in figure 4.2. On the plus side, the vast majority of American partisans reject partisan violence. Worryingly, though, a substantial number don't. In 2017, 12 percent of partisans said it was at least occasionally OK to send threatening messages to the other party's public officials. Nearly as many (8 percent) said it was acceptable to harass ordinary partisan opponents on the internet in a way that makes them feel frightened. The difference in threatening leaders versus citizens is not statistically distinct, meaning partisans are similarly supportive of threatening both leaders and ordinary citizens—the latter are not immune. This is important given recent research suggesting that most animosity in standard partisan hostility measures is directed at opposing leaders and not ordinary voters (Druckman and Levendusky 2019).

The last two items involve explicit support for violent partisan acts. When asked whether it would be justified for their own party to use violence in advancing political goals today, 8 percent of partisans said it would be at least "a little bit" justified. However, when asked how they would feel if the opposing party were to win the 2020 presidential election—a hypothetical but realistic scenario given recent alternation in party control of the presidency—15 percent chose violence. The thought of losing the next presidency nearly doubled the number of partisan violence supporters in 2017.

Overall, the results are sobering, showing levels of partisan hostility and openness to violence that go far past what previous public opinion research has documented. These 2017 data provide essential benchmarks for radical partisanship. But do these numbers capture a sudden upward spike responding to the 2016 presidential election, which Donald Trump made norm defying and extraordinarily hostile? Or do they reflect longer-term partisan hostility that scholars have been underdocumenting with mild measures (e.g., Iyengar, Sood, and Lelkes 2012; Mason 2018)? And how have these levels changed since these 2017 data? We save those tests for chapter 5.

Partisan Symmetry

We also wait to investigate the correlates of radical partisanship—who they are (chapter 6). But one burning question deserves an answer now: are Democrats and Republicans equally radical on partisan moral disengagement and violence? Our review of big social-partisan trends and recent violence in the first three chapters might lead us to expect more of both from Republicans, but that is not what we find in 2017. Instead, ordinary Democrats and Republicans are remarkably similar in partisan moral disengagement and violent views, despite the greater prevalence of right-wing violence (Lowery et al. 2018). And, as a spoiler for trends in chapter 5, partisan parity generally holds in most of our surveys through fall 2020, but with new gaps emerging after the 2020 election.

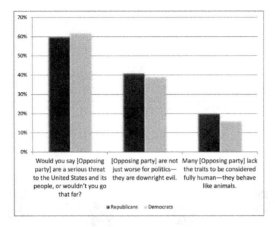

FIGURE 4.3. Partisan symmetry in moral disengagement. *Note*: Data from our 2017 election survey. The threat item is dichotomous. The other two sets represent the percentage of partisans who "somewhat" or "strongly" agreed with the item.

Figure 4.3 shows 60 percent of Republicans and 62 percent of Democrats agree that the other party is a serious threat to the United States. When asked if the other party is "downright evil," about 39 percent of Democrats and 41 percent of Republicans agreed. Finally, we find about 20 percent of Republicans and 16 percent of Democrats characterized their partisan opponents as behaving "like animals."

Similarly, figure 4.4 shows that Republican and Democratic views about partisan violence were statistically indistinguishable in 2017, even for the 2020 election item in which a small gap appears. Twelve percent of Republicans and Democrats believed it was at least occasionally acceptable to send threatening messages to leaders in the other party. Slightly fewer partisans found it acceptable to frighten ordinary partisan opponents on the internet, with 7 percent of Republicans and 8 percent of Democrats agreeing it was at least occasionally acceptable. Likewise, 8 percent in both parties believed it was at least "a little" justified for their own party to use violence in advancing political goals today. Finally, 12 percent of Republicans and 18 percent of Democrats approved of violence at least "a little" if the other party were to win the 2020 presidential election. That party difference is not statistically significant.

Why didn't we find partisan asymmetries—with Republicans endorsing greater radicalism—given social-partisan trends and recent violence? This is a major puzzle that we begin to answer throughout the rest of the

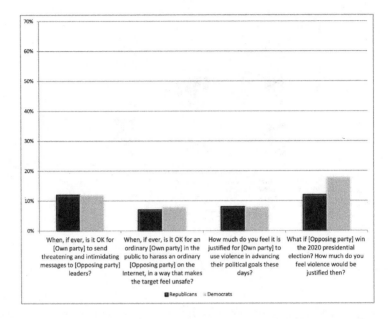

FIGURE 4.4. Partisan symmetry in support of partisan violence. *Note*: Data from our 2017 election survey. Figure represents the percentage of respondents for each question who answered with a response other than "never."

book. First, it is important to note the political context, which affects comparisons, as we will show. In particular, this survey and most of the others were conducted when Democrats were out of power. The presidency, the Senate majority, and the courts were all controlled by the Republican Party until 2021, and Republicans controlled the House of Representatives in our early surveys starting in 2017. In particular, the 2016 presidential election was a devastating and shocking loss for most Democrats, and an astonishing win for Republicans, and it is in this context that we first asked about partisan moral disengagement and violence. Chapter 9 examines the influence of political power and change on radical partisanship in greater detail.

As for asymmetries in violent acts despite symmetries in attitudes, there is surely a key role for enabling leaders. Any inflammatory rhetoric from top Democratic leaders pales in comparison with the incendiary content produced by top Republicans. Chapter 10 considers the rhetorical role of leaders, and chapter 7 addresses the link from radical attitudes to aggressive behaviors. Chapters 5 and 9 show that the January 2021 Republican attack on the Capitol roughly corresponded with the first asymmetries we saw in our radical partisanship surveys (in February), though that February also coincided with several other inflammatory events.

How Do Radical Views Relate to Other Measures?

Beyond the Partisan Cold Shoulder

These new radical questions go far beyond traditional measures of partisan hostility, often called affective polarization. However, it is important to determine whether these attitudes are an extension of "normal" animus or something else entirely. Partisan hostility is most often measured with "feeling thermometers," in which survey respondents rate both parties on a 0 to 100 scale that ranges from cold/unfavorable to warm/favorable (see Iyengar et al. 2019). The differences in ratings for one's own party versus the other indicate the level of hostility. A second measure addresses social polarization by asking how happy or unhappy respondents would feel if a close family member married someone from the opposing party (see Klar, Krupnikov, and Ryan 2018).

Table 4.2 compares these two standard measures of polarization with an average of the three partisan moral-disengagement items and an average of the four partisan violence items. A correlation of 1.0 means the measures perfectly align, an estimate of 0.0 indicates no straightforward relationship at all, and negative estimates indicate measures that move in opposition to each other.

As expected, moral disengagement is moderately correlated with both measures of affective polarization, indicating a substantial relationship but also clear empirical differences. However, we were surprised to find no relationship between standard affective polarization measures and violent partisan attitudes. Thus, while moral disengagement may be a more extreme extension of affective polarization, the risk for partisan violent views is unrelated to the most common measures of partisan hostility. In other words, the measures researchers have used for decades fail to track

TABLE 4.2 **Correlating radical partisanship and affective polarization**

	Moral disengagement index	Violence index
Party thermometer difference	0.43	-0.02
Unhappy with marriage to opposing partisan	0.30	0.06

Note: Data from our 2017 election survey.

the likelihood of violent views, confirming our empirical blindness without these new measures.

From Moral Disengagement to Violent Attitudes

One major argument we made early on is that partisan moral disengagement provides the psychological rationale that makes physically harming opponents easier on the ego. Does moral disengagement cause violent views, or do violent views force a moral rationalization? Probably both. In any case, we might expect a strong correspondence between the two. But the mix of correlations in table 4.2 might lead us to expect no relationship.

Instead, we find that violent partisan attitudes are substantially related to partisan moral disengagement, even though the average level of partisan moral disengagement is nearly ten times higher than the average level of support for partisan threats and violence among our 2017 respondents. The correlation between the two constructs is a robust 0.21, confirming our theoretical expectations that moral disengagement facilitates violent views—or that endorsing violence might encourage partisans to adopt morally disengaged rationales. However, we can go beyond that average relationship by building from our theoretical framework for aggressive behavior.

We test many traits that distinguish radical partisans in chapter 6, but we introduce one here—trait aggression—to clarify the relationship between moral disengagement and partisan violence. Aggressive personality is a trait indicating an individual's propensity for aggressive interpersonal behavior. Importantly, it involves behavioral tendencies in everyday life, not politics, though we expect it to have political consequences. Chapter 6 tests trait aggression's independent influence on radical partisanship, anticipating higher levels among aggressive people. Here, we think moral disengagement may translate more readily into violent views among more aggressive people.

We measured trait aggression in 2017 with two questions commonly used by psychologists for this purpose: (1) When provoked, how likely are you to hit someone? and (2) How hard is it for you to control your temper? We average the responses into a single scale from least to most aggressive.[6] Most people fall toward the bottom of the scale, but many are scattered up at the top.

Figure 4.5 shows the strength of the relationship between moral disengagement and violent partisan attitudes at varying levels of trait aggression.[7] Among people very low in trait aggression, partisan moral

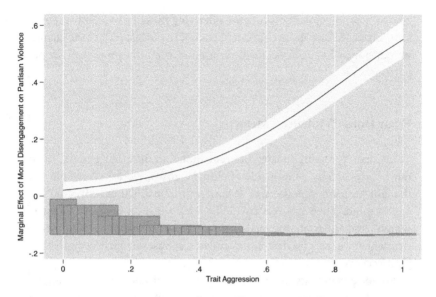

FIGURE 4.5. Relating moral disengagement and violent views by level of trait aggression. *Note*: Data from our 2017 election survey. The solid line estimate is drawn from models regressing support for partisan violence on the interaction of trait aggression and moral disengagement. "Interflex" interaction STATA package was used to generate this figure (Hainmueller, Mummolo, and Xu 2019) with kernel smoothing estimator. Shaded area represents 95 percent confidence interval. Bars represent the average level of aggression at each of the evaluation points in kernel-weighted locally linear regressions.

disengagement is unrelated to violent partisan views. These least-aggressive people rarely endorse violence no matter their level of partisan moral disengagement. However, more aggressive people appear to translate moral disengagement into violent partisan attitudes far more readily. Moving from least to most morally disengaged corresponds to an average shift across half the partisan violence scale among the most aggressive people. In sum, the link from moral disengagement to the belief that violence against political opponents is justified is mostly limited to the most personally aggressive partisans.

We find this interesting for two reasons. First, as we expected, moral disengagement does appear to open a door to political violence, particularly among those who are already somewhat comfortable with behaving aggressively in everyday life. Second, the strong role of trait aggression indicates that when respondents report that they approve of violence, they are not "just saying that." That is, they are not peaceful people who just enjoy reporting violent attitudes. Underlying these pro-violent responses are truly aggressive motives and tendencies. In the last part of the chapter, we consider what Americans have in mind when they say they support partisan violence.

What Does "Violence" Mean?

"Violence" probably means different things to different people. In the third wave of our panel study (February 2020), we asked people who thought partisan violence was at least a little justified exactly what they had in mind. Their answers covered a wide range of behaviors. Our research assistant content-coded their open-ended responses into categories, which we later used as closed-ended responses in our November 2020 election survey.

Some respondents indicated that they would approve of *any* level of violent action, including the most extreme: "any kind, I'm a fan," "Anything at this point. We are trying to stop an emerging dictatorship," "revolution," and "remember 1776?" Some mentioned historical methods like "tar and feather," "hanging," and "pitchforks, guillotine if necessary," so some partisans have mental models that include mythologized historical examples like the American Revolution. Others said, "gun violence" and one said "rape." One responded, "Protesting them without violence unless provoked . . . then start putting buckshot in their asses." Among the violence endorsers who gave substantive responses (about three-quarters gave an answer), only 13 percent mentioned some kind of lethal violence, including 10 percent who said "any" violence, 1 percent who indicated some kind of mass death event, and 2 percent who made other lethal comments.

We were surprised by the low level of lethality among partisans who endorsed violence. That seemed reassuring, at least compared with a starting point of 15 percent or more of all partisans endorsing violence in some cases: it seems the vast majority of them were not thinking about *lethal* violence. That puts the overall number of partisans endorsing at least some violence *and* explaining it in lethal terms at perhaps 2 or 3 percent, setting aside the quarter of nonsubstantive comments. Of course, the prompt to elaborate on a violent response might make some people skittish about explaining what they just avowed. Even that latter alternative explanation, if true, would be an interesting indicator about social desirability—or perhaps fears of legal liability or getting on an FBI watch list—despite our explicit reassurances that their answers would remain anonymous.

Some of the nonlethal responses focused on punching or pelting opponents: "beating the hell out of right-wing fascists is OK," "punching them in the face like they do us," "pushing, shoving, rock throwing," "rotten eggs in the cases of communists like Sanders and Cortez," "throwing eggs mixed with cow shit," and "KNOCK PEOPLE LIKE ADAM SCHIFF ON THEIR ASS AND WOMEN LIKE NANCY PELOSI SPIT ON." In total, around 30 percent of partisans who endorsed violence (and told us what they meant) chose some kind of physical aggression against opponents, which translates to roughly 6 percent of all partisans. A few respondents even made clear that the specific acts they endorsed were the upper limit of their support: "sometimes leaders of both parties need to be punched out. . . . I don't believe in shooting, or stabbing anyone, but maybe getting the snot beat out of them is sufficient."

Five percent talked about property destruction: "vandalism, rioting," "against property—never persons," and "destroy buildings like democrats do but there must be no persons or animals in the buildings." Finally, 13 percent mentioned verbal aggression like "berating them in public" and another 6 percent said protests, which we wouldn't classify as violence.

We organized these responses into seven general categories. In the postelection wave of our 2020 election survey, we asked people who approved of "violence" which forms would be justified: (1) widespread violence by armed groups that kills lots of people, (2) violence by armed individuals that might kill a few people, (3) punching people, fistfights, beating them up, (4) destruction of property, (5) verbal insults and harassment, (6) something else, or (7) none of these are justified. We asked respondents to choose as many of these options as they believed were appropriate. Figure 4.6 presents the distribution of responses.

The closed-ended responses largely affirm the analysis of open-ended replies in the preceding survey. Only 7 percent of partisans who approved of violence were thinking about mass killing, and just 17 percent were thinking about lethal violence that kills a few people. Most focused on fights, harassment, harming property, or something else we did not include. A full third of partisans who initially approved of violence seemed to blanch when they read these options—they rejected all of them.

Finally, we can clarify who partisans have in mind as targets when they endorse violence. In contrast with the threat questions, we did not

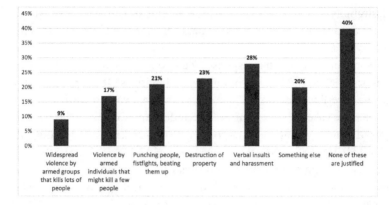

FIGURE 4.6. Types of violence acceptable for those who approve of violence. *Note*: Data from our 2020 election survey, postelection. Among those who say violence today is at least a little bit justified. *N*=127.

specify whether leaders or citizens would be targeted. In wave 2 of our panel study (September 2019), we asked whether partisans were thinking mostly about voters, leaders, both, or neither when they endorsed "violence today." Forty-six percent focused on leaders alone, 25 percent said both voters and leaders, and another 12 percent said voters exclusively. Twenty percent said they had "neither" leaders nor voters in mind as targets, perhaps thinking of property destruction instead. In contrast with support for partisan threats, partisans who endorsed violent acts were far more discriminating in targeting leaders than ordinary voters.

Overall, it seems most partisans who endorse violence are not thinking maximally of partisan civil war, but some are thinking of lethal violence, and the lower level of violence that more have in mind could certainly escalate into broader and deadlier conflicts. As we will see in chapter 9, it does not take much for violent attitudes and behaviors to escalate.

Are They Serious?

We've heard from some people who are reluctant to believe ordinary partisans are serious in their extreme hostility. They suggest many of these partisans are using extreme responses as an expressive outlet to indicate more mundane dislikes in hyperbolic form (Schaffner and Luks 2018). Or they suggest that these responses are just survey trolls who enjoy giving extreme responses in order to shock researchers (Lopez and Hillygus

2018). These are worthy considerations, but we doubt they explain most of the partisan hostility we find.

One sign that these aren't just trolls or expressive responses is that our respondents appear to be very sensitive to the extremity of the questions. Very few respondents gave the most extreme responses across more than a few items. For example, in the September 2019 wave of our panel, only 10 people out of 2,356 gave the most violent response on all four of our standard partisan violence questions. If it just feels good to say, why wouldn't more say it consistently across items?

We also asked respondents directly about the degree to which their answers were serious. After responding to our radical partisanship items, the final question asked, "We have asked a lot of tough questions about disliking political opponents. Do you say negative things about them because it feels good, or do you only say things about them you firmly believe?" They could choose one of five responses: (1) just feels good to say, (2) mostly feels good, but also a little belief, (3) both equally, (4) mostly believe, but also a little bit feels good, (5) firmly believe. In our 2017 study, 47 percent of our sample chose "firmly believe" or "mostly believe," and another 30 percent said, "both equally." Only 4 percent of violence endorsers said their answers were entirely expressive, or "just feels good to say." In other words, the majority believe in their answers, *and* feel good saying it.

Subsequent chapters provide more evidence of serious responses. Consistent with figure 4.5 above, we find that aggressive personality is the strongest predictor of radical partisan views, even more so than strength of partisan social identity. In other words, people who report behaving aggressively in everyday life (e.g., physical aggression, argumentativeness, socially hostile attitudes, and frequent anger) are most likely to give hostile and violent responses to our partisan questions. They have no expressive partisan motive to misreport their interpersonal aggression levels early on in the survey, long before we've asked them our more hostile partisan questions. We also find correspondence between aggressive personality and self-reports of aggressive political behavior in chapter 7, and observed partisan aggression corresponds with violent partisan views. Each of these results is consistent with our view that most radical partisans mean what they say.

Conclusions

The results in this chapter confirm our expectations for detecting substantial levels of radical partisanship in recent years, as predicted by the historical, societal, and psychological alignments we described in the preceding chapters. These results also provide benchmarks for further investigation in the following chapters, including change over time, the influence of political contexts and events, reactions to leaders, and measured links between violent attitudes and aggressive behaviors.

Taken together, our 2017 survey results showed the underlying potential for mass partisanship to grow violent, and not just among a few extremists. Large numbers of partisans—even majorities in some cases—hold morally disengaged views of their opponents, and roughly 10 to 15 percent endorse threats and violence against their partisan opponents. In addition, we showed that conventional measures of partisan hostility fail to capture the dynamics of violent partisanship, and we found that moral disengagement substantially corresponds with violent views, especially among the most *interpersonally* aggressive people. We also made the case that these views should be taken substantively and seriously. Reassuringly, though, not everyone who endorses partisan violence is calling for a civil war—a large majority of the partisans who endorse violence seem to have nonlethal acts in mind.

It bears restating that we do not consider peaceful mass demonstrations, political protests, or even disruptive collective action to be violent, even if some in the public do. As Eric Nordlinger (1972) wrote in his book *Conflict Regulation in Divided Societies*, broader social conflicts can be avoided "even if there are marches, demonstrations, expressive rioting, strikes, destruction of property, arson and looting." He continues by noting that "American political scientists are wont to be overly sensitive to such hostile and remonstrative acts, consequently labelling as violent many civil disorders in which no lives are lost. Such disorders may more meaningfully be viewed as measures of the conflict's intensity rather than as indicators of a regulatory failure" (11–12).

As of this writing, the American government is still somewhat successfully "regulating" the deep conflicts inherent in American society. Despite widespread protests over racist police brutality in the summer of 2020, protesters were largely peaceful, even when police and other government security forces weren't.[8] The January 6 insurrection was certainly an acute failure to regulate political conflict, but most of the perpetrators are facing arrest and prosecution by government agencies. Nonetheless, the Republican efforts to reject the legitimate outcome of the 2020 election added unprecedented partisan strains that are likely to continue for years if not decades to come.

In the next chapter, we examine how recent events have shaped levels of partisan moral disengagement and approval of partisan violence. Since 2017, we have repeated these measures multiple times each year all the way through February 2021. How did these radical views of ordinary partisans change throughout the Trump administration and in the aftermath of large-scale violence surrounding the 2020 presidential election?

CHAPTER FIVE

Trends: Stumbling toward a Breakdown

Leave Democrat cities. Let them rot. — Retweet by President Donald Trump, August 16, 2020[1]

[A] nationwide review conducted by ABC News has identified at least 54 criminal cases where Trump was invoked in direct connection with violent acts, threats of violence or allegations of assault. — ABC News Report, May 30, 2020[2]

Our survey collections on radical partisanship span nearly all of the Trump presidency. Those frequent observations are important checkpoints for evaluating how these attitudes evolved during a period when the president himself used dehumanizing and violent language directed at his partisan opponents. The battle for power during these years was particularly intense. Trump was impeached twice during his single term, a first for an American president. The Democratic Party began the Trump administration entirely out of power, with Republicans controlling the presidency, the Senate, the House of Representatives, and the federal courts. Democrats regained control of the House in 2018, beginning a return to more substantial power following the 2020 election. While this might have been an exceptional time in American politics, it is also an instructive time to observe the influence of political events and leaders on radical attitudes. In this chapter, we document what happened to these radical attitudes during a time of radical partisan governance.

We begin by exploring violent political attitudes from before the Trump administration, in hopes of identifying longer-term trends for context. Although none of our radical partisan questions were asked before 2017, we found a few questions about violence that offer a sense of prevalence in earlier years. We then document stability and change in our radicalism measures at several points from 2017 into 2021. We find substantial increases in morally disengaged and violent partisan attitudes over this time, especially in February 2021. Democrats and Republicans generally moved together over this time (with some small exceptions), but by early 2021, many more Republicans embraced radical partisanship than Democrats on all dimensions.

Political Violence across Decades

Chapter 4 documented levels of radical partisanship from our first survey in 2017. What about extreme partisan views from before the Trump era? American public opinion surveys have rarely asked about support for political violence (and nearly never for partisan moral disengagement), making long-term trends difficult to track. However, we found a few key exceptions to provide some benchmarks for general comparison, bearing in mind that different wordings and sampling methods prevent us from treating them as equivalent.

The first evidence we found is a single item measured by Herbert McClosky and Alida Brill in their book *Dimensions of Tolerance: What Americans Believe about Civil Liberties* (McClosky and Brill 1983). In 1978 and 1979, they asked a national sample of Americans whether "using violence to achieve political goals" was "sometimes the only way to get injustices corrected" or "wrong because there are many peaceful ways for people to get their views across" (75). Only 6 percent of Americans then said violence is sometimes necessary.

Two decades later, a 1997 Pew Research Center telephone poll found that 27 percent of US adults said, "Violence against the government may be justified in some cases," while 71 percent said, "Violence against the government is never justified" (Kohut et al. 1998, 52). This was a year after Bill Clinton's reelection as president and a year before his impeachment along partisan lines for lying to investigators about his sexual misconduct. How would the public answer today? For greater comparability than our core questions can provide, we repeated Pew's question in our November 2020 web-based survey. Twenty-eight percent of US adults said violence is at least sometimes appropriate against government, a result nearly identical to that of the 1997 Pew study. However, only 49 percent said "never" in 2020, compared with 71 percent two decades before. The remaining 23 percent in 2020 chose the "don't know" category—far more than the 6 percent in the 1997 study. The degree to which this difference is due to substantive change or differences in survey methodology is unclear. Whether the 2020 numbers indicate more support for violence or not depends on how we treat the "don't know" category. Support for political violence stayed the same, but rejecting violence also declined a great deal.

Just over a decade after Pew's political violence question, during Barack Obama's presidency, two 2010 Knowledge Networks (GfK) web-based surveys by Nathan Kalmoe found 73 percent and 76 percent of American adults agreed (strongly or somewhat) that "citizens upset by government should never use violence to express their feelings," while 25 percent and 26 percent either disagreed or indicated neutrality (Kalmoe 2014). Democrats and Republicans in the public did not differ in rejecting political violence. Notably, 2010 was a particularly vitriolic midterm election year, with many Republicans furious about the new law extending health insurance access to most Americans, enacted by the nation's first Black president. Even so, these numbers are remarkably close to those of the 1997 Pew survey, despite slightly different wordings and diverging sampling methods.

We repeated the 2010 "never use violence" question in a January 2020 survey with a national quota sample from the Lucid survey company. Although the sample is probably less representative than GfK and YouGov data, we found a nearly identical 27 percent who disagreed with rejecting violence or felt neutrally about it.

In sum, two similar questions on violence against the government appear to show stable responses from the public across twenty-three years of surveys and a dramatically polarizing political environment, at least prior to the 2020 election. Large portions of the public have endorsed political violence for decades, at least since the 1990s. Whether the much smaller percentage in the 1970s is a substantive change or is due simply to survey method differences is hard to know. In any case, support for political violence among a sizable minority of the public is not new.

Our only benchmark for partisan moral disengagement comes from a Pew Research Center survey in 2014, which asked partisans who rated opponents "very unfavorable" whether their opponents' policies "are so misguided that they threaten the nation's well-being." (This question inspired our own question about national threat, though with slightly different wording and without making the question conditional on an "unfavorable" rating.) In 2014, Pew found 27 percent of Democrats and 37 percent of Republicans saw the other party's policies as a threat to the nation. For comparison, our 2017 election survey found about 60 percent in each party who said the other party was "a serious threat to the United States and its people." That is a big jump in three years, but again it is hard to definitively know how much substantive and methods differences account for the change.

Recent Trends in Radical Partisanship

Our surveys from 2017 through early 2021 provide our strongest evidence for trends over time. There, we asked identical questions in YouGov surveys that hold sampling methods constant.[3] That window in time captures an absolutely vital period in American political life as democracy slid backward and violence escalated, culminating in the January 2021 Republican attack on the US Capitol. How did radical views change across this uniquely disruptive American presidency?

Our starting point in November 2017 was one year after Donald Trump's election and one year before the congressional midterm elections of 2018. During this time, Democrats widely protested many discriminatory actions by the Trump administration, including the "Muslim Ban" Executive Order signed by Trump as one of his first acts as president.

Figure 5.1 shows trends in partisan moral disengagement from November 2017 to February 2021. In general, levels of partisan moral disengagement have been gradually increasing during that time, with a notable jump in 2021. Belief that the opposing party is "a serious threat to the United States and its people" increased from 61 to 72 percent of partisans across the series. Similarly, the percentage of partisans who reported "strongly" or "somewhat" believing that the opposing party is "downright evil" increased from 40 to 59 percent across the four years. Dehumanizing partisan opponents is least common, but the share of partisans who believed out-party citizens "behave like animals" also increased, from 18 to 36 percent. Put differently, the prevalence of dehumanizing attitudes more than doubled over the four-year time span.

Figures 5.2 and 5.3 depict changes in support for partisan threats and violent acts. We expected violent trends to increase in the 2020 election year as partisan vitriol reached a fever pitch. The sudden onset of the COVID-19 virus created even greater stakes, with hundreds of thousands of Americans killed because of inadequate federal and state government action, causing an economic crisis greater than any since the Great Depression. Just as important, Black Lives Matter protests over unjust killings of

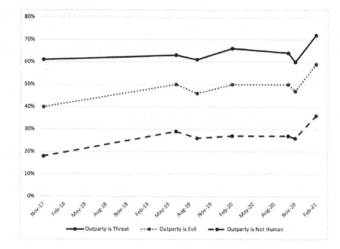

FIGURE 5.1. Trends in partisan moral Disengagement, 2017–21. *Note*: Each survey is marked by a dot. Results are weighted.

Black Americans by police and civilians were met by violent reaction from right-wing extremist groups and police, leading to several deaths. During this time, President Trump and Republican media outlet Fox News publicly rationalized right-wing violence—including murders[4]—encouraging their Republican followers to see the violence as not just excusable, but necessary.

We begin these trends with partisan threats. Figure 5.2 presents the percentage of partisans who "somewhat" or "strongly" approve of sending threatening messages to opposing leaders and regular citizens. The trends are not always rising here, unlike for moral disengagement. We see a clear rise in support for threats against elite and mass targets just before the 2018 election (up to 19 and 12 percent, respectively), followed by a decline immediately after the election. Notably, the high preelection levels appeared during a fall campaign that included nonlethal mail bomb attacks targeting journalists and Democratic leaders. Chapter 9 considers whether the attacks may have elevated violent views and especially support for threats against leaders.

Donald Trump was impeached by the US House of Representatives for the first time in mid-December 2019, and most of the respondents in that Voter Study Group survey answered in the three weeks prior to that vote. Our February 2020 survey was in the field in the week after Trump's first Senate acquittal by Republicans, and our February 2021 survey collection occurred in the three days following Trump's second impeachment acquittal for inciting the January 2021 insurrection. Not only were both impeachments threats to Trump's power (including future eligibility to hold public office), but many Republicans viewed them as illegitimate efforts, similar to their reactions to elections they had lost.

We see two other similarly sized spikes in support for threats in the lead-up to Trump's first impeachment in December 2019 and in the aftermath of his acquittal in a *second* impeachment trial in February 2021 (but not after his first acquittal). That final peak in support for partisan threats in February 2021 also corresponds with the aftermath of the violent insurrection of January 6, and the January 20 inauguration of Joe Biden as president.

Figure 5.3 depicts partisan violence views across the four-year span. The overall impression is a gradual rise in support for violence today, in contrast with the largely flat trends in threats, which had temporary spikes. The "violence today" trend starts at 8 percent, hovers around 10 percent through the middle surveys, and finishes markedly higher around 17 percent in the last two surveys. We also notice local peaks before the first presidential impeachment in December 2019, after the November 2020 election, and in the postinsurrection and postinauguration period of February 2021. When asked to imagine losing the upcoming presidential

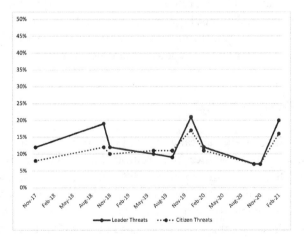

FIGURE 5.2. Trends in approval of partisan threats, 2017–21. *Note*: Each survey is marked by a dot. Results are weighted. For better readability, violence trends have a smaller *y* axis than the moral disengagement trends.

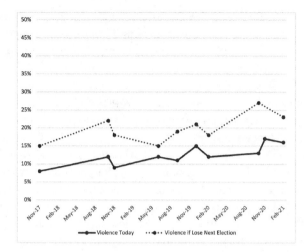

FIGURE 5.3. Trends in approval of partisan violence, 2017–21. *Note*: Each survey is marked by a dot. Results are weighted. Election loss includes all partisans asked to evaluate that scenario. (Those asked about winning are excluded here.)

election, trends in violent views followed patterns like those for "violence today," starting at 15 percent and ending near 25 percent, with peaks just before the 2018 and 2020 elections, and in the February 2021 aftermath. Chapter 9 returns to these abrupt high points to investigate the provocative roles of political events. For now, it is sufficient to say that the leaps in approval of threats against leaders and citizens seem to coincide roughly with elections, other threats to power, and violent events.

Radical Trends by Party

Next, we look at these radical attitudes by party, which can help us understand some of the political context around these numbers. Democrats and Republicans have generally not differed much in radical attitudes for most of the four-year period, but we identify some important exceptions here. We emphasize, again, that parity does not indicate Democrats and Republicans feel this way for the same reasons. On the contrary, we find divergent reasons behind these attitudes in chapter 6. Regardless, it is important to begin by learning the prevalence of these attitudes in each party over time. This is because risks may grow asymmetrically over time, and asymmetries may serve as clues to understanding how events influence ordinary people in each party. Here, we focus on divergences from the average trends discussed above.

Moral Disengagement by Party

We begin with moral disengagement. Figure 5.4 shows similar trends across the three items, and similar levels of moral disengagement for both

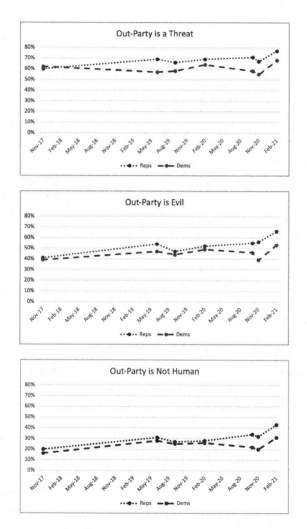

FIGURE 5.4. Trends in moral disengagement by party. *Note*: Each survey is marked by a dot. Results are weighted.

Democrats and Republicans until a statistically significant divergence in views beginning in late 2020 amid a global pandemic and the most contentious American election campaign in decades. Those gaps are notable, though they are differences in degree rather than kind—Democrats were still close behind on each measure.

The partisan gap for viewing the other party as a threat first opened significantly in mid-2019 at 8 points, rose to around 12 points in late 2020, and then shrank to 9 points in February 2021 as partisans in both parties perceived the greatest threats to date. A similar gap in seeing opponents as evil appears at the same time. It grows to 17 points right after the 2020 election as Republicans' views held steady and Democrats' views became substantially milder. But after the insurrection, Biden's inauguration, and Trump's second impeachment acquittal, both parties register their highest belief that the others are evil, with Republicans 13 points more likely to say so than the majority of Democrats who say the same. Just dwell on that for one moment—over *half* of Democrats and *two-thirds* of Republicans believed the other group was evil in February 2021.

Partisan dehumanizing views followed a similar pattern from late 2020 onward, with 12-point gaps in each of the last three surveys. Republicans remained more willing to dehumanize Democrats after the 2020 election and 2021 inauguration of Joe Biden, even as partisan dehumanization levels in both parties surged 10 points in the last survey—agreeing that the other partisans "lack the traits to be considered fully human—they should be treated like animals."

Violent Views by Party

We turn next to trends in violent partisan attitudes by party. As with moral disengagement, the overall impression in figure 5.5 is of party similarity rather than difference. But if partisan moral disengagement tended to be more prevalent among Republicans, these measures show that, when violent partisan attitudes significantly diverged, it tended to be more prevalent among Democrats—at least until voters ousted Trump from office.

Threats against citizens and leaders from the other party were endorsed at similar levels by Democrats and Republicans in 2017 and 2018, even as those levels rose a bit. Democrats expressed more support than Republicans for both kinds of threats in September 2019, but Republicans significantly leapfrogged Democrats in December 2019 as Trump's first impeachment neared. For Republicans, approval for threatening Democratic leaders and citizens peaked at 28 percent and 24 percent, respectively.

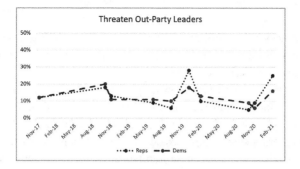

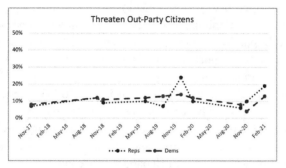

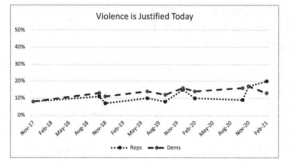

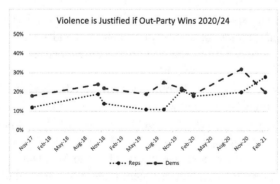

FIGURE 5.5. Trends in approval of partisan violence by party. *Note*: Each survey is marked by a dot. Results are weighted.

No differences recur until 2021, when Republicans exceeded Democrats with 25 percent approving of threats against leaders and 19 percent for threatening Democratic citizens.

When it comes to attitudes toward political violence "today," 2017 was the lowest point of approval for both Democrats and Republicans, with 8 percent believing that political violence was at least "a little bit" acceptable. Democrats significantly exceeded Republicans by a few points in November 2018 and again in September 2019. After Biden was elected, Trump was impeached for the second time, and Trump supporters violently stormed the Capitol, partisan patterns of violence reverse. By February 2021, Republicans were significantly more likely to favor immediate violence, as their support rose to a record 20 percent and Democratic support fell to 13 percent.

When we asked partisans to imagine their party losing the next presidential election, Democrats generally supported violence more than Republicans during the Trump administration. We see significant gaps between 8 and 14 points in 2018, early 2019, and late 2020, but partisan differences reverse in February 2021, when Republicans become 8 points more likely to endorse violence than Democrats, conditional on losing the 2024 presidential election. We discuss the influence of partisan control of government on these attitudes further in chapter 9.

Violent Views in February 2021

In this chapter, we have observed an alarming rise in several forms of partisan radicalism from late 2017 to early 2021, especially among Republicans. To further clarify where we stand at the end of these trends, we asked questions about three new topics to assess violent partisan attitudes in our February survey: approval of the January US Capitol attack, support for similar attacks on state capitol buildings, and—most explicitly—approving assassination of opposing partisan leaders.[5] Figure 5.6 shows the results.

To start, 12 percent of Republicans answered the Capitol question with "don't know" compared with only 1 percent of Democrats who said the same. Nineteen percent of Republicans supported the Capitol attack "somewhat" or "strongly" compared with 6 percent of Democrats. After armed takeovers of state capitol buildings in Michigan and Oregon, and armed protests outside government buildings in several other states, one-quarter of Republicans said it was at least "a little bit" justified for

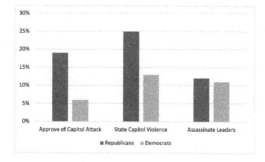

FIGURE 5.6. Broader support for partisan violence. *Note*: Data from our February 2021 survey. Percent replying "somewhat" or "strongly" approve. Weighted results.

their party "to use violence to take over state government buildings to advance their political goals these days." Just 13 percent of Democrats said the same.

There was no ambiguity in our final question: "How much do you feel it is justified for [Own party] to kill opposing political leaders to advance their political goals these days?" Twelve percent of Republicans and 11 percent of Democrats said assassinations carried out by their party were at least "a little bit" justified. This was the only question in the February 2021 survey that did *not* show significantly higher radicalism among Republicans than Democrats. Generalizing to the population of American partisans means roughly twenty million who endorse assassinating US leaders.

While these last questions are not trends, they help us understand the degree of radicalism seen at the end of our trends in February 2021. Where partisans go from there is an open question. Early signs from Republican leaders and voters in the months since do not look encouraging, but we will be monitoring in any case.

Conclusions

We see nothing today like the levels of partisan violence that plagued the distant American past. Nonetheless, levels of partisan moral disengagement and support for partisan violence have clearly grown, and ethnopartisan alignments of political parties suggest more conflict ahead. Recent violence may be a prelude to far worse if these trends continue, most of all among Republicans, whose political power is increasingly threatened by democracy and whose constituent social groups are losing their disproportionate dominance in all facets of political, social, and economic life.

In this chapter, we followed trends in partisan moral disengagement and violent attitudes among Democrats and Republicans. High levels of moral disengagement are generally and gradually rising, especially among Republicans. Support for partisan violence today and violence conditional on losing the next presidential election also seem to be rising relatively linearly over the past several years. By contrast, partisan threats against leaders and citizens appear to be more strongly responsive to momentary events without much general rise over these years.

We generally saw similar levels of partisan moral disengagement and support for violence in both parties. In the first few years, Republicans were occasionally more likely to endorse morally disengaged views and Democrats were sometimes more likely to endorse partisan violence. But in February 2021, with its several provocations, Republicans leaped above Democrats in endorsing both moral disengagement and partisan violence. We concluded our analysis with additional evidence of worrisome support for violence, especially among Republicans—a substantial minority endorsed the US Capitol attack, supported similar attacks against state capitols, and some even backed assassinating opposing partisan leaders.

In chapter 6, we will see that, even when people in each party hold similarly radical views, their radicalism is motivated by very different group orientations, consistent with broader social-historical changes in the bases of each party. And chapter 7 will begin to address how these increasingly violent partisan views relate to low-level aggressive political behavior, in ways that may help explain rising trends in the prevalence of more violent and threatening partisan behaviors.

CHAPTER SIX

Who Are the Radical Partisans?

They were yelling Democrats are f—ing idiots and Democrats are demons. . . . It makes me feel angry that this is allowed and that our police are allowing this kind of hate-filled atmosphere to take over. — Nancy Nichols, attendee at a Democratic protest in Texas, August 27, 2020[1]

The Democratic Party's candidates weren't just offering a different idea for governance; they were threatening the place of whites in the social order. — Seth Masket, political scientist, November 16, 2020[2]

When someone shows you who they are, believe them the first time. — Maya Angelou

In June 2020, a group called the Transition Integrity Project gathered more than one hundred political practitioners (including current and former senior government and campaign officials) to engage in a "war game" tracing potential outcomes after the 2020 election. In virtually every scenario, the simulated result was disruption and chaos. For our purposes, one prediction stood out. The report warned that, "[the] potential for violent conflict is high, particularly since Trump encourages his supporters to take up arms."[3] Political violence researchers were sounding alarms about growing risk factors even sooner, including a 2019 report from the Carnegie Endowment for International Peace that warned "we have the tinder for political violence" (Kleinfeld et al. 2019). Indeed, on January 6, 2021, hundreds of Trump's supporters took violent action aimed at overturning the election result in an assault on the US Capitol, following months of death threats against election officials.

The insurrectionists endangered lawmakers and injured police at the Capitol as they temporarily succeeded in halting congressional certification of the election. They threatened the lives of Democratic congressional leaders, the vice president of the United States (a fellow Republican), and others among the minority of Republican leaders committed to an orderly transition of power, who refused to overturn the results of a legitimate election for partisan gain.

Most Republicans in the public did not participate in the Capitol attack, of course, but many were sympathetic to it. Hours after the attack, a flash poll showed 45 percent of Republicans who knew of the attack expressed support for storming the Capitol (Walker 2021). By early February—after the full scale of the harm was known and a few (but not many) Republican leaders had condemned the attack—our own survey found Republican support for the Capitol assault still at 25 percent. Who condones partisan violence like this? Beyond that attack, who are the radical partisans who believe partisan violence today is justified and who vilify their opponents to the greatest extremes? This chapter begins to identify those answers.

We focus our investigation on a range of individual-level political and personal traits that are plausible candidates for influencing radicalism. Social identification with the party is an obvious motive for radicalism, along with a general tendency to think and act aggressively in everyday life (trait aggression). We also consider intersections of partisanship with important group orientations that have reshaped the parties on a societal scale, including attitudes about ongoing racial inequities and women's place in the world. We expect partisans whose social views align with their party to be more hostile toward their opponents.

Overall, we find that Democrats and Republicans hold radical partisan attitudes for some common reasons—attachment to party and tendencies toward interpersonal aggression, for example. But what distinguishes them? We find that partisan moral disengagement (but not violent views) is closely related to racially resentful and sexist attitudes among Republicans, but not among the fewer Democrats who share those views. In fact, anti-Black views among white Democrats work to *reduce* extreme hostility toward Republicans. This, we believe, signals the centrality of traditional social hierarchies in structuring radical partisan animosity, with Republicans staunchly defending the elevated status of white men while Democrats increasingly push back against the forces of systemic racism and patriarchy.

Getting to Know the Radical Partisans

Who are these radical partisans? Some of them are your neighbors, family, co-workers, and friends. Let's meet some of them from the profiles of real respondents in one of our 2019 surveys.

Meet Mike.[4] He's a conservative Republican from Tennessee who feels about as close to the party as most of his fellow partisans. He's white, fifty-three years old, and divorced—perhaps related to his extremely sexist views. He never attended college, he's currently unemployed, and he demurred when we asked his income level. He has no particular religious attachments, and he holds extremely negative views of Black Americans. He's a little bit less aggressive in everyday life than the average person, which may partly explain why he *claims* he has never publicly insulted or physically assaulted anyone over politics. In response to someone who shared a Biden tweet criticizing Republicans, he replied, "You're an idiot, as well as part of the problem." Mike is sure Democrats are a national threat, that they're evil, and he even thinks they're a little less than human. In 2019, he thought "a moderate amount" of violence by Republicans would be fine to advance political goals, but he said "a great deal" of violence was called for if Democrats won the 2020 presidential election.

Nia is a twenty-seven-year-old Democrat from Connecticut. She's very liberal, and she says being a Democrat is very important to her. She's Black and Catholic. She graduated from college a few years ago, and she's currently a single graduate student. Nia probably doesn't make much money as a graduate student, but she lists her family income as over $150,000, which might mean she lives with well-to-do parents or a partner. She considers herself to be very aggressive when provoked by other people, but she doesn't get into verbal or physical altercations with other people over politics. She holds positive views of other women and recognizes systemic inequalities by race. In her view, Republicans are evil, and they pose a clear threat to the United States. She also thinks violence by Democrats is a little bit justified today, but she doesn't see any additional justification for violence on the basis of how the 2020 election goes. She called Trump "immature" in response to a tweet of his about fistfighting Biden.

John is a moderate Democrat from Maryland. At seventy-four years old, he's retired, having earned a high school degree in his younger days. He declined to give his income, if any beyond Social Security. He's more attached to his party than most Democrats, he has more sexist views of women than most, and he has a bit of an aggressive streak. A Protestant and married, he lists his race as "other." He strongly believes that Republicans pose a threat to the nation, that they are evil, and that they lack the traits to be considered fully human, but he thinks violence is never appropriate, not even if Democrats lose the 2020 presidential election. He hasn't insulted, threatened, or assaulted any people over their politics.

When he saw a tweet by Trump claiming he could beat Biden in a fistfight, he replied "in your dreams . . . wake up."

Amy is a forty-two-year-old white Republican who lives in California. She's a politically conservative Catholic. She's married and working, with a postgraduate degree and a family income over $100,000 per year. She feels as attached to the Republican Party as anyone can feel, and she tells us she's a lot more aggressive than most people in everyday life. Like Mike, she thinks Democrats are a national threat, that they're evil, and she somewhat agrees that they're less than human. She applauded a tweet by Trump alleging election fraud, writing "very good" in reply. However, she doesn't think violence by Republicans is OK, regardless of who wins the 2020 election.

Having met a few radical partisans, what do we see? Like many of our survey respondents, they embrace partisan moral disengagement, but despite holding such hostile views of opponents, not all of them endorse partisan violence. They don't seem particularly unusual in many respects (though we shouldn't forget the extremity of their views).[5] Yet, despite their diverse backgrounds, you may have noticed they also share some traits that we expect make them more likely to hold radical views, as we turn to a more systematic analysis. What kinds of people embrace radical partisan views and who considers these views beyond the pale?

Partisan Attachments and Trait Aggression

To start, because radical partisanship is partisan by definition, we should expect that those with stronger social attachments to their party will be more likely to espouse radical partisan views than those with only weak attachments. As we described in chapter 3, people are motivated to respond to threats with aggression when they feel strong psychological attachments to their group. In today's politics, the threat feels nearly constant in the minds of many partisans. Every election, legislative bill, and court ruling is viewed as a status competition. News coverage tends to emphasize those partisan outcomes over policy substance (Dunaway 2008; Hitt and Searles 2018; Lawrence 2000). On the other hand, healthy democratic parties are supposed to manage hostility and channel potentially lethal conflicts into nonviolent politics, and so we might expect some countervailing force among strong partisans attentive to their group's norms. (Of course, that potential moderating influence requires parties to fulfill their pacifying role instead of enflaming their followers with radical rhetoric.)

Chapter 3 also described how individual predispositions for interpersonal aggression (trait aggression) in everyday life extend into the political world, and chapter 4 presented initial evidence of trait aggression's moderating power in the relationship between moral disengagement and violent views. Here, we expect our tests to show that partisan attachments and trait aggression are two of the most powerful predictors for radical partisanship (we will test racial and gender attitudes later).

We measured partisan social identification with four survey items, including "To what extent do you feel like a Democrat/Republican?" and "Agree/Disagree: When I talk about Democrats/Republicans I tend to say 'we' rather than 'they.'" Leonie Huddy and her colleagues (Huddy, Mason, and Aarøe 2015) used these items to discover that people with stronger partisan social attachments reacted more angrily toward threats to their party's status. On a scale of 0 to 1, the average party identification score was around 0.7 for both parties in our three-wave panel surveys. We measured trait aggression with a four-item index (Kalmoe 2015) that we described in chapter 4, and we found no partisan differences on interpersonal aggression. We use our Wave 1 (June 2019) questions for the predictors and our outcome measures for radical partisanship from Wave 3 (February 2020). Doing so takes a few steps toward sorting out the causal order of these relationships, though not definitively in that regard.

Predicting Partisan Moral Disengagement

How do partisan social identity and trait aggression relate to partisan moral disengagement? We create an average moral-disengagement score for each person by combining the three moral-disengagement questions. In addition to partisan social identity and trait aggression, our analysis includes strength of ideological self-identification, college education, sex, and age.[6] We include the three sociodemographic measures because we expect people with more education, women, and older people may be less drawn to radical partisanship. These latter traits also tend to coincide with trait aggression and partisan attachment, and so accounting for those factors helps us identify the independent influence of each one. Since partisan social identity and radical outcomes are measured with wording conditional on partisanship from the survey in which they are measured, our analysis focuses on the 94 percent of Wave 1 partisans who identified with the same party in Wave 3.

The statistical model summarized in figure 6.1 confirms our expectations that partisan moral disengagement is strongly related to both

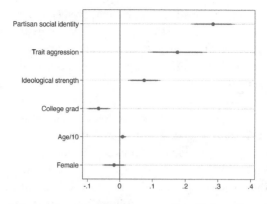

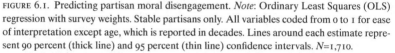

FIGURE 6.1. Predicting partisan moral disengagement. *Note*: Ordinary Least Squares (OLS) regression with survey weights. Stable partisans only. All variables coded from 0 to 1 for ease of interpretation except age, which is reported in decades. Lines around each estimate represent 90 percent (thick line) and 95 percent (thin line) confidence intervals. *N*=1,710.

partisan social identity and trait aggression. (Readers unfamiliar with statistical regression models may want to follow the endnote for a quick primer. See the online appendix for full model results.)[7]

Partisan social identification is the strongest predictor of partisan moral disengagement in our model, roughly twice as large as other factors. A person with the strongest party attachment has a partisan moral-disengagement score that is 28 points higher, on average, than a partisan with the weakest attachment. Trait aggression's relationship with moral disengagement is also substantial as expected, at about two-thirds that size. Stronger liberal or conservative identity also predicts significantly more partisan moral disengagement compared with weak identifiers, and college graduates have significantly lower levels than people with less formal education, on average. Age and sex are unrelated here.

We also looked for differences between Democrats and Republicans in the direction and strength of these predictors. The results were largely similar, but we also found a few small differences. Partisan social identity and trait aggression factors predict partisan moral disengagement equally well for each set of partisans. Ideological strength (largely conservative) looks more powerful at reinforcing moral disengagement for Republicans than Democrats, while the lower levels among college graduates also appear more distinctive for Republicans, perhaps as a cross-cutting force due to the party's growing hostility toward higher education (Parker 2019; see online appendix for results).

Predicting Violent Partisan Attitudes

We repeated these tests to predict violent partisan views, measured as an average of our four partisan violence questions in Wave 3. Figure 6.2 shows a summary of the results. These factors collectively predict violent partisan views just as well as partisan moral disengagement, but the lower average levels of support for violence mean smaller coefficients for the estimated relationships.

As we predicted, partisan social identity and trait aggression relate significantly and substantially to violent views, but their relative strength is reversed compared with the results for moral disengagement. What stands out is the strength of trait aggression. The most interpersonally aggressive people are 17 points more likely to approve of partisan violence than those who are not aggressive at all, from a baseline level just 4 points above zero. Trait aggression is by far the most powerful predictor of violent partisan views. This makes sense, considering that aggression and violence are generally related. The result also provides further validation for our measures of violent partisan attitudes by connecting them with nonpolitical aggressive *behavior* in everyday life.

Partisan social attachments also predict violent partisan attitudes well. A partisan with the strongest party attachment approves of violence about 7 points more than a partisan with the weakest attachment, on average. Older people are also significantly less likely to endorse partisan

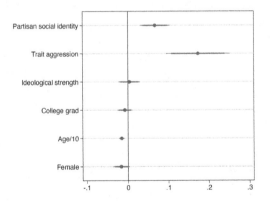

FIGURE 6.2. Predicting support for partisan violence. *Note:* OLS regression with survey weights. Stable partisans only. All variables coded from 0 to 1 for ease of interpretation except age, which is reported in decades. Lines around each estimate represent 90 percent (thick line) and 95 percent (thin line) confidence intervals. *N*=1,710.

violence. Ideological strength has no relationship here, nor do the other sociodemographic factors. Even more so than for moral disengagement, these predictors for violent partisan attitudes are similar for Republicans and Democrats.

Beyond these tests in our panel surveys, we replicated these models in several of our other surveys, and our main factors here do similarly well at predicting partisan moral disengagement and support for partisan violence in every test.

Racial Resentment, Hostile Sexism, and Radical Partisanship

Having examined basic predictors for radical partisanship, we now consider the conditional effects of animosity toward Black Americans and women. In recent research, one significant predictor of partisan animosity has been "social sorting." Republicans and Democrats have grown increasingly socially divided along racial, religious, and other lines in recent decades. These social divisions between the parties have reduced the prevalence of "cross-cutting" identities that tend to dampen intergroup partisan conflict (Mason 2018). It is easier to view opposing partisans with extreme hostility when we can find nothing in common with them than when we can relate.

Even more than the demographic categories of race and sex, party sorting on racial and gender worldviews means conflict over the status of women and people of color in social hierarchies now substantially contributes to the hostile partisanship currently on display in the American political arena, including affective polarization on party feeling thermometers (e.g., Abramowitz and Webster 2018). It is a fight for the soul of America, as Joe Biden has put it, between those who believe in founding democratic *ideals* and those who want a country dominated by people who *look* like the founders. Do those same dynamics enflame radical partisan views?

Racial Resentment and Moral Disengagement

We begin with racial resentment and partisan moral disengagement. We measure racial attitudes with the common "racial resentment" scale, in which some whites deny systemic barriers as explanations for ongoing racial inequality and point to supposed Black cultural inferiority related to work ethic instead (Kinder and Sanders 1996). This is one of the primary conflicts between Democrats and Republicans today. Importantly, the scale was conceptualized for white Americans (Kinder and Sanders 1996), and so we focus on white respondents here.[8]

Our survey respondents indicated their agreement or disagreement with four statements, including "Generations of slavery and discrimination have created conditions that make it difficult for Blacks to work their way out of the lower class" and "It's really a matter of some people not trying hard enough; if Blacks would only try harder they could be just as well off as whites." We only asked about these statements in Wave 3 of our panel.

Notice that what we are testing is whether a person's *racial* attitudes can affect their moral disengagement from their opposing *party* members. Given that the Republican Party is largely made up of white Americans, and Republicans misperceive a *predominantly* Black Democratic Party (Ahler and Sood 2018), we should not be surprised to see racial and partisan attitudes interrelated. In fact, Westwood and Peterson (2020) have recently demonstrated that many Americans automatically think about race when they think about party, and vice versa.

This scale increasingly distinguishes the views of white Democrats and Republicans, particularly during and after Obama's presidency, when the public increasingly associated the Democratic Party with Black Americans (Tesler 2016). We find enormous gaps in racial resentment between white Democrats and white Republicans in our survey. On a 0 to 1 racial resentment scale, average white Democrats score 0.28, while average white Republicans score 0.71. This substantially informs our understanding of partisan behavior going forward. But we're most interested in how racial resentment relates with partisan moral disengagement over and above the predictors we have already identified.

We expect this relationship to differ by party. For white Republicans, anti-Black racism coincides with their partisanship, while the same views for white Democrats clash with their party. Thus, we expect racial resentment to boost moral disengagement for Republicans but that the same views *reduce* moral disengagement for Democrats. Figure 6.3 presents the average values of partisan moral disengagement by party and level of racial resentment, after accounting for the influence of the other factors modeled in figure 6.1. As we predicted, the relationship between racial resentment and moral disengagement is vastly different for partisans in each party.

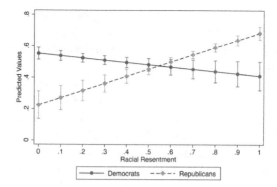

FIGURE 6.3. Predicted levels of moral disengagement across racial resentment, by party. *Note*: Predicted values taken from the model in the appendix. Lines around each point estimate are 95 percent confidence intervals. All other variables are held at their means or modes. White respondents only. N=1,322.

Here, we find racial resentment far surpasses the strength of our key predictors—partisan social identity and trait aggression—in accounting for why white Republicans vilify Democrats. This is our first empirical indicator that radical American partisanship is driven by vastly different things for the two parties, though it is wholly in line with our historical-social-psychological expectations. Republicans who don't believe in systemic racism, and who believe that Black Americans' struggles are due to their own individual faults, are most likely to despise Democrats. In contrast, the (numerically fewer) Democrats who deny systemic racism are significantly *less* likely to despise Republicans. For them, sharing a key belief associated with Republicans makes Republicans seem less despicable.

For white Republicans, racial resentment is consistent with their party identity, and it therefore generates much higher levels of partisan moral disengagement, shifting their views by 46 points across the scale. Republicans at the highest levels of racial resentment are 17 points more morally disengaged than the few white Democrats who are high in racial resentment. Thirteen percent of white Republicans have the highest score possible on racial resentment. The *least* racially resentful Republicans, meanwhile, have moral-disengagement levels 30 points *below* Democrats who are low on racial resentment. Only 12 percent of white Republicans score in the bottom half of the scale, however, so this distinction applies to very few people. For those few, low racial resentment likely works as a cross-pressure—the progressive racial attitude makes them more open to seeing Democrats as worthy of care. We find the reverse among Democrats, for whom denying systemic racism is incongruent with their party. Those who do deny systemic racism are significantly *less* likely to vilify Republicans (by about 14 points) than Democrats who recognize racial disparities due to discrimination.

This finding upends a common theme in political punditry—that all partisans are equally driven by "sectarianism," or party loyalty. It is not simply that all partisans hate the other party because they want their own party to win. It isn't even because they are well sorted by race demographically. Instead, there is a uniquely powerful relationship between white Republicans' hatred of Democrats and their resentment toward Black Americans. For white Democrats, racial resentment works in the other direction, with the highest moral disengagement found among the *least* racially resentful Democrats, consistent with their party's reputation for racial justice.

This distinction between white Democrats and Republicans is one to keep in mind while interpreting the other results in this book. Partisans of both parties may vilify their opponents to similar degrees, but white Republicans are doing so largely in defense of a racist system that they refuse to acknowledge, while white Democrats vilify more when they recognize racism's role in holding Black Americans back.

RACIAL RESENTMENT AND PARTISAN VIOLENCE.   Now, we apply the same test for violent partisan attitudes. Will we see the same partisan divergence with racial resentment on violent views as we did for partisan moral disengagement? The short answer is no. Figure 6.4 shows no significant relationships for white Republicans or white Democrats. Strength of partisan identity, trait aggression, and age are the only significant predictors of violent partisan attitudes, along with sex. In these models, white women were significantly less likely to endorse partisan violence compared with white men.

Overall, then, our results suggest that racial resentment operates differently across our two dimensions of radical partisanship. Racial animus among white Republicans is strongly related to vilifying Democrats, and white Democrats with more progressive racial views are likelier to vilify Republicans, but racial resentment does not have the same relationship with violent partisan views. Beyond these tests in our panel surveys, we found the same racial resentment patterns in our 2020 election survey. There, we also substituted an alternative measure of white racial attitudes and found comparable results (the FIRE scale, DeSante and Smith 2020).

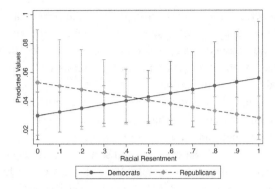

FIGURE 6.4. Predicted levels of violent partisan views across racial resentment, by party.
Note: Predicted values taken from the model in the appendix. White respondents only. All
other variables are held at their means or modes. $N=1,322$.

HOSTILE SEXISM AND MORAL DISENGAGEMENT.   We turn next to the relationship between sexism and radical partisanship. Given a major partisan divide over traditional social hierarchy, we expect sexist ideas to contribute to partisan moral disengagement and violence in ways like racial
resentment. We expect antifeminist gender attitudes consistent with Republican identity and at cross-purposes with Democratic identity to result
in more radicalism among sexist Republicans and less radicalism among
sexist Democrats. Here, we test how hostile sexism relates to moral disengagement for each party.

We measure hostile sexism by asking respondents about their agreement with three statements, including "Women seek to gain power by getting control over men" (Cassese and Holman 2019). We average the three
answers to form the hostile sexism measure. As others have found, we
see average differences in hostile sexism between ordinary partisans in
each party. On a 0 to 1 scale, Democrats score an average of 0.3, while
Republicans average 0.6. Notably, many women hold hostile sexist attitudes too (0.40), nearly as much so as men (0.49). Our question, then, is
whether sexism works similarly or differently on moral disengagement by
party (or not at all). Figure 6.5 summarizes the results of a model identical to the one in figure 6.3, except that it replaces racial resentment with
hostile sexism.

Much like what we saw with racial resentment, we find the relationship
between hostile sexism and moral disengagement differs substantially
by party. Hostile sexism is only related to moral disengagement among

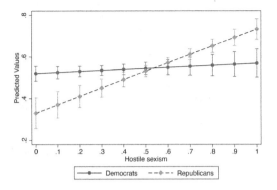

FIGURE 6.5. Predicted levels of moral disengagement across hostile sexism, by party. *Note*: Predicted values taken from the model in the appendix. Lines around each point estimate are 95 percent confidence intervals. All other variables are held at their means or modes. *N*=1,710.

Republicans—and powerfully so—shifting them 40 points up the disengagement scale. Republicans' feelings about the status of women are strongly related to their feelings about Democrats, with those highest in hostile sexism vilifying Democrats most. Not only is the relationship strong, but it also far exceeds the strength of the relationship for partisan social identity. We find the same for Republican men and women in additional tests. Republicans with the lowest levels of sexism, by contrast, are significantly *less* morally disengaged than low-sexism Democrats, though only 7 percent of Republicans score in the bottom quarter of the scale. We expect this is because feminist views are a cross-pressure for Republicans, which allows less sexist Republicans to see Democrats as more like themselves. In contrast with Republicans, Democrats have similar levels of partisan moral disengagement across all levels of hostile sexism. These null patterns hold for Democratic men and women.

Taken together, this is evidence that sexism itself is a Republican-associated trait that can either reinforce or diminish the links between Republican identity on moral disengagement. It also bolsters the idea that the main divide between Democrats and Republicans is not simply blind partisanship—instead Republicans are especially engaged in an identity-focused battle to maintain white male supremacy. Democrats do not share this motivation, and feminist attitudes (or at least views that are not antifeminist) do not prompt an equal and opposite reaction among Democrats. In additional tests with our 2020 election survey (not shown

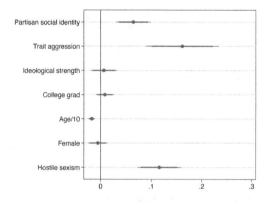

FIGURE 6.6. Predicting violent partisan views. *Note*: OLS regression with survey weights. Stable partisans only. All variables coded from 0 to 1 for ease of interpretation except age, which is reported in decades. Lines around each estimate represent 90 percent (thick line) and 95 percent (thin line) confidence intervals. $N=1,710$.

here), we found the same patterns for hostile sexism and partisan moral disengagement.

SEXISM AND PARTISAN VIOLENCE.   We expected the relationship between hostile sexism and support for partisan violence would look like the results for moral disengagement above, or maybe like the null results for racial resentment and violence. Instead, we found that partisans who endorse hostile sexism are significantly more likely to endorse partisan violence regardless of party. We tested whether the parties differed in the strength of that relationship and found mixed results—in the Wave 3 data, the relationship appeared to be stronger among Democrats—a surprise. However, when we replicated the test in our 2020 election data, we found the same main relationship for hostile sexism and violence with no difference by party. Thus, we are confident that hostile sexism is strongly and positively related to holding violent partisan views, and we doubt that there is a partisan difference.

Given our conclusion that the results do not generally differ by party, figure 6.6 summarizes the results of a model that replicates figure 6.2 while adding hostile sexism as a new predictor of partisan violence. As we described above, our main new finding here is that hostile sexism generally predicts greater support for partisan violence. Even when accounting for the significant role of partisan social identity and trait aggression, those who are highly sexist tend to approve more of partisan violence. The relationship even rivals that of the strongest predictor—trait aggression—and if anything, the higher prevalence of hostile sexism at all levels makes its practical relationship more important. A shift from the lowest to highest levels of sexism yields a 12-point increase in support for partisan violence, which would triple the level relative to the mean.

In retrospect, this relationship is not at all surprising. Scholars who specialize in violence against women frequently find that sexism is associated with general acceptance of violence in interpersonal relationships (Forbes, Adams-Curtis, and White 2004; Herrero, Rodríguez, and Torres 2017). Given an interpersonal link between sexism and aggression, we should not be surprised, then, to find our evidence connecting sexism with partisan violence for Democrats as well as Republicans. This is much like the role of trait aggression—indeed, that factor even has a "hostility" toward others component—but it appears that hostile sexism in particular opens the door to more violence against out-group partisans even after accounting for trait aggression's influence. Here, both Democrats and Republicans who are high in hostile sexism are also more approving of using violence against their *partisan* opponents.

Integrating Our Findings on Group Attitudes

Overall, racism and sexism both contribute to radical partisanship, but in different ways for each party. And for Republicans, those relationships far outstrip the strong expected links partisan radicalism has with partisan social identity and trait aggression. When it comes to moral disengagement, hostile group attitudes toward traditionally subordinate groups increase Republicans' moral disengagement but do not do so for Democrats. In fact, racially resentful Democrats are *less* likely to vilify Republicans owing to that shared anti-Black orientation with Republicans.

We see a different picture for violent partisan attitudes—more partisan similarity than difference. Racial resentment doesn't predict violent partisan attitudes overall nor when considered separately by party, though its unique role in spurring moral disengagement among Republicans may also indirectly influence violent attitudes among Republicans. Sexism proves to be substantially related to greater support for partisan violence in *both* parties. We cannot definitively say why this is so. We think it may relate to the long tradition of violence against women of all races and its immediate connection to violent impulses regarding political power. In any case, the finding deserves additional attention, and we intend to explore it further in subsequent research.

Conclusions

Who are the radical partisans? What traits predict who is likely to hold radical partisan views? Here, we found that strong social attachment to one's political party and a predisposition for interpersonal aggressive behavior strongly and consistently predicted partisan moral disengagement and violent partisan views. However, additional tests showed that attitudes related to systemic racism and hostile sexism rivaled and even surpassed the powerful relationship that radical partisanship has with the strength of partisan social identity and trait aggression. Those results drive home the inextricable links between group attitudes and radical partisanship, connecting individual-level political psychology to the sweeping social-historical account of parties in chapter 2.

For Republicans, denying systemic racism and holding sexist views of women has become consistent with the party's identity, and that consistency encourages Republicans with those views to see Democrats as more threatening, evil, and inhuman—extreme outsiders who endanger the long-standing dominance of white men by sociopolitical discrimination and violence. People in higher-status groups are generally the least motivated to acknowledge inequality that advantages their own group (Saguy and Dovidio 2013), and that denial has major consequences for moral disengagement.

For Democrats, racism and sexism are cross-pressures on a Democratic identity increasingly oriented toward dismantling barriers to racial equality and women's equality. Cross-pressures of that sort reduce the "othering" of Republican partisans. Put differently, our findings show that hostility toward social out-groups joins in-group party attachments as wellsprings for partisan moral disengagement (Kane, Mason, and Wronski 2021).[9] This divide is not only polarizing the nation in the traditional sense of the word—it is also radicalizing the nation's partisan conflict.

Democrats and Republicans often shared similar levels of radical partisan attitudes in recent years, as we saw in chapter 5, but they are radical on behalf of starkly different visions of America. One side pushes for equality by dismantling systemic discrimination against marginalized groups while the other pulls the country backward in defense of privileges for high-status groups. What the two parties fight over matters, not just the fact that each is fighting. We cannot have a full and open debate about the state of American democracy without acknowledging that moral difference. White, Christian, heterosexual men have held the highest status in American society since the founding of the nation. What Americans are confronting, now, is whether that status hierarchy should persist.

These group orientations matter for partisan hostility because of Republicans' increasingly strong association with old-fashioned hierarchical worldviews on race and sex. Such party-group alignments are not new nor immutable, however. In fact, Democrats were the party of relatively regressive views on race and sex in the nineteenth century (Edwards 1997), but those roles have flipped following twentieth-century partisan realignments. Different alignments in the future would almost certainly lead to different relationships for radical partisanship.

Hardly any Americans have taken violent partisan action yet, but in an unsettled social-political environment that includes radical encouragement from political leaders (see chapter 10), more partisans *will* violently lash out, and many more will support or even enable those actions. Identifying the types of people most drawn to radical partisanship was crucial here for identifying risk factors, given what we now know about the prevalence of morally disengaged and violent attitudes among American partisans. That imperative is even greater given evidence in the next chapter that links violent partisan attitudes to aggressive political behaviors in the real world.

PART II

Radical Behaviors and the Impact of Conditions and Events

CHAPTER SEVEN

From Radical Views to Aggressive Behavior

I wanted to knock him out so badly. I couldn't believe he didn't go to sleep. He must've had a good chin because I thought I was hitting him good. — A twenty-nine-year-old Trump supporter who assaulted a sixty-one-year-old anti-Trump protester in 2019.[1]

I'm there for the greatest celebration of all time after Pence leads the Senate flip!! OR IM THERE IF TRUMP TELLS US TO STORM THE FUCKIN CAPITAL IMA DO THAT THEN! . . . I'm with a group going to fight, not hang out. — Facebook message from a fifty-one-year-old Trump supporter before the January 2021 riot, arrested for violence at the US Capitol[2]

There is no question that violent views can lead to violent partisan behaviors, as we saw in the attack on the US Capitol in 2021 and in the armed takeover of the Michigan State Capitol in early 2020, among other violent actions. In both high-profile cases, Republican leaders incited their followers and used violent rhetoric to mobilize them into action. Beyond those spectacular incidents, we regularly see news stories of partisans throwing punches at rallies and protests, like the assault case in the epigraph above, and we know Americans send thousands of death threats targeting politicians each year. Well into this project, some dismissed those accelerating cases as isolated incidents, either not part of a pattern or too rare to worry much about. The 2021 insurrection helped many Americans recognize the threat of violence and the larger threat of Republican authoritarianism more generally.

"Aggressive behavior" is distinct from the lethal and crippling harms of "violence." Aggression includes (1) physical harms that fall short of death or maiming, (2) threats of harm, and (3) verbal aggression like insults (Anderson and Bushman 2002). Beyond altercations at political events, political aggression manifests in everyday interactions—a bumper sticker that fuels aggressive driving, a T-shirt that leads one person to block a grocery aisle and another to push that person out of the way, or a political comment that motivates violent replies on social media. Previous studies have found partisan harm in the form of material discrimination like college scholarship allocation (Iyengar and Westwood 2015), but our investigation into aggressive *physical* harm in politics goes much further.

No one knows how common these kinds of behavior are—whether anecdotes and episodic news stories reflect substantial patterns of partisan-motivated aggression. What are the rates of physical and verbal aggression of the sort that don't get criminally charged? And, critically, do the radical partisan views we documented in prior chapters correspond with more aggressive partisan *behavior*? This chapter begins to answer these vital questions with tests that focus on two sets of aggressive behavior measures: self-reports and direct measures of physical harm. We conclude by considering how our findings correspond with prominent cases of political aggression and violence.

From Attitudes to Behaviors

The sociologist Charles Tilly (2003) writes, "Most holders of views that justify violence against one sort of human or another never actually abduct, maim, or murder anyone" (8). Our evidence supports that conclusion: millions of Americans endorse partisan violence today, but vanishingly few have carried out violent attacks or murders, even as rates of both rise. However, we also don't believe that violent partisan attitudes are mere expressions—signifying nothing but partisan disdain. We do expect to find evidence that violent attitudes lead many people to act out aggressively in ways that fall short of serious bodily harm. These milder but more common forms of partisan aggression harm individuals and endanger democracy, not least because they have the potential to spark larger conflagrations.

It turns out that the same things that predict conventional political actions like voting can also predict and explain aggressive behavior and violence. Voter turnout is a function of (1) individual traits that affect motivation and ability (e.g., interest, knowledge), (2) institutions that help or hinder voting (e.g., laws that create or remove barriers to participation), and (3) mobilization by leaders, groups, and interpersonal networks (e.g., Rosenstone and Hansen 1993; Brady, Verba, and Schlozman, and 1995). Similarly, aggressive behavior and violence are shaped by (1) individual motives and capacity (e.g., violent attitudes, physical ability), (2) institutions (e.g., a law punishing violent behavior, opportunities to hurt victims), and (3) mobilization through incitement and recruitment by leaders, groups, and acquaintances. The broader norms that partisans set matter too, as part of a broader culture that may encourage violence.

These factors work interactively, not just independently. In voting drives, some citizens are responsive to mobilization efforts while other citizens are not. The same is true for violence: some people are more susceptible to violent appeals. By recognizing that behavior is a product of more than just individual attitudes, this framework helps to explain how it is that while millions of people hold violent views, only a small portion of them get into fights over politics, and very few of them carry out violent attacks in today's social-political environment.

Patterns like this fit well with psychology research more generally, in which the strength of links between attitudes and behaviors is highly conditional (see Guyer and Fabrigar 2015 for a review). The anticipated costs and benefits of acting on attitudes matter a great deal (Ajzen and Fishbein 1977), whether for mundane behaviors like voting or extreme behaviors like violence. Expecting legal and social sanctions surely plays a big role in preventing violent political attitudes from becoming aggressive or violent behavior for many people, along with the risk of bodily harm. Put another way, we would see far more aggressive and violent political behavior if the legal and social sanctions against those behaviors disappeared, as they did in many historical eras. Tilly (2003) describes those easy societal transitions from peaceful coexistence to violence and back again: "The most plausible behavioral accounts of such rapid switching center on the lifting and reimposition of social controls, following the assumption that impulses to attack remain more or less constant" (230).

Some forms of physical aggression also require physical abilities beyond the reach of many Americans, though some more lethal forms make it easier (e.g., guns, bombs). Others may doubt their ability and opportunity to successfully carry out extreme forms of action (e.g., assassinations), and that may decrease their willingness to risk the costs that accompany the attempt. In contrast, people who frequently behave aggressively in everyday life (e.g., shouting matches, fistfights) may feel more capable of and comfortable with engaging in aggressive *political* behavior.

In sum, these frameworks lead us to expect that *partisans who behave aggressively* are much likelier to endorse political violence, even as *most partisans who sincerely hold violent views* will not behave aggressively or violently—at least not without political leaders and social groups making even more explicit mobilizing and normalizing efforts around political violence than we see today. This is yet another reason to emphasize that the Republican Party's inclination to ignore the 2021 Capitol insurrection gives implicit license for its partisans to engage in increasingly aggressive behavior.

Self-Reports of Aggressive Political Behavior

Measuring aggressive behavior naturally poses methodological and ethical challenges. First, assessing *behavior* in surveys is hard. Surveys generally rely on self-reports, which are often unverifiable and sometimes inaccurate. Ethically, we do not wish to cause real harm for the sake of research (and we might be barred by regulatory agencies from doing so). Nonetheless, measuring political aggression rates and learning how violent attitudes relate are urgent concerns.

Though imperfect, the most straightforward way to map real-world aggressive political behavior is simply to ask. We start from the victim's perspective, with the expectation that people will be more willing to report aggression done to them rather than aggression that they have done to others. In our 2020 preelection survey, we asked respondents if they had ever been insulted, threatened, or physically attacked because of their political views.[3] They responded yes or no for each outcome. Of course, the half of the public *not* politically targeted may mostly be people who don't talk about politics with others out of reticence or indifference. So we also assessed the rates of victimization among people who *do* talk about politics. We don't have general political discussion items in this survey, but we do have indicators of whether people ever post about politics on social media.[4] Figure 7.1 shows the results.

Political victimization is prevalent in the US. Forty-seven percent of all respondents said they had been insulted because of their politics, 15 percent reported being threatened, and 3 percent said they had been physically attacked. With 255 million adults in the US, that translates to roughly 120 million insulted over politics, 38 million threatened, and 8 million physically attacked (though bear in mind that small percentages like those for physical attacks could be disproportionately inflated by measurement error; see Ansolabehere, Luks, and Schaffner 2015).

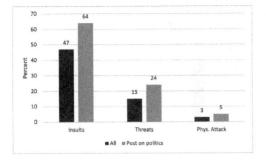

FIGURE 7.1. Self-reported victimization by aggressive political behavior. *Source*: 2020 Cooperative Election Study (CES) preelection survey. All: *N*=1,000. Post on politics: *N*=344.

Among the one-third who reported posting about politics on social media, 64 percent said they had been targeted with political insults, 24 percent said they had been threatened, and 5 percent reported being physically attacked over politics—all three substantially and statistically more than the general public. These victimization reports—if accurate—shine harsh new light on the levels of aggressive behavior in US politics.

Perpetrators

What about *perpetrating* political aggression? We asked about insulting, threatening, and physically attacking others because of their politics right after the victimization items in the 2020 preelection survey ("Do you ever . . ."). We also asked similar questions in Wave 3 of our panel survey (February 2020) with subtle but possibly consequential wording differences ("Have you ever . . .").[5] We do not see one as better than the other, and we present both for a fuller picture. It is important to note that the election study was done in October 2020, while the panel study was done in February 2020, so we cannot tell whether different observed levels of aggression are due to differences in question wording, time, or something else. For both versions, we gave respondents frequency scales ranging from "never" up to "often" or "every day," but we'll focus on "never" responses versus the rest. Figure 7.2 shows the results from the two surveys in 2020.

How many American partisans report that they behave aggressively in politics? The first thing that jumps out is the high rate of professed aggressive behavior, especially for insults. Twenty-seven percent of partisan

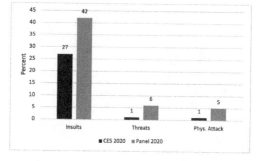

FIGURE 7.2. Self-reported aggressive political behavior among partisans. *Note*: 2020 Cooperative Election Study (CES) preelection survey (*N*=837 partisans), Wave 3 panel study (*N*= 2,188 partisans). Different question wordings.

respondents said they had insulted someone over politics in the Cooperative Congressional Election Study (CES) and 42 percent said the same in the panel study. Among them, most said they had done so only occasionally. Unsurprisingly, fewer said they had threatened someone because of the person's politics (1 percent and 6 percent), and similar numbers said they had been in a political confrontation that got physical at least once (1 percent and 5 percent).[6] Aggression rates were similar for Democrats and Republicans. Notably, victimization reports were much more prevalent than perpetrator reports from the same respondents. That is probably due to some perpetrators targeting multiple people, but people are also less likely to perceive their own behavior as aggressive compared with the same behavior by political opponents.

Aggression is also often reciprocal, and that holds true for political aggression in particular. We find that perpetrators often report being victims of aggression in the CES study, though we cannot tell whether they started the conflict or responded in kind. Seventy-seven percent of political insulters said they had been insulted compared with 38 percent of those who did not report insulting others. Forty-two percent of threateners said they were threatened, compared with 14 percent of nonthreateners. Finally, 38 percent of physically aggressive people in politics reported being physically attacked compared with 2 percent of those who didn't physically assault others over politics.[7] In general, partisan aggression seems to coincide with partisan victimhood.

Who do aggressive partisans target? Our panel study asked a follow-up question: whether their targets were "mostly regular people," "mostly famous people," or both. The answers are important given research that suggests most affective polarization (measured using feeling thermometers) is directed at opposing leaders and not average voters (Druckman and Levendusky 2019).

What did we find? Forty-two percent who acknowledged insulting people said they mostly targeted ordinary people, while 18 percent said they mostly targeted famous people. Forty percent said they targeted both groups. In other words, political aggression appears to be aimed more at ordinary people, even when famous targets are accessible on social media and via public information. In contrast with the findings on affective polarization, when we ask about abusive behavior, we see that people are more interested in targeting their fellow citizens.

Who Behaves Aggressively in Politics?

In chapter 6, we found several factors predicting support for partisan violence. As a reminder, we found that trait aggression and strong partisan social identification were potent predictors of violent partisan attitudes, along with hostile sexism. By contrast, education, age, sex, and racial resentment did not correspond with violent views after accounting for other explanations. Do those same patterns hold for aggressive political behavior?

We investigate this question using our panel study—the same data we used for our attitudes tests in chapter 6 for close comparison. Figure 7.3 shows the results of models predicting each form of political behavior. As a reminder, the results show the relationship of each factor with the outcome, after accounting for the influence of all the other factors.

The factors predicting aggressive political behavior look much the same as those predicting violent partisan attitudes. Trait aggression is far and away the strongest predictor of aggressive political behavior, as it was with violent partisan views. People who behave aggressively in everyday life behave more aggressively in the political domain too. For example, the most aggressive partisan is about 30 points more likely to insult someone than a nonaggressive partisan. Likewise, highly aggressive partisans are about 10 points more likely to threaten or physically attack other people because of politics, in comparison with nonaggressive partisans.

But even holding trait aggression constant, we again find a potent positive relationship between partisan social identity and all three aggressive behaviors. Those who are the most strongly attached to their party are

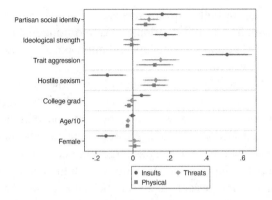

FIGURE 7.3. Predicting aggressive political behavior among partisans. *Note*: OLS régression with survey weights. All variables (except age) coded from 0 to 1 for ease of interpretation. *N*=2,187partisans. Outcomes measured in Wave 3. All predictors are from Wave 1 except hostile sexism (Wave 3). Full results in the online appendix. Error bars indicate 95 percent (thin) and 90 percent (thick) confidence intervals. Although our Wave 3 outcomes are binary, we estimate OLS models for easier interpretation. Results with probit models and CES 2020 replications are similar.

significantly more likely to insult, threaten, and physically attack people over politics.

Hostile sexism, interestingly, is related to more threats and physical aggression but less insulting behavior. As we note in chapter 6, the general relationship may be due to the high correlation between sexism and violence in American society—while insults are not as violent as threats and attacks. We leave it to future research to examine why that particular difference arises.[8] Overall, we find that self-reported aggressive political behavior and professed violent attitudes are associated with very similar traits—especially aggressive personality, strong partisanship, and hostile sexism.

Linking Violent Attitudes to Aggressive Behaviors

Given similar predictors, we expect to find a strong positive relationship between partisan violence and self-reported aggressive political behavior. A link from violent views to aggressive behavior would help to validate the importance of the violent views that we observe in our surveys.

Behaviorally aggressive partisans are *massively* more likely to hold violent partisan attitudes.[9] Figure 7.4 shows the relationships clearly. Americans who never insulted anyone over politics (darker gray bars) averaged a score of 0.04 on our 0–1 violent partisan attitudes index. Those who had insulted people (light gray bars) scored slightly higher, at 0.11. The gap is much larger when it comes to making threats—with scores ranging from 0.04 among those who never threaten anyone over politics to 0.44 among those who do. Endorsement of partisan violence is *ten* times higher for those who had threatened people over politics. The same chasm appears when comparing people who had and hadn't gotten into physical altercations over politics—a twelve-fold difference (0.04 versus 0.48).

In sum, a majority of Americans say they have been insulted because of politics, especially if they are politically active on social media. About 15 percent report being threatened because of their politics, and 5 percent say they have been physically attacked (as of October 2020). We also find substantial portions of Americans who report insulting others over politics (25 or 42 percent, depending on the measure and the date of the survey), and a small percentage who report threatening and physically attacking behaviors against political opponents (1–5 percent). Even the small percentages potentially represent the behaviors of hundreds of thousands—even millions—of Americans engaged in extreme political behavior that goes unnoticed in news and scholarship.

Partisan strength and trait aggression were strongly related to all three aggressive behaviors, as they were with violent partisan attitudes, and those violent attitudes were strongly related to aggressive political behavior. In sum, people who approve of partisan threats and violence are

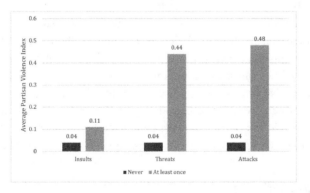

FIGURE 7.4. Relating aggressive political behavior and support for partisan violence. *Note*: Violent partisan attitudes (four items) coded 0–1. Wave 3 panel study. *N*=1813. All paired differences are statistically significant.

substantially more likely to insult opponents, threaten opponents, and even physically attack them.

Of course, anonymous self-reports could result in undercounts due to social desirability or even legal concerns, or they could include over-counts from unserious responses, but, as with most behavioral research, self-reports are a good place to start. One challenge with interpreting rare survey responses (e.g., threats, physical aggression) is that they could reflect mistaken clicks in online surveys or misreadings rather than real reports (Ansolabehere, Luks, and Schaffner 2015). But if self-reports of rare aggressive political behavior are just survey errors, they should have no relationship to the factors we tested. Instead, we find strong relation-ships, bolstering the validity of these reports. We go further in the next section with directly observed measures of aggressive political behavior.

Direct Measures of Partisan Aggression

Psychologists who study aggressive behavior face steep investigative chal-lenges, given the ethical problems from staging opportunities to observe physical aggression. (Mostly) gone are the days when Stanley Milgram led participants to believe they were administering potentially lethal electric shocks on others as the victims screamed. Instead, psychologists have de-veloped creative solutions for directly observing milder forms of physical harm in controlled settings.

One of the most common research designs for aggressive behavior to-day involves uncomfortable noise blasts—an extension of the Taylor Ag-gression Paradigm that originally used fake electrical shocks (Bond and Lader 1986; Bushman 1995; Taylor 1967). These methods give participants an opportunity to deliver painfully loud noise blasts to their lab opponents' ears or feed hot sauce to lab opponents who say they really can't handle spicy foods. No one is actually blasted or spiced, as participants are told in the debriefing, and the perceived harm meted out is mild enough not to deeply trouble the participant. We conducted two studies that employed variations on these aggression measures, aimed at ordinary partisans.

Painfully Loud

Our noise-blast tests appeared at the end of Wave 2 in our panel study (September 2019).[10] We explained to the national adult sample that we were planning a study on our university campuses that pitted Democrats and Republicans against each other in a game. Respondents were told that when a person lost a round, they would "get blasted with noise (a horn sound) for 5 seconds." They were further informed that "brief exposure to the higher noise levels will not cause any permanent injury, but it starts to get uncomfortable."

We asked half of our survey participants to assign noise levels for one pair of competitors in the upcoming study—one Democrat and one Republican. The other half was randomly assigned to choose the noise level for just one target, from one party or the other. Participants knew the *specific* noise level they chose would be administered to those individual targets, and not just an average noise level diluted across all such survey responses, which is critical for a valid measure of clear harm.[11]

The two-target design allows us to see if each person treats Democrats and Republicans differently (within-subjects), while the one-target design experimentally infers that any systematic differences across the entire sample that are correlated with partisanship are due to partisan bias (between-subjects design). Although we had some concern that a direct comparison might cause respondents to treat the parties equally because of social desirability, we need not have worried.

The noise scale was labeled in decibels, but we also provided descriptors for how participants would feel at each level and relatable examples of common noises at each level. The noise options ranged in increments of 10 decibels, from "70 (moderate—dishwasher)" to "130 decibels (painfully loud—jet engine)."[12] This design enabled us to observe the perceived application of physically uncomfortable stimuli against ordinary partisans within the context of a nationally representative survey—the first such test of which we are aware. Naturally, the indirectness of this aggression differs from in-person versions of the traditional Taylor paradigm, and that physical, social, and temporal distance may make aggressive responses more likely than in-person interactions.

The Direct Measure: Partisan Noise Blasts for Both Parties

First, we present the results of the two-target exercise, in which each respondent assigned a noise level to both a Democrat and a Republican. As we expected, partisans were significantly more likely to assign the maximum "painfully loud" option to the opposing party rather than to their own. On average, partisans assigned the most painful noise to their own party 2 percent of the time and assigned this painful noise to the opposing party 6 percent of the time—a statistically significant 4-point difference ($p<.001$). Figure 7.5 shows the full distribution of noise-blast responses by party. Republican and Democratic participants show the same partisan discrimination in meting out more painful noise at 130 decibels to the opposing party than to their own. We see some variation at the lower end of the spectrum, with Republicans somewhat more likely to assign the quietest sound to their fellow Republicans, while Democrats and Republicans are equally likely to assign that quietest sound to Democrats.

What types of partisans tended to hurt their opponents more with painful noise blasts? Figure 7.6 shows the factors that predict aggressive partisan bias. Overall, the predictors are weaker than for self-reported behaviors, but two main factors stand out here as they did with other radical outcomes: partisan social identity and trait aggression. The most

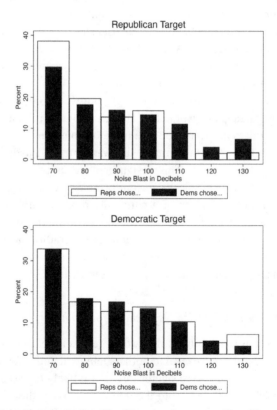

FIGURE 7.5. Noise blasts by partisanship of target and aggressor. *Note*: Wave 2 panel study. Half sample. Partisans only.

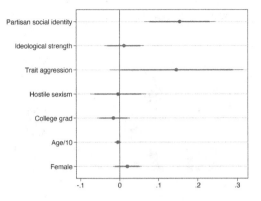

FIGURE 7.6. Predicting partisan bias in painful noise blasts. *Note*: Wave 2 panel study. Half sample. Partisans only. OLS regression with survey weights. All variables (except age) coded from 0 to 1 for ease of interpretation. N=2,187. All predictors are from Wave 1 except hostile sexism (Wave 3). Full results in the online appendix. Error bars indicate 95 percent (thin) and 90 percent (thick) confidence intervals.

strongly identified partisans (the half above the median in social identity) were especially likely to choose physical harm for their partisan opponents in comparison with weakly identified partisans. The difference is substantively similar for trait aggression but less precise, reaching only marginal significance (p<.10).

Validating Measures

The noise-blast measures also provide important observed behavioral validation for our four-item partisan violence index and our self-reported aggressive behavior items. First, the partisan violence scale significantly predicts more painful noise blasts toward opposing partisans. Among the roughly 80 percent of respondents who entirely rejected partisan violence, only 3 percent chose the painful option for opponents but not for their fellow partisans. Among the remaining fifth who express at least some openness to partisan violence, the number who chose to hurt the opposing partisan and not their own party member rose to 13 percent (p<.001).

In sum, the results from our nationally representative noise blast provide directly observed measures of physically aggressive behavior that disproportionately targets partisan opponents, all in the context of a survey. Although our design diverges from the in-person format of the traditional approach, our participants still made choices they expected would make an opposing partisan more physically uncomfortable than a person from their own party.

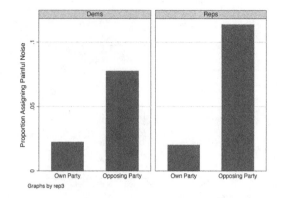

FIGURE 7.7. Effects of target partisanship on painful noise blasts (one-target experiment). *Note*: Wave 4 panel study, February 2021. Partisans only. *N*=1,420.

The Experiment: Partisan Noise Blasts for One Party

The one-target noise-blast experiment shows much the same. Respondents choosing the "painfully loud" option differed significantly depending on the partisanship of their target: 2 percent chose the "painfully loud" outcome for their own party member compared with 9 percent assigning noise levels for out-partisans ($p<.001$). The bias for Republican respondents was substantively larger (more than 9 percent) than for Democrats (more than 6 percent), but that 3-point difference was not statistically significant ($p=.11$). Figure 7.7 shows the proportions of partisans assigning painful noise to each group.

In contrast to the two-target tests, this rougher test did not yield any statistically significant differences for party social identity, trait aggression, or other factors. The impact of our partisan violence index was similarly insignificant. We expect that this is because the two-target (within-subjects) design is more statistically efficient than the between-subjects design.

Perpetrators in Real-World Violent Attacks

Each of our measures and tests for mild and moderate aggressive political behavior is revealing, but we recognize they do not directly capture the kinds of rarer, more extreme behaviors Americans are most worried about. We are not well equipped to analyze violent political crimes with individual-level observations (we don't expect to find many militia members taking online political surveys), so we summarize the work of other scholars here to provide some context.

The United States is experiencing a swift rise in the number of far-right terrorist attacks and plots. According to a June 2020 report by the Center for Strategic and International Studies, "right-wing attacks and plots account for the majority of all terrorist incidents in the United States since 1994, and the total number of right-wing attacks and plots has grown significantly during the past six years. Right-wing extremists perpetrated two-thirds of the attacks and plots in the United States in 2019 and over 90 percent between January 1 and May 8, 2020" (CSIS 2021). These numbers do not include hate crimes, which are also on the rise predominantly among right-wing and white supremacist perpetrators. A 2019 FBI report found hate crimes in the US at a sixteen-year high in the year 2018 (FBI 2019). They also found that hate crimes involving vandalism declined, while hate crimes involving physical assault increased.

What about the participants in the 2021 US Capitol insurrection in particular? The political scientist Robert Pape (2021; Pape and Ruby 2021) analyzed the 377 people arrested for that violent attack in the first three months after.[13] He found most were middle-class, middle-aged white men who had no known ties to right-wing extremist groups already linked to violence. Only about one in ten had militia ties, though an NPR report found that 14 percent were current or former members of the US military or law enforcement.[14]

In other words, most resembled ordinary Trump supporters, which Pape interprets as a dangerous sign for the future—a normalization of radicalism. Those profiles contrast with those arrested for right-wing violence in the past, nearly half of whom were affiliated with supremacist gangs or far-right militias. Likewise, only 9 percent of January 6 arrestees were unemployed and two-thirds were over thirty-five, in contrast with past attackers, one-quarter of whom were unemployed with over 60 percent under thirty years old. Forty percent held white-collar jobs. Notably, however, past and present right-wing profiles were almost entirely white and male.

The predominance of men in the Capitol attack (85 percent) reflects men's general propensity to commit violent crimes. For example, in 2012, 74 percent of people arrested for any crime were men, 80 percent arrested for violent crimes were men, and 89 percent of people arrested for murder were men (FBI 2013). The predominant whiteness of the insurrectionists

(95 percent) is lopsided like Republican voters (82 percent), but even more so, and men of all races and ethnicities tend to vote more Republican than the women in each group.[15]

Finally, on geography, Pape found that about half of arrestees from the Capitol attack were from counties where Biden outpolled Trump, including some of the largest metropolitan areas, which have large numbers of Trump voters, even if they are far outnumbered by Biden voters. Neighborhood-based partisan segregation could still play a role in those places (Brown and Enos 2021), and their social circles might be echo chambers, but the attackers' broader communities were not overwhelming Trump bastions—far from it. Like their other traits, their geographic origins were similar to most Americans.' Importantly, Pape finds insurrectionists were more likely to come from counties where white populations are shrinking in comparison with the number of nonwhite residents, which could trigger racial threat for those who dread that change (Bai and Federico 2020; Craig and Richeson 2014b).

How do these characteristics fit with the risk factors for aggressive political behavior and violent partisan attitudes we identified above? Of course, partisans' violent acts suggest they probably hold tolerant attitudes toward violence. And we can safely assume most insurrectionists held strong personal attachments to the Republican Party's titular head, Donald Trump, even if their relationship with the leaders of other factions in the party were strained. Big parties are always factional, which adds interesting nuances to our general party focus. Elsewhere, we have written on how partisan hatred can be directed at in-party leaders who appear disloyal to the party (Mason and Kalmoe 2018), as many of the insurrectionists felt toward Vice President Pence that day for not working to overturn the election.

Trait aggression is harder to judge from afar. Young, less educated men tend to be slightly higher in aggressive personality than others—especially in terms of physical aggression—but not as much as many people may guess (Kalmoe 2015). Their political violence probably corresponds with more general aggressiveness, but we can't know that for sure, and inferring it from their specific aggressive political acts seems too tautological.

Finally, their older age continues to stand out compared with our estimates of both mild aggressive behavior and past criminological studies. An NPR report found that most are charged with breaching the Capitol building rather than individual violent acts, which may reduce the role of factors that normally predict violent behavior. The one in six individually charged with a violent crime were somewhat younger than the rest, by our quick calculations—thirty-seven years old for those who were charged with violence versus forty-two years for the other arrestees. All of those arrested for violence to date appeared to be men by name and photo.[16]

Our brief consideration of recent political violence highlights the real-world challenges of predicting it: the strongest motivators of aggressive political behavior are unknown for most people outside a survey. However, some signs may serve as proxies for the factors we identified. Strong political commitments are often visible with signs, bumper stickers, social media posts, and other comments, but plenty of nonviolent people use those. Political expressions that indicate support for violence are especially worrisome. And political activism in combination with a criminal record of violent felonies or misdemeanors may be the most volatile mix. To our knowledge, no researchers have systematically examined the criminal records of the insurrectionists for a test in this case.

Tens of millions of people fit the rough profiles of the Capitol insurrectionists, and only a tiny fraction of them acted, but it was enough to cause several deaths, pose mortal threats to lawmakers, and create existential challenges for American democracy. This is one of many reasons why we believe documenting violent partisanship in the public is so important—to discern who and how many are likely to take further steps to violent intention and then action. Violent partisan attitudes measure risk for aggressive and violent individual partisan behavior, but aggregate levels in representative surveys seem to serve as a useful national barometer for mass political risks of violence as well.

Conclusions

In this chapter, we moved from violent partisan views to aggressive partisan behavior—from attitudes to actions. Hostile partisan views are not just extreme expressions of general partisan dislike. Instead, they motivate real-world behavioral aggression in verbal and physical forms. These are mundane (but still serious) forms of interpersonal behavior that are surprisingly prevalent. People who would never pick up a gun to kill their opponents today are much more willing to take mild actions that physically hurt opposing partisans. These aggressive behaviors may not attract as much attention as shootings or bombings, but their relative commonality greatly expands their impact.

Overall, we provided a look at how much aggressive political behavior exists in our politics today. Self-reports and observed aggression in our noise-blast tests show partisan-motivated physical aggression is generally confined to a small percentage of partisans, who nonetheless could represent hundreds of thousands or even millions of American partisans. The use of verbal political insults was quite common, however. The numbers who reported being victimized by aggressive political behavior were far higher than the numbers who reported being perpetrators. We also showed how politically aggressive behaviors are motivated by partisanship and that they often gain more impetus from violent partisan views, strong partisan identities, and aggressive personality traits—in addition to views about gender social hierarchy that have long been linked to violent behavior.

In the next chapter, we turn to the historical and political circumstances that lead Americans to express support for political violence. There, we find that Americans aren't pacifists when it comes to violence against government—under the right (or wrong) conditions, large majorities endorse mass political violence, at up to three times the number who say partisan violence is appropriate today.

CHAPTER EIGHT

Historical Precedents and Reasons for Violence

But when a long train of abuses and usurpations, pursuing invariably the same Object evinces a design to reduce them under absolute Despotism, it is their right, it is their duty, to throw off such Government, and to provide new Guards for their future security. — US Declaration of Independence (1776)

If we don't do something real soon, I think you'll have to agree that we're going to be forced either to use the ballot or the bullet. It's one or the other in 1964. It isn't that time is running out—time has run out! . . . If we don't cast a ballot, it's going to end up in a situation where we're going to have to cast a bullet. It's either a ballot or a bullet. — Malcolm X, "The Ballot or the Bullet" (1964)

A small but substantial minority of Americans believe violence against their opponents is appropriate today. Does that mean the vast majority *always* oppose political violence, or is their opposition conditional? What about support for widely celebrated mass violence, like the American Revolution, or responses to abusive conditions common in rationales for political violence, like those cited by the Declaration or Malcolm X? In this chapter, we examine the political conditions—historical and hypothetical—under which Americans consider political violence to be legitimate. Put differently, does 16 percent support for partisan violence ever grow to 76 percent? (It does.)

Answering these questions places today's violent partisan views in context by identifying circumstances that win substantially greater support for violence. It also shows the latent potential for substantial growth in violence among Americans today, as it often grew in our national past. But instead of interpreting these views as principles that citizens consistently apply to evaluate the political world, we see these attitudes primarily as socially constructed products of political culture. Most people follow cues from trusted others about how to think about politics. In this case, they learn which violence is acceptable from leaders and peer groups on the basis of national and partisan identities, among others.

We begin with public views of historical political violence in two national surveys. Next, we examine the conditions that legitimize violence according to these respondents. Finally, we consider the justifications ordinary Americans give for political violence in their own words. Each element substantially contextualizes and clarifies our main findings on violent partisan views today.

Endorsing Historical Violence: Four Cases

No American event looms larger in public consciousness than our violent origin story—the Revolutionary War. The national founders aired their colonial grievances against the British monarchy and declared their national independence for the stated purpose of establishing a limited form of what we now call liberal democracy: "We hold these truths to be self-evident, that all men are created equal, that they are endowed by their Creator with certain unalienable Rights, that among these are Life, Liberty and the pursuit of Happiness.—That to secure these rights, Governments are instituted among Men, deriving their just powers from the consent of the governed."[1]

What the founders created with violence was more democratic than most governments at the time, though not recognizable as democracy in a modern sense, with only about 6 percent of the population eligible to vote and enslaved Black Americans composing 18 percent of the nation.[2] Nonetheless, the principled claims provided an air of moral righteousness to their efforts, and those claims provided later generations of democratizers with vital rhetorical firepower justifying violence, citing founding principles. The Revolutionary War was also a form of partisan warfare between Whig Patriots and Tory Loyalists, as we described in chapter 2. What does the public think about the American Revolution's violence today?

Our expectations should be set by the reality that few prominent politicians would dare to publicly criticize the American Revolution, and they pledge allegiance to the founding documents that rationalize that violence. Politicians don't oppose it, of course, because our broader political culture generally reveres this violence (no pun intended).[3] As a result, we expect to see that the American Revolution generates the most public support for political violence. And that's exactly what we see.

In our 2020 election study, we asked a nationally representative sample of one thousand Americans, "Was it OK in the 1700s for American colonists to fight a war against the British government for independence, to begin establishing a more democratic government?" Seventy-six percent said that violence was definitely or probably appropriate (41 percent and 35 percent, respectively), and 18 percent said it was probably not OK. Only 6 percent of respondents said, "Definitely not." Here, we see an inversion of violence views compared with our questions about modern partisan violence: the percentage that *rejects* the American Revolution's violence is similar in size to the number who *endorse* partisan violence today.

Support for American Revolution violence is relatively bipartisan, consistent with the national consensus: 78 percent for Democrats and 84 percent for Republicans. That makes sense given that the parties and the broader political culture generally send unified signals to the public on the subject. Even so, Republicans were more likely to *definitely* endorse that violence (58 percent) than Democrats (35 percent). Bigger gaps appear by race when comparing white Americans (81 percent definitely/probably) to Black Americans (61 percent) and other people of color (70 percent). We shouldn't be surprised that people from groups that were subjugated under the new American government are less sanguine about its revolutionary violence, despite strong national cultural pressures otherwise. Women, who similarly had few recognized political and legal rights until the twentieth century, are also less supportive of the Revolution's violence (68 percent) than men (85 percent), though women are generally less likely to support wars and other state violence (e.g., Kalmoe 2013).

The Confederate Rebellion

Our second historical case is the American Civil War, in which white Democrats in eleven Southern states rejected Republican Abraham Lincoln's presidential election because of his party's antislavery views, and they launched a failed rebellion against democracy that killed three-quarters of a million Americans. In contrast with the American Revolution, the rebellion has a far more mixed representation in political culture, with white Southerners as its strongest traditional advocates. Our question explicitly mentioned rejecting the election of an antislavery president.

In our 2020 survey, 37 percent endorsed the Southern rebellion's violence (15 percent definitely, 22 percent probably). One-third of Americans "definitely" opposed it, and another 30 percent said it was "probably not OK." Democrats were 24 points more likely to definitely *reject* that violence (43 percent) than Republicans (19 percent). Interestingly, white Southerners were no more likely to endorse the violence than other whites, with 39 percent of whites in support. By contrast, 79 percent of Black Americans opposed Confederate violence—an 18-point racial gap in opposition. These results by party and race may indicate a growing nationalization of Confederate support among bigoted white Americans (and particularly among Republicans). Women were more likely to choose one of the "probably" options than men, but their responses were not appreciably different as an average.

Twentieth-Century Political Violence

Next, we move to two cases of twentieth-century political violence, both far smaller in casualties than the prior ones, but still politically important: violence by Vietnam War protesters in the 1960s and 1970s, and the Oklahoma City bombing in 1995 by antigovernment white supremacists. We did not have space for these questions on our 2020 election survey, but we asked about them in a January 2020 survey with a nationally diverse sample of 1,982 American adults.[4]

American involvement in the Vietnam War began with bipartisan support among leaders and voters. Only a small group of Americans stood in opposition. Within a few years, however, most Democratic Party leaders had turned against the war, and their voters followed (Zaller 1992). Half a century later, a 23-point partisan divide over the war still remains (Rakich 2019). During the war, some fringe antiwar groups planned and carried out bombing attacks designed to hinder the war effort, usually meant to destroy unoccupied offices but still producing casualties. One such attack was the midnight bombing of an army research center in an academic building at the University of Wisconsin in 1970 that killed a graduate student. What do Americans think of those attacks today?

In stark contrast to the American Revolution and even the Southern rebellion, Americans strongly reject this antiwar violence, at rates similar to rejection of partisan violence today. With three response options, 10 percent of Americans said "yes," that violence was OK, 11 percent said "maybe," and 72 percent said "no," not OK. As with general war views,

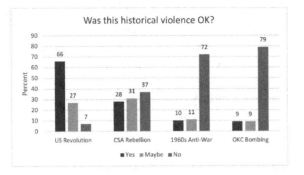

FIGURE 8.1. Support for historical political violence. *Note*: January 2020 Lucid survey.

Republicans were more likely to reject antiwar violence (79 percent) than Democrats (69 percent). Whites (79 percent) were more opposed to this violence than people of color (56 percent), and women were slightly more likely to reject this violence (74 percent) than men (70 percent).

Last, the Oklahoma City bombing in 1995 killed 168 people and destroyed a federal government building. Two white supremacists motivated by antigovernment fervor carried out the attack. This violence was far more recent than that of the other events. Over half of American adults today were adults then too, many with vivid memories of the attack and its aftermath. Once again, Americans broadly reject this violence, though perhaps not as much as we would expect. Only 9 percent say "yes" it was OK, 9 percent say "maybe," and 79 percent say "no," not OK. Despite the ideological valence of the attack, we find no partisan differences in rejection between Republicans (82 percent) and Democrats (79 percent) and only slightly larger rejection from women (81 percent) than men (76 percent). People of color took a more accepting view of this violence (62 percent said "no") than whites (86 percent).[5]

Figure 8.1 displays the results for all four historical violence questions in the Lucid survey. This summary shows the wide range in public support for political violence depending on the historical case.[6]

We draw a key lesson from these historical views: Americans *do* endorse political violence in some cases—they aren't absolute political pacifists—but not in others. Support and opposition to political violence is highly dependent on the political context. Opposition to American Revolutionary violence was under 10 percent, whereas opposition to twentieth-century terrorism by the Left and the Right hovered roughly around 75 percent, similar to levels in our questions about partisan violence today. Put differently, large majorities of Americans support the rebellious violence of the Revolution, even as large majorities reject partisan violence today. Of course, Americans aren't especially well versed in history, and so some of these historical attitudes may not be as grounded as they first appear, but they do show that Americans alter their views on violence depending on context.

Circumstances Legitimizing Violence

Political philosophers have long pointed to abuses against the governed as a motive for violent reaction, but more recent political theory suggests that popular sovereignty (the idea that the people are the source of all legitimate political power) is another essential pivot point between just and unjust political violence. Do ordinary Americans see it the same way?

We asked our January 2020 survey participants whether political violence would be appropriate under a range of scenarios including practices that prevent free and fair elections, deny equal rights, or undermine the rule of law, plus two policy conditions: banning guns and banning abortions. Table 8.1 gives the full question wording, and figure 8.2 shows the results.[7]

These results are especially notable because, stripped of historical cues, 40–50 percent of Americans regard violence as out of the question under

TABLE 8.1 **Question wording for political conditions legitimizing political violence**

No free elections	The government does not allow free elections for people to choose their leaders.
Unequal votes	Free elections are held, but some people's votes count more than others' in deciding the outcome.
Dangerous party	Free elections are held, but a party that some people think is dangerous to the country wins power.
Imprison critics	The government harasses and imprisons people who criticize the government's leaders.
Corrupt gov't	The government is corrupt—people get special treatment by giving leaders money.
Race/rel. discrim.	The government discriminates against citizens based on race and religion.
Lawless rulers	Leaders from the governing party disobey the laws while prosecuting their political opponents who do the same.
Ban guns	The government bans possession of all firearms, including rifles, shotguns, and handguns.
Ban abortion	The government bans all abortions for any reason, including life-threatening conditions for the mother.

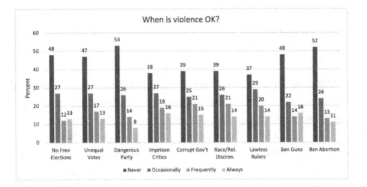

FIGURE 8.2. Political conditions legitimizing political violence. *Source*: Lucid January 2020 survey.

each of these extreme political circumstances. For them, even serious abuses against political opposition and social groups and the absence of elections do not justify violence. We know this isn't just pacifism, because only 7 percent of the same respondents said the violence of the American Revolution was not OK.[8] In other words, most who totally reject violence here did not reject violence for the Revolution. This reminds us of a common pattern in public opinion: most Americans depend on cues from political leaders, communities, and culture to figure out where they stand on political issues. Americans are told and taught that the American Revolution's violence was legitimate and that the Oklahoma City bombing was not. The political conditions alone are much harder for most people to evaluate when stripped of those contextual cues, except when those scenarios are a common trope in political rhetoric—for example, 23 percent of Republicans support violence if all guns are banned.

The range of responses across items is notably smaller here than in the historical cases above. Even so, we see two roughly distinct sets of support for political violence. About half of respondents say violence is at least occasionally OK in the first set of questions. That set includes questions about the absence of free elections, unequal votes, a dangerous party gaining power, and both policy conditions. Considered separately by party, Republicans were 5 points more likely to say violence was "always" OK in the absence of democratic elections (16 percent) compared with Democrats (11 percent), but Republicans were 7 points likelier to say "never" on violence when a "dangerous" party gets power. Republicans were also 13 points more likely than Democrats to answer "always" on violence for a gun ban (23 percent versus 10 percent). In contrast, Democrats were no more likely to answer "always" on the abortion ban than Republicans.

A second set of questions yields substantially more political-violence endorsement, with support levels closer to 60 percent on average (more than 10 points higher than the first set). These questions focus on imprisoning critics, government corruption leading to special favors, racial and religious discrimination, and government leaders who escape prosecution for crimes while prosecuting their opponents. The only item among these that had substantial partisan differences involved the lawless governing party, with Republicans "always" supporting violence (18 percent) at rates 6 points above Democrats (12 percent).

Comparing these two sets of responses, Americans in early 2020 saw more legitimacy for violence in response to government abuse than they did in response to threats to free and fair elections, by a margin of 10 points or more. We investigate this tendency further in chapter 9 by directly comparing perceptions of electoral integrity with support for partisan violence.

Legitimizing Violence in Their Own Words

In September 2019, we asked our panel, "Under what circumstances, if ever, would it be OK for Americans to use lethal violence against their government or against political opponents?" In contrast with most of our questions, this one was open-ended, allowing respondents to provide their own words and interpretations to the question. These items followed our partisan violence items, which may have influenced responses in ways that might help us better understand what people were thinking when they answered our closed-ended questions about violence. So what did they say?

Similar to our analysis above, roughly half rejected violence completely under any political circumstances they could imagine, with statements like "None. There are better ways to resist evil." A handful said only personal self-defense could legitimate violence: "It's never okay to use lethal violence unless in self-defense if there's a threat of personal harm."

Many respondents who did think violence might sometimes be justified referenced rights, the Constitution, and authoritarian abuses, resembling the categories above, which were asked in a different survey than this one. They said things like "if Constitutional rights are violated," "if they try to take our guns," "if an election is obviously rigged/stolen and the party which benefited from cheating refuses to investigate," "only if there was a coup," "if Trump loses the election and refuses to vacate the office," "only if they try to rule us like a dictator," "if they are Nazis or attempting to eradicate specific populations" (and so on). Very few sounded open to violence under circumstances we would associate with conventional democratic politics.[9]

Conclusions

The results in this chapter help to contextualize our survey responses about violence throughout the book. Our five-year data collection project is limited to that time and context. How do Americans think about political violence beyond our immediate context?

The evidence here shows that the public's views about political violence depend substantially on political contexts—and probably depend on opinion leadership about those scenarios. Large majorities endorse the political violence of the American Revolution, inverting support and opposition rates we see in our contemporary partisan violence questions. Far fewer condone other historical episodes of antigovernment violence, and that support varies by partisanship and by social positions like race and sex in each case. We also found differences in support for political violence in extreme hypothetical scenarios. When it comes to legitimating conditions for violence, Americans see rights-based grievances as more provocative than election-based violations when considering violence in both open- and closed-ended questions.

In mapping support for violence across scenarios, we do not mean to imply that most citizens are reasoning their way into or out of violence on the basis of principles. Instead, our evidence is consistent with our broader claims that widespread support for violence is primarily driven by opinion leaders nationally and locally. Majority support for the Revolution's violence, for example, probably reflects a political culture in which most mainstream politicians and local social networks celebrate that violence uncritically rather than using a reasoned evaluation of principles. That provides important clues for understanding the nature of violent views today.

We continue to investigate the effects of context and events in violent partisan views in chapter 9, with particular attention to the role of election campaigns, election results, and reactions to violence as potential radicalizing factors for the public's violent partisan attitudes.

CHAPTER NINE

Reactions to Election Losses and Violent Events

Where Joe Biden sees American darkness, we see American greatness. . . . The hard truth is . . . you won't be safe in Joe Biden's America. . . . The choice in this election is whether America remains America. — Vice President Mike Pence, 2020 Republican National Convention Speech

We are up BIG, but they are trying to steal the election. We will never let them do it. — President Donald Trump, tweet, November 3, 2020

Political-violence researchers often point to the importance of provocative events that spark broader conflicts in contentious times, as we noted in chapter 3. In extraordinary times, many people—even presidents— may feel compelled by circumstances to react with violence. Here, we test whether shocking political events during and immediately after the Trump presidency served as sparks that changed levels of radical American partisanship. We analyze the influence of two contexts in turn: (1) the effects of losing elections framed in apocalyptic and illegitimate terms (as in the quotes above), and (2) reactions to violent political events. Each holds the potential to radicalize partisans even further.

The first section considers the impact of losing elections on radical partisan views. Election losses cause great partisan anger, sadness, and fear—and loss *could* motivate attraction to conspiracy theories that explain away identity-threatening outcomes (e.g., Miller et al. 2016). Losses could directly enflame partisans on their own, but partisan leaders also serve as guides for their followers' reactions—ranging from grudging acceptance to open rebellion. We approach these questions several ways. First, we look at self-reports in which partisans express greater support for violence if they imagine the other party winning the next presidential election. Then we assess pre- and postelection change in radical attitudes on the basis of whether a person's party has gained or lost ground (and whether they are aware of that change). Finally, we test how views of election legitimacy in 2018 and 2020 affect the link between loss and radical partisan views. We expect election loss to radicalize people the most when joined by a belief that the election was illegitimate.

The second half of the chapter tests the effects of violent political events, which have the potential to spark cycles of violent retribution. First, we ask partisans directly how they would respond to violence by the other side. Next, we examine the change in radical views before and after violent attacks carried out in the middle of the 2018 election campaign. The events of that year create a natural experiment in the middle of our survey collection that enable us to test the effects of partisan terrorist attacks. Then, in a different direction, we test whether reminders of past political violence against partisan leaders change how American partisans think about radicalism. Public reactions to partisan violence in 2021 provide a final perspective on radical reactions to violence.

Together, these tests provide a clearer view of how radical partisanship changes (or doesn't) as political events alter the partisan context.[1] In that way, this chapter builds on the contextual evidence we presented in chapter 8, and the findings provide more clues about the roles party leaders play in enflaming or pacifying their followers, which we investigate further in chapter 10.

Winning and Losing Elections

Democracy depends on political elites and ordinary people having confidence in fair elections, especially so for the losers whose consent is the bedrock of stable democracy (Anderson et al. 2005; Przeworski 1991). Parties that lose a legitimate election are expected to accept the results, acquiesce to governance by the opposition, and turn their focus to winning the next election. Winners, for their part, are expected to respect the formal and informal limits on their power that might otherwise be used to gain unfair advantage in future elections. If this system breaks down, losers may turn to disruption or even violence to contest the result, and empowered winners may take authoritarian steps against their opponents or against electoral mechanisms to reduce the chance of losing future elections.

Electoral defeat is generally more provocative than electoral victory (Kaplan 1993; Scrivens 2020). The history of nineteenth-century racial-partisan violence in the US from chapter 2 suggests that whites who lost elections or status responded the most violently, though they remained violent even after reestablishing total white supremacy (Francis 2014). Radical political groups in the late twentieth century were more likely to use violence under a president who was hostile to the group's aims (Hewitt 2000). Barack Obama's 2008 presidential win spurred a rise in violent right-wing rhetoric and ultimately caused a resurgence in white supremacist terrorism (Sela, Kuflik, and Mesch 2012; Simi 2010). And reminders of shifting racial demographics are sufficient to spur whites who fear status loss to embrace white nationalism and even violence (Bai and Federico 2020; Craig and Richeson 2014a; Wetts and Willer 2018). However, winning can sometimes embolden voters, as evidenced by the increase in hate crimes by Trump supporters against minority groups in the aftermath of Trump's 2016 presidential victory (Edwards and Rushin 2018).

Election losses evoke strong partisan emotions because of the implications for national party status, while policy wins and losses have far more muted effects (Huddy, Mason, and Aarøe 2015). However, the strategic incentives for party elites to use inflammatory rhetoric and mobilize violent action are a bigger source of danger than direct individual reactions. Even when party leaders do not intend to cause violence, the rhetoric they use to mobilize nonviolent political action—vilification, threat, and apocalyptic stakes—serve as potent ingredients for violent attitudes, as we showed in chapter 4. These forms of moral disengagement make it easier for partisans to endorse—and carry out—violent acts. So how do ordinary partisans respond to electoral defeat?

Future Presidential Losses

Our most controlled method of assessing partisan reactions to election wins and losses involves asking respondents to imagine a future presidential election win or loss. In that way, we can uniformly test the effects of wins and losses for both parties—as long as the election outcome is uncertain enough to make either outcome plausible. We focus on the presidency as the most singularly powerful office in government. The downside of hypothetical question wording, of course, is that those designs lose some real-world validity owing to their artificial nature—partisans are

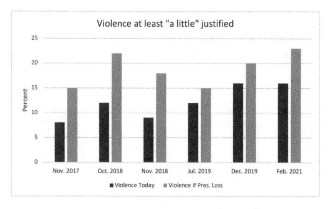

FIGURE 9.1. Observational tests of anticipated election loss legitimizing violence. *Note*: Partisans only. Results weighted. All paired differences are statistically significant. (Nov. 2017: *N*~780, Oct. 2018: *N*~815, Nov. 2018: *N*~689, July 2019: *N*~1814, Dec. 2019: *N*~4898, Feb. 2021: *N*~798). We find no significant differences by party in the gap between "violence today" and "violence given election loss."

imagining realistic circumstances but not experiencing them. We address that issue in the following section.

In every survey we've fielded asking about partisan violence, we've followed up the question about violence *today* with a question asking respondents their attitudes about violence conditional on the result of the next presidential election. In six surveys, we asked all respondents whether violence would be OK if the opposing party won the next presidential election. As we first indicated in chapter 4, people tend to be more accepting of violence when they imagine a future election loss, in comparison with when they are thinking about "today." Figure 9.1 shows consistently greater percentages endorsing violence at least "a little" in each survey when considering a presidential loss. Although the size of the difference varies from 3 to 10 percentage points, all the differences between "violence today" and "violence if your party loses the upcoming presidential election" are statistically significant.

In three other surveys, we randomized whether respondents were asked about their own party winning or losing the presidency in the next election. These comparisons are more direct tests of electoral effects than the observational comparisons above. Figure 9.2 shows those results. In each case, anticipating losses yields more violence endorsement than anticipating electoral victory, with effects ranging from 5 to 15 percentage points.[2]

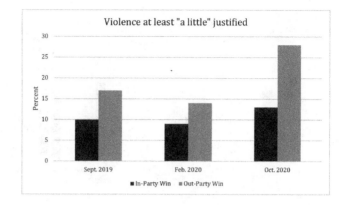

FIGURE 9.2. Experimental tests of anticipated election loss legitimizing violence. *Note*: Partisans only. Unweighted for the experiments. All paired differences are statistically significant. (Sept. 2019: *N*=1931, Feb. 2020: *N*~1813, Oct. 2020: *N*=836).

Finally, we test these election effects among panel respondents who randomly evaluated an in-party win in one survey wave and an out-party win in the other. Eighty-one percent gave the same response to both (almost all of those said "never"), while 16 percent indicated violence would be more appropriate if the other party wins than if their own party wins—a statistically significant increase.[3]

In sum, experimental, cross-sectional, and panel tests all show notable rises in support for partisan violence in the face of anticipated presidential loss. Of course, these are imagined scenarios rather than real reactions, and they may not correspond well with how people respond to real losses of political power. For that reason, we test reactions to actual transitions of partisan power next.

Losing Political Power

We expect to find that those who win power will be less inclined to violence than those who don't. The winners can change the law, and, if necessary, command the state's violent agents. For nearly all our time series, Republicans held total or near-total control of federal government, including Congress, the courts, and the presidency. Democrats gained control of the US House of Representatives in 2019 following the midterm elections, which allowed them to block Republican legislative efforts. However, Republican legislative action was minimal compared with unilateral presidential action, which minimized the substantive impact of that change. The 2020 elections saw Democrats win the presidency and a majority of the US Senate while retaining a House majority. The Republican supermajority controlling the Supreme Court and lower courts remained, however—a consequence of Republican court-packing combined with the Constitution's undemocratic Electoral College and the US Senate's lopsided overrepresentation of small, white, disproportionately Republican states.

For most of our series, Democrats and Republicans were indistinguishable in their support for violence today, as we showed in chapter 5 on radical trends. But when small gaps appeared during Trump's presidency (two of nine surveys), Democrats were slightly more approving of violence than Republicans (July 2019, September 2019). That could suggest partisan equality in violent views, or it could also reflect the influence of the power context at a time when Democrats were disempowered. We have only one data point after Democrats gained presidential and congressional power—February 2021. There we see the first clear partisan gaps in violent views, with Republicans substantially more violent than Democrats, by nearly 10 percentage points. That large shift provides real-world evidence that changes in presidential power affect which party holds more violent views.

We see a similar shift in moral-disengagement views: Republicans had been either equal with Democrats or slightly higher in moral-disengagement trends while in power. Those gaps were larger in February 2021: Republicans were 9 points higher than Democrats in seeing opponents as a national threat (77 percent of Republicans agreed), 14 points higher in thinking the other party is evil (67 percent of Republicans agreed), and 12 points higher on believing partisans on the other side behave like animals (33 percent of Republicans agreed). The growing gap was notable, given that Democrats also expressed more moral disengagement after the 2020 election—the Republican rise just outpaced theirs. Of course, rising perceptions among Democrats that Republicans are a national threat were arguably legitimate reactions to that party's election rejection and the Capitol attack.

More specifically, we can compare levels of support for violence after the presidential power transfer with the forecasts participants made, to see whether respondents' hypothetical responses matched their real-world reactions to loss. By the time the dust (and tear gas) settled after the inauguration, our February 2021 survey showed the same patterns our respondents forecast in the fall. In October 2020, 14 percent of Democrats said violence would be at least "a little" OK if Biden won the election, and in February 2021, 14 percent of Democrats said violence was OK today. Likewise, 18 percent of Republicans in October 2020 said violence would be OK if they lost the election, and in February 2021, 20 percent said violence was OK today.

Of course, by February 2021 a number of concurrent events had taken place beyond the presidential election outcome, and so we cannot definitively separate the effects of a shift in partisan presidential power from the effects of Trump's second impeachment, the January insurrection at the Capitol, and extremist rhetoric from Republicans generally.[4] Notably, the other peak in violent views occurred just before Trump was impeached and threatened with (unlikely) removal the first time. We await our next surveys to establish whether the notably greater Republican radicalism persists well into Biden's presidency or diminishes as the election, insurrection, and impeachment fade. In the meantime, we examine changes in violent views among individuals surveyed before and after the election, looking for diverging reactions by party.

Reactions to Partisan Power Shifts in Panel Survey Data

We can examine election panel surveys that allow us to directly measure individual-level change in radical partisan views before and immediately after elections. Our two election panels bookend the 2018 midterm election and 2020 presidential election, testing whether wins and losses changed radical partisan views. Naturally, we expect stronger reactions to presidential elections than to midterm elections (which generally receive less attention, and where victory can be a matter of interpretation). However, our postelection data in 2020 cover a period of time in which 61 percent of Republicans in our sample said Trump won and another 21 percent said they weren't sure who won (mid-November to early December). Only 17 percent of Republicans said Biden won at that time. Another caveat is that both of our postelection surveys occurred before the official power transfers, which could matter as well. Both factors make it harder to cleanly measure a potential loss effect, but we try nonetheless.[5]

Figure 9.3 shows results that offer mixed support for our expectations. Democrats reclaimed the majority in the US House of Representatives from Republicans in the 2018 midterms. Democratic power gains in 2018 did not clearly push Democrats and Republicans in opposite directions on violence immediately after the midterm election. In fact, any change seemed to move both parties in the same direction, if at all.

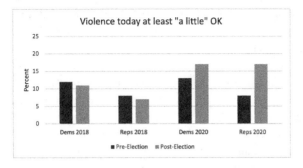

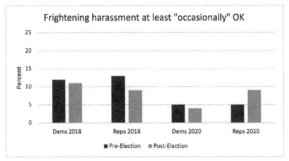

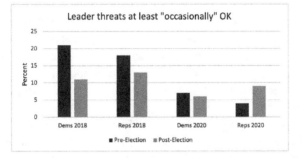

FIGURE 9.3. Support for partisan violence before and after the 2018 and 2020 election. *Note*: Includes only partisans who completed both surveys. 2018: *N*=685, 2020: *N*=752. Results weighted. Violence today: Republican rise in 2020 and Republican decline in 2018 are significant changes. Harassment: Republican decline in 2018 is marginally significant. Republican rise in 2020 is marginally significant. Leader threats: Democratic decline in 2020 is marginally significant. Republican rise in 2020 is significant. The 2018 Democratic and Republican decline is significant.

In 2018, Republican support for violence today and for frightening harassment against ordinary partisans declined slightly following the election result, while Democratic support held steady. Support for threatening opposing leaders fell substantially for both parties after the 2018 election, especially for Democrats. We discuss the elevated preelection levels of support for threats below in our analysis of partisan reactions to the violence that took place while that survey was in the field.

In our 2020 election panel, the figure shows that support for violence "today" rose in both parties after Biden won and Trump refused to accept the result, though only the 9-point rise for Republicans was statistically significant. Democrats showed a marginally significant decline in support for leader threats and no change in citizen harassment while Republican support for those things rose significantly by 5 and 4 points, respectively.

Overall, we conclude that election context affects whether election outcomes drive change in radical partisan views. The observations most consistent with our expectations occurred around the 2020 presidential election, with losses by Republicans leading to sharp rises in violent and threatening views. Not only was this a more intensely watched contest, but it was also a different time in the country. This demonstrates the difficulty in analyzing election effects during a mess of radical events. We will take on those other radical events below.

Election Legitimacy Beliefs and Violent Views

Losing an election is one thing. Losing because of election fraud is another. Violence is more likely in places where elections are illegitimate (or absent altogether), as one of democracy's main functions is to limit political unrest. Consequently, we expect doubts about election legitimacy (whether true or not) will produce more support for political violence, consistent with recent cross-national research (Dyrstad and Hillesund 2020). However, many people may believe elections are wholly corrupt and still view violent measures as beyond the pale, or they may acknowledge the fairness of elections but still endorse violence for partisan advantage or vengeance. Here, we assess the relationship between beliefs about election legitimacy and radical partisan views.

False beliefs about election fraud are common, especially among election losers (Miller, Saunders, and Farhart 2016; Sinclair, Smith, and Tucker 2018), and general conspiratorial beliefs correspond with more violent political attitudes (Uscinski and Parent 2014). What's different recently is that the Republican Party—and President Trump in particular—loudly, consistently, and baselessly claimed fraud to explain every electoral loss in 2016, 2018, and 2020, leading ordinary Republicans to follow their leaders in believing the lies. In fact, the "Stop the Steal" slogan used by Trump supporters in 2020 had been coined by Trump ally Roger Stone's political action committee in 2016—in anticipation of a Trump loss that never occurred.[6] As a result, the level of election distrust among Republicans in 2020 far surpassed previous years. Those inciting words led to violence by Republican followers who believed their leaders' carefully crafted lies.

Here, we investigate the legitimacy-violence relationship more systematically in the general public with our 2020 election survey. In anticipation of Trump's delegitimizing efforts, our 2020 election study focused almost exclusively on election rejection and violence in both waves before and after the vote. Overall, we find that the specific belief that the opposing party would (or did) cheat in the 2020 presidential election strongly and consistently predicted specific forms of violent resistance against the other party's (re)elected president. Let's take a look at those results in detail.

Our Methods

We measured specific views on 2020 election cheating before and after the vote by asking, "Do you think either party [will try to cheat/cheated in trying] to win the presidential election?" with yes/no responses for each. We focus on views of the opposing party. In October 2020, 80 percent of Democrats and 73 percent of Republicans said "yes," that they believed the other party would try to cheat in the imminent election.

Beyond our usual violence questions, we also asked a range of election-rejection questions in case the opposing party wins. These were hypothetical before the election. When repeated only for Republicans after the election, the questions were no longer hypothetical. Three of these were violent: "if [own-party candidate[7]] loses the election," should: "the military stage a coup to overthrow the president by force?" "governors call up their state's National Guard troops to resist federal orders?" or "citizens prepare weapons to resist the federal government in their communities?" We asked each question on a 4-point scale from "definitely yes" to "definitely not." In the postelection survey, we asked the same questions, only of Republicans, starting with the preamble "After the presidential inauguration in January . . ." Notably, these questions include partisan violence carried out by government officials too, and not just citizens. Figure 9.4 shows the distribution of individual responses.[8]

Across both parties, support for military coups, governors' resisting federal orders, and citizens' using weapons to resist the federal government was generally low, but not nearly as low as we would have hoped.

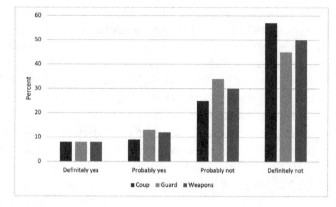

FIGURE 9.4. Support for specific partisan violence if one's own party loses. *Note*: October 2020 survey. Results weighted. Partisans only.

About 17 percent of partisans thought that a military coup was probably or definitely necessary if their party lost the presidential election. About 21 percent believed that their governor should probably or definitely call up the National Guard to resist the federal government, and about 20 percent probably or definitely approved of armed rebellion by citizens. Overall, about a fifth of American partisans were ready for a full-blown violent rebellion against the newly elected president and his government.

Finally, using the same response scale, we asked everyone in the 2020 postelection survey, "Should military and law-enforcement officials side with [own-party candidate] to make sure he is sworn in as president in January?" Ninety percent of Democrats said "definitely" or "probably" yes, as they should with a legitimately elected president. But 48 percent of Republicans said the military and law enforcement should unlawfully install Trump as president instead.

Legitimacy-Violence Relationships

To test the relationships between violent attitudes and perceptions of election legitimacy, we take the average of three of our standard violence items—harassing regular partisans on the internet, threatening leaders, and approving of violence today—creating an "index" of the three items. We call this the partisan violence index. We do the same with the three violent "election rejection" items—approval of a military coup, a governor's use of the national guard, and an armed citizen insurrection. We call this the specific violence index. We also look at the familiar item about violence in the case of losing the next election and perceptions about the other party cheating. Table 9.1 shows the basic two-way correlations between beliefs about cheating and violent partisan views.

In the month before the 2020 election, the belief that one's partisan opponents would cheat in the upcoming election was not significantly related to our three-item partisan violence index. It was, however, related to support for violence if the other party were to win the upcoming presidential election. In other words, the belief that the other party will cheat is not related to violence today—but it is related to violence if the cheating successfully ensures the cheater's victory. Furthermore, the worry about partisan cheating before the election is significantly related to support for military coups, governors' rejecting federal election outcomes, and armed citizen rebellion (the specific violence index) in both parties.

After the election, we see some relationship between the idea that the other party had cheated in the election and our three-item partisan violence index. This is different from what we saw in the preelection survey. Once the election is over, a sense that the other party cheated is related to support for threats to citizens and leaders, as well as partisan violence in general. Furthermore, for Republicans who believed that Joe Biden won the presidential election because Democrats cheated, we see an increase in the specific violence index—support for military coups, governors' rejecting federal election outcomes, and armed citizen rebellion.

What do these results mean substantively? Three examples illustrate the pattern. Twenty-nine percent of partisans who expected opponents to cheat in the 2020 presidential election endorsed general violence in the case of a presidential loss, compared with 19 percent who didn't expect

TABLE 9.1 **Relationships between election confidence and violent partisan views**

	2020 presidential election		
Preelection	Partisan violence index (3)	2020 Pres. loss violence item	Specific violence index
Opponents will cheat	−.05	**.13***	**.22***
Postelection	Partisan violence index (3)		Specific violence index (GOP only)
Opponents cheated	**.07^**		**.16***

Note: Pearson's *r*. Bolded items are consistent with our expectations. * *p*<.05, ^ *p*<.10 (two-sided)

cheating—a difference of 10 percentage points. Second, 22 percent of partisans who expected cheating endorsed an armed citizen insurrection, compared with 13 percent who didn't expect cheating. Finally, after the election, 10 percent of Republicans who thought Democrats cheated endorsed a military coup to keep Trump in power, compared with half that number among those who didn't believe Democrats cheated.

The implications from these tests go beyond the simple legitimacy-violence relationship. Here, we found that specific partisan violence items performed consistently better than three of our general partisan violence items that guide much of the book. Both are substantially correlated, yet the analytical distinctions point to the importance of fielding questions at varying levels of specificity. Notably, our fourth "general" item focused on hypothetical 2020 presidential election loss performed similarly to the specific violence items, though not quite as strongly. Practically speaking, scholars and practitioners should monitor both general and specific violent partisan attitudes to assess contemporary threats—both are valuable, with general violent views sounding warnings for larger shifts on specific violence.

Effects of Violence Targeting Partisans

Perhaps nothing is more radicalizing than exposure to violence (Bliuc et al. 2019; Getmansky and Zeitzoff 2014; Kaakinen, Oksanen, and Räsänen 2018; Lyall, Blair, and Imai 2013), and US politics have grown more violent. Likewise, psychological and sociological research shows that interpersonal aggression is usually a response to some perceived or real provocation (Anderson and Bushman 2002), and targeted violence is the most intense form of political provocation. Victimization seemingly legitimates retaliation—a pattern researchers have also found in the psychology of violent white supremacists.[9] But these comparisons may seem ill-suited to our focus on the public in general. How do ordinary partisans respond to violence targeting partisans?

Do violent attacks increase desire for retribution among the targeted party? Do copartisans of the attacker see violence as more legitimate? Or does the reality of political violence cause partisans on both sides to retreat and reject violence? The answers are critical for understanding how increasing violence will affect the public and whether America is at risk for spiraling cycles of violence.

We begin to find answers with three kinds of evidence: (1) asking partisans directly about support for violence as a response to violence by the other side, (2) a natural experiment analyzing violent responses to partisan mail bombs and a hate crime shooting during one week of the 2018 midterm campaign, and (3) experimental reminders of gun violence targeting partisans in the past. Of course, we have already identified more support for partisan violence in February 2021, following the Capitol attack, though that comparison is conflated with many other events, making it less clear cut than we would prefer.

Direct Questions and Perceptions of Violence

The most direct way to test how partisan violence changes views about partisan violence is simply to ask. The pro-democracy survey organization Bright Line Watch (BLW) conducted a survey in October 2020 that included our four familiar threat and violence items, plus a fifth: what if the opposing party engages in violence? About 15 percent of partisans in their survey chose something other than "never" for the "violence today" item, rising to 25 percent if the opposing party wins, and jumping to 41 percent if the other party uses violence. In short, the number of partisans open to violence leaps dramatically in response to a hypothetical violent provocation.

We repeated the Bright Line Watch question in our 2020 postelection survey. Recall that our "violence today" question in that survey found 17 percent of both parties endorsing violence at least "a little." In comparison, 39 percent of Democrats and 48 percent of Republicans endorsed violence if the other side was violent first, and that partisan difference is statistically significant. This direct-ask approach probably demonstrates the clearest effect of reactionary violence, though it has the disadvantage of being a hypothetical scenario.

Reactions to Violent Partisan Events

Unfortunately, we happened to find unusually relevant real-world circumstances for testing the effects of partisan violence on support for partisan violence, in the form of a natural experiment. Sixteen mail bombs targeting Democrats and mainstream media figures were discovered between October 22 and November 1, 2018, during the 2018 midterm election campaign. The bombs were sent by an obsessive Trump supporter, and the targets included Barack Obama, Joe Biden, and Hillary Clinton among several others. Luckily, none of the bombs detonated, and so there were no casualties. Then, in the same week, a shooter (motivated by

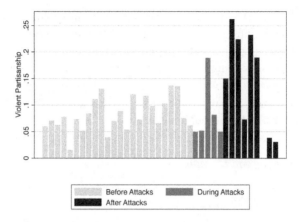

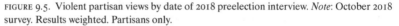

FIGURE 9.5. Violent partisan views by date of 2018 preelection interview. *Note*: October 2018 survey. Results weighted. Partisans only.

anti-Semitic conspiracy theories commonly promoted by Fox News and President Trump) killed eleven worshippers at a synagogue in Pittsburgh. In other words, two major partisan-linked terrorist attacks took place in the same week.

The attacks occurred in the middle of our preelection midterm survey. Eighty percent of our responses came before the news of the first mail bomb broke late on October 22. Eleven percent of our responses came during the time between that date and the synagogue shooting, and we collected 9 percent of our responses after the shooting. That distribution gives us an opportunity to test how these violent events affected violent partisan attitudes.[10]

Figure 9.5 illustrates the weighted means for our four-item partisan violence index as a function of the date of the interview, grouped by the time before, during, and after the attacks.[11] Violent partisan views before and during the week of the bomb attacks appear relatively stable or rising slightly. The week the bombs were discovered was back to the slightly elevated level. The three days immediately following the synagogue shooting mark some of the highest levels of violence support that we record (three of the top seven recorded rates). Notably, the highest approval of violence by far is two days after the synagogue shooting.

The days immediately after the synagogue shooting saw a 5-point rise in violent views on average, which is two to three times greater than the baseline level immediately before. However, that spike diminishes quickly over subsequent days. This is an important point. Support for partisan violence increases in the immediate aftermath of partisan terrorist attacks—but also has a very rapid decay rate. This is both disturbing and reassuring information—violence does beget violence but only for a short period of time.

We certainly do not wish to overclaim. There are clear trends here toward violent attitudes after violent events. We consider the evidence *suggestive* of inflammatory reactions to real-world partisan violence, not decisive. However, it does fit with our direct questions about violence in reaction to violence, and it is consistent with other research finding inflammatory effects from violence in other contexts.

This pattern of initially violent responses followed by declines also fits with polling data in the aftermath of the 2021 Capitol attack. A survey by YouGov in the evening after the attack showed 45 percent of Republicans supported the attack. Polling a few weeks later showed Republican support for the attack had declined to about 15 percent, similar to our measure of partisan violence "today." There are many reasons why initial Republican support may have declined, including learning more about the seriousness of the attack and hearing some Republican leaders denounce the attack. However, it is also consistent with an initial rise in support for violence immediately following an attack.

Reminders of Past Partisan Violence

Finally, we consider how reminders of past violence targeting partisans affects radical views. In January 2011, Democratic US representative Gabby Giffords was shot in the head at a meet-and-greet event in her Tucson, Arizona, district. The shooter killed five attendees, including a federal judge, and fourteen constituents were injured. Giffords barely recovered, and with substantial disability. The shooting was not apparently motivated by partisanship, but it spurred a heated debate about the role of violent rhetoric in politics. Gifford's district had been included in a Republican electoral map shared widely that put gunsights over the places Republicans wanted to "target" in the 2010 midterm election. Tea Party rhetoric against health care during the eighteen months before the election was unusually extreme, including veiled threats of political violence if Republicans didn't get their way (i.e., "Second Amendment remedies").[12]

Six years later, a gunman approached a baseball practice in Alexandria, Virginia, where Republican members of Congress were preparing for their annual charity baseball game. The gunman—who had a history of domestic violence—opened fire with an assault rifle, critically wounding two, including Louisiana congressman Steve Scalise, and injuring two others. Police killed the gunman when they arrived on the scene. That attack *was* apparently motivated by partisan animus against Republicans—as the shooter had worked on Bernie Sanders's 2016 Democratic primary campaign and had made public statements critical of Donald Trump and Republicans.

The stark realities of violence might not be foremost in people's minds when we ask them questions about partisan violence. What happens when we remind them of specific recent acts of violence against partisan leaders? We embedded a randomized experiment in our 2017 election survey, just five months after the Scalise shooting. One-third of respondents read a brief description of the Gifford's shooting, one-third read a description of the Scalise shooting, and one-third saw no reference to partisan shootings. Both shooting statements indicated the victim's party.[13]

Our first purpose was to examine direct responses to the partisan shootings. In both shooting conditions, we asked, "Thinking back on that event, how do you feel about it?" Participants chose from a 5-point response scale, from "very negative" to "very positive." The answers largely resemble the responses we get when we ask about rejecting general partisan violence. Roughly 80 percent of respondents described one or the other shooting as "very bad." But, as we anticipated, the target's partisanship made a substantial difference in reactions to real shootings of partisan leaders.

Figure 9.6 shows the differences. Democrats were 9 points more likely to describe the Democrat Gabby Giffords's shooting as "very bad" compared with the Republican Steve Scalise's shooting, and Republicans were 10 points more likely to see Scalise's shooting as worse than Giffords's. The difference for Democrats was statistically significant, and the difference for Republicans was marginally significant.

Our second goal was to test whether reminders of actual shootings of partisan leaders changed how Americans thought about violent partisanship. We tested the effects of *any* reminders of partisan shootings on responses to our four-item partisan violence index. Democrats were no more or less likely to endorse partisan violence when hearing about either shooting compared with no text. Republicans, on the other hand, were significantly more likely to endorse partisan violence when hearing about shooting attacks on leaders in either party.[14] Diminishing sample

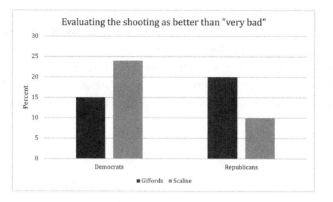

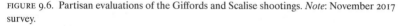

FIGURE 9.6. Partisan evaluations of the Giffords and Scalise shootings. *Note*: November 2017 survey.

sizes prevented a test for differences dependent on the partisan identity of the target. From these experimental tests, we conclude that exposure to violence is enflaming to some—consistent with our expectations. Why we did not find the same reaction from both parties in this final test is unclear. It may simply be that the Scalise shooting was more recent in time and therefore still a radicalizing memory for Republicans.

Conclusions

In this chapter, we considered how regular events like election losses and rare events like violent attacks affect public support for partisan violence. We also tested how beliefs about election legitimacy affect support for partisan violence. These results help us understand how and when changing circumstances might spur more radical partisanship in the public, especially when egged on by political leaders. Consistent with the cross-national research we reviewed in chapter 2, our evidence from American radical partisan attitudes suggests that partisan conflict around elections and immediately after violent partisan attacks poses greater threats for violent partisan behavior than previously thought (e.g., Harish and Little 2017; Lyall, Blair, and Imai 2013; Wilkinson 2004). The changes we observed in violent and inflammatory views occur among large swaths of the partisan public and not just among a handful of extremists.

Overall, we conclude that baseline levels of radical mass partisanship are sensitive to changing political circumstances. Although we posit a substantial role for political leaders in these effects, our evidence also shows violent reactions among partisans even in the absence of enflaming leadership. Our next chapter more directly tests the effects of leaders' messages on radical partisan attitudes. How does their rhetoric fan or douse the partisan flames?

PART III

Communicating Radicalism

CHAPTER TEN

Words Matter

And we fight. We fight like hell. And if you don't fight like hell, you're not going to have a country anymore. . . . So we're going to, we're going to walk down Pennsylvania Avenue. I love Pennsylvania Avenue. And we're going to the Capitol, and we're going to try and give . . . our Republicans, the weak ones because the strong ones don't need any of our help. We're going to try and give them the kind of pride and boldness that they need to take back our country. So let's walk down Pennsylvania Avenue. — President Donald Trump, speech to supporters at the White House, 1:10 p.m. ET, January 6, 2021

Insurgent words turn into violent acts—on the steps of the Reichstag, and now in the #Capitol. — German foreign minister Heiko Maas, 2:30 p.m. ET, January 6, 2021[1]

The words of a president matter, no matter how good or bad that president. At their best, the words of a president can inspire. At their worst, they can incite. — President-Elect Joe Biden, televised speech during the Capitol attack, 4:05 p.m. ET, January 6, 2021

Trump's brazen language was always intended to provoke. As the 2020 election approached, the president's routinely aggressive rhetoric grew even more belligerent. He threatened violence against Americans demonstrating peacefully for racial justice and police reform, he encouraged violence against protesters by police, and his subordinates ordered unidentified federal security forces to violently clear protesters so the president could stage a photo op (Chappell 2020). One news organization found fifty-four distinct criminal cases in 2020 in which Trump himself was directly invoked by citizens criminally charged with political violence (Levine 2020). In September 2020, Trump declined to promise a peaceful transfer of power in the case of his electoral loss, and during the first presidential debate, he declined to condemn right-wing violence, telling the Proud Boys right-wing militia to "stand back and stand by" instead.[2]

Then Trump called on thousands of his supporters to gather at the White House on January 6, 2021, in Washington, DC, to oppose the 2020 election result. It was the day when Congress would officially recognize Joe Biden's election victory at the US Capitol just down the road. Few serious people doubt that Trump's violent antielection rhetoric directly caused the violent attack on the Capitol that day. Inciting the insurrection was what the US House of Representatives impeached him for (the second time). Even Republican Senate minority leader Mitch McConnell did not dispute Trump's responsibility for the illegitimate violence: "The mob was fed lies. They were provoked by the president and other powerful people, and they tried to use fear and violence to stop a specific proceeding of the first branch of the federal government which they did not like."

We see no need to relitigate Trump's effects on inciting that violent behavior—his effect is obvious. However, we remain interested in the broader role elite messages play in the public's radical partisan attitudes and the extent to which we can *directly* measure those effects on attitudes. That is the focus of our final empirical chapter here. How do Trump's inflammatory messages affect support for partisan violence and radical partisanship among ordinary people? And, if he chose to break character with pacifying rhetoric, would his followers respond? What about potential effects from Joe Biden's rhetoric or exposure to inflammatory partisan media?

Here, we begin to unpack the role of opinion leadership in a more targeted way, with experimental exposure to specific messages, along with more cumulative observational tests from surveys that include self-reported media use. Notably, the messaging interventions we test here are limited to a single message exposure from one source, whereas widespread shifts in radical attitudes probably require consistent messaging from a large faction of party leaders, like the language of Trump and his allies. Nonetheless, we believe evidence of *any* effects from limited exposure to violent or pacifying language plausibly suggest larger effects if this language is repeated regularly by party leaders—particularly from top party leaders like Donald Trump and Joe Biden.

Indeed, we find powerful evidence that their words matter.

Inflammatory Messages from Top Party Leaders

In most cases of widespread violence through history and around the world, leaders, influential citizens, and peer groups advocated directly for violence, while also providing rationalizations that facilitated moral disengagement (Humphreys and Weinstein 2008; Kalmoe 2020). Indeed, most people seem naturally opposed to political violence when it does not have widespread endorsement from leaders and political culture more generally, and they broadly support political violence when those same leaders, peer groups, and social networks advocate it. We know that partisan opinion leadership is the most important force in shaping ordinary political views (Bakker, Lelkes, and Malka 2020; Karpowitz, Monson, and Preece 2017; Lenz 2012; Zaller 1992). Does opinion leadership work similarly for radical partisanship? Case studies certainly seem to suggest so.

No American leaders have greater impact on the party faithful than presidents and presidential candidates. The first wave of our panel (June 2019) included experimental treatments with real-world inflammatory quotes from Donald Trump and Joe Biden. Trump was the incumbent Republican running for reelection in 2020, essentially unopposed for the nomination by his party, and Biden was the prior vice president and one of the front-runners for the Democratic presidential nomination in a crowded field of high-quality candidates (he went on to win the nomination and the 2020 election). We focused on three types of messages: harsh criticism that contains vilifying elements of moral disengagement (similar to our national threat question), violent rhetoric (limited to interpersonal aggression between the candidates), and rhetoric that delegitimizes elections. One of the challenges in our experiments was that we would repeatedly design a message with the most extreme example we could find, and then Trump went further not long after.

Table 10.1 shows the specific wording for the texts. We randomly assigned each survey respondent to read one message, except for the control group, which saw none. These texts for Biden and Trump are not identical in every way, but we wanted to use real quotes to increase external validity, even while sacrificing some direct comparability within the category.[3] Of course, these tests involve a single exposure to a quote, and the message is mediated by us rather than observed directly in video or audio, which may reduce the effects we see.

After the message, we asked respondents a series of questions, including our standard items about partisan moral disengagement and partisan violence.[4] Throughout, we only measure the effects among partisans. Previewing our results, we find very few substantial effects of these inflammatory messages on individual radical attitudes.

TABLE 10.1 **Enflaming experimental messages**

Harsh rhetoric	Democratic presidential candidate Joe Biden said the following about Republican President Donald Trump: "This president is doing great damage. We are so concerned with stopping his attack on American values, on our principles." Republican President Donald Trump said the following about Democratic presidential candidate Joe Biden: "The Democrats have become too extreme. And they've become, frankly, too dangerous to govern. They've gone wacko."
Violent rhetoric	Democratic presidential candidate Joe Biden said the following about Republican president Donald Trump: "They asked me if I'd like to debate this gentleman, and I said no. I said I wish I were in high school, I'd take him behind the gym and beat the hell out of him." Republican President Donald Trump said the following about Democratic presidential candidate Joe Biden: "He is trying to act like a tough guy. Actually, he is weak. In a fistfight with me, he would go down fast and hard, crying all the way."
Election delegitimizing rhetoric	Democratic presidential candidate Joe Biden claimed Republican laws make voting more difficult for racial minorities: "You've got Jim Crow sneaking back in. You know what happens when you have an equal right to vote? Republicans lose." Republican President Donald Trump alleged fraud by Democrats in recent elections: "In addition to winning the Electoral College in a landslide, I won the popular vote if you deduct the millions of people who voted illegally."
Control	[nothing]

Note: Each text began "Read the comment below and answer the questions that follow."

Enflaming Partisan Moral Disengagement

We tested the effect of inflammatory messages from Biden and Trump on partisan moral disengagement with the three-item index we introduced earlier. Unexpectedly, reading any of the inflammatory partisan messages significantly *decreased* moral disengagement by 5 points, on average, compared with no message. Perhaps the incivility was distasteful enough to make many partisans rethink endorsing similar sentiments themselves, even when delivered by one of their party's major leaders. These effects occurred for both Biden's and Trump's messages compared with the control, and results were similar whether the respondent shared the speaker's partisanship or not. In sum, the morally engaging results might suggest a kind of backlash effect against the hostility in those inflammatory messages. More people react against the direction of the message than in line with it, though we certainly would not recommend it as a strategy for deradicalizing the public. We did not find significant differences between the various inflammatory messages.

Enflaming Violent Partisan Views

The average combined effect of reading any one of the inflammatory messages did not significantly increase support on the partisan violence index in the sample as a whole. However, Biden's reminder of Republicans' efforts to disenfranchise Black Americans significantly elevated radicalism among Democrats—in this case, increasing approval of violence among Democrats by 4 points compared with no message. Here, in the only message that links antidemocratic Republican actions and racial inequality, we see violence emerge as more popular among Democrats. Matters of racial equality remain fundamental to the story of partisan radicalism.

The "violent" messages did not have enflaming effects on violent views, but note that the candidates talk about physically fighting *each other*, which is a far cry from indirectly or directly advocating for widespread partisan violence. That probably weakens the impact of our messages by comparison. We cannot say from this evidence how people would react if one or both candidates called for lethal attacks against opponents, especially if the messages were repeated and joined by a chorus of fellow partisans. In other contexts, however, those circumstances have been associated with mass partisan violence—including violent actions beyond violent attitudes.

Overall, we were not able to provide much direct evidence of inflammatory messages inducing more radical partisan attitudes. Only one of Biden's uncharacteristic inflammatory messages had radical effects, and not Trump's routine vitriol. Note, too, the message that enflamed Democrats was an accurate description of Republican attempts to disenfranchise Black voters, recalling a long history of racial authoritarianism and violence. This isn't "uncivil rhetoric" that often receives blanket condemnation. This involves naming the threat as an essential step toward democratization and social justice.

On one hand, we take it as a positive sign that some of these other inflammatory messages may be relatively ineffective, at least when read just once. On the other hand, a single quote from a leader in a survey is a mild stimulus for the outcomes we study. The world since our studies has provided far stronger messages with radicalizing potential, regularly repeated by Republican leaders and media outlets. In retrospect, the messages we tested were all far milder than Trump's language inciting his supporters on January 6, 2021, delivered to an audience of die-hard believers literally ready to fight. Each caveat is important for generalizing our tests and for recognizing their limits. We certainly don't see our results here as strong evidence against inflammatory effects in general—just a limitation of our methodological scope.

Pacifying Messages from Top Party Leaders

The second wave of our panel in September 2020 tested Biden and Trump messages that might reduce radical and violent partisanship. We focus on two types of messages. First, some political leaders explicitly reject physical aggression and violence in politics. At times when violence threatens democracy, it is essential for leaders and citizens to reinforce norms against violence. We expect that top party leaders can reduce public support for violence with an explicit rejection of political violence, and perhaps reduce moral disengagement with that language as well.

Second, previous scholarship shows that appeals to superordinate identities can pull people out of intergroup conflict (Sherif 1961). By highlighting common identities and goals, groups can work together—thereby uniting them morally and psychologically. Political scientists recently found this pattern specifically for partisan hostility (measured with feeling thermometers) using appeals to shared American identity (Levendusky 2018). We extend those tests with similar appeals examining their effects on our radical partisanship items.

Table 10.2 shows the texts we used, all based on real quotes, though some were lightly edited to better suit our purposes for length and conceptual content.[5] Notably, the Trump quotes are from White House press releases with statements attributed to Trump, not things he publicly said aloud.

Pacifying Moral Disengagement

We find substantial evidence that pacifying messages from top party leaders have significant pacifying effects, with leaders seeming to hold more power to pacify than to enflame with a single message. The appeal to common national identity significantly reduced moral disengagement among partisans of both parties by 4 points compared with the no-message control. The results are substantively similar for Democrats and Republicans and in messages from Trump and Biden. In other words, opposing leaders can reassure fearful opponents by affirming shared national identity over

TABLE 10.2 **Pacifying experimental messages**

Superordinate American identity (national unity) Rhetoric	Democratic presidential candidate Joe Biden said the following about divisions in the country: "Americans have never let their country down. I know why we're strong. I know why we're united. We always move forward. That's why I am more optimistic about our future, now more than ever." Republican President Donald Trump said the following about recent political divisions: "No matter who we are or where we're from, we all salute the same great flag. As one people, let us move forward to rediscover the bonds of love and loyalty that bring us together as Americans."
Antiviolence Rhetoric	Democratic presidential candidate Joe Biden said the following about divisions in the country: "Violence directed at anyone because of their political opinions is never acceptable, regardless of what those beliefs might be." Republican President Donald Trump said the following about divisions in the country: "I condemn in the strongest possible terms all acts of violence. That has no place here."
Wave 2 control	[nothing]

Note: Each text began "Read the comment below and answer the questions that follow."

partisanship, and leaders in one's own party can guide their followers to less vilifying views.

Among the moral-disengagement questions, the superordinate message effect is strongest for seeing the opposing party as a national threat. The appeal to national unity decreases threat perceptions by 8 points. The antiviolence message may also reduce perceptions of national threat by 5 points, a marginally significant difference. Once again, these effects are similar for partisans from both parties, in messages coming from Trump or Biden. In sum, party leaders' talking about peace and unity seems to reduce partisans' perceptions of the other party as a national threat.

Pacifying Violent Partisan Views

After seeing the extent of radical partisanship, many people have asked us: what can be done about it? We present our most important practical evidence in the book here, showing how top party leaders can successfully reduce violent partisan attitudes with their messages, especially among the partisans who are most likely to hold violent views (and perhaps act on them).

People with strong partisan social identity have some of the highest levels of endorsement for partisan violence. That makes it easier to pacify them compared with low-identification partisans who already reject

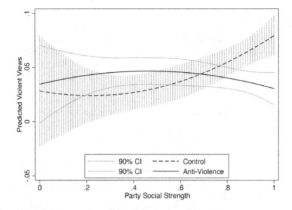

FIGURE 10.1. Effect of antiviolence messages on violent partisan views by partisan social strength. *Note*: Wave 2 panel. Predicted values for the partisan violence index drawn from a quadratic fit of partisan social identity for each treatment group. Regions around estimates indicate 90 percent confidence intervals.

violence. More generally, we know partisans who are most attached to their party are most responsive to messages from their own party's leaders.

We do not find statistically significant pacifying effects on violent attitudes across the whole sample, but we do find significant and substantial pacifying effects of antiviolence rhetoric among strongly identified partisans in both parties.[6] Figure 10.1 shows the effects of the antiviolence message (from either leader) on political-violence attitudes compared with the control condition—across all levels of partisan identity strength and among both parties. We use a flexible fit line here to estimate the relationship (quadratic) because a linear fit leaves the misimpression of a backfire effect among low-strength partisans, when a better fit shows no effects for the low-strength group.

The dashed line for the control condition shows us what we already knew from chapter 6. Partisan identity strength is a strong predictor of violent political attitudes without the intervention of messages from party leaders. As partisan strength increases, approval for political violence also increases, on average. In contrast, the solid line for the antiviolence message flattens out, indicating that antiviolence messages from top party leaders neutralize the higher levels of violent views normally seen among strongly identified partisans. In the absence of messaging, the strongest partisans are the most radical, but when they receive pacifying messages, the strongest partisans are pacified. (Note that the upper levels of partisan strength are highly populated.) Thirty-five percent of partisans have strength scores at 0.9 or above where the antiviolence message effect is statistically significant, and 21 percent of partisans in our survey max out with a strength score of 1. The region where the confidence intervals do not overlap tells us the difference is statistically distinct.

This is a crucial result. Two obvious questions follow: Does the message effectiveness depend on the party of the leader? And does it affect partisans in both parties equally? In additional tests (not shown here), we find that Democrats respond similarly to both Biden's and Trump's antiviolence messages. For added statistical power, figure 10.2 shows the combined effect of Trump and Biden messages for Democrats, with the strongest 20 percent of partisans expressing significantly less support for partisan violence after reading an antiviolence message. Consistent with what we have seen before, stronger partisan identity is related to greater approval of political violence in the absence of any messages at all (dashed line). However, when Democrats read antiviolence messages from Biden *or* Trump, this relationship disappears as strongly identified Democrats move away from violent partisan views (solid line).

What about Republicans? We see similar patterns of response to both the Biden and the Trump messages, but the Trump message definitely produces a stronger effect. We show the effect of each leader's antiviolence message on Republicans in figure 10.3. Again, the dashed line for the control condition shows the familiar positive relationship between partisan identity strength and approval of partisan violence. However, the solid

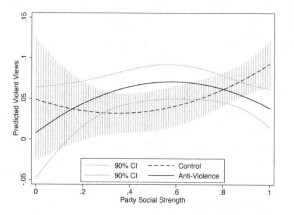

FIGURE 10.2. Effect of antiviolence messages on violent partisan views by partisan social strength—Democrats only. *Note*: Wave 2 panel. Predicted values for the partisan violence index drawn from a quadratic fit of partisan social identity for each treatment group. Regions around estimates indicate 90 percent confidence intervals.

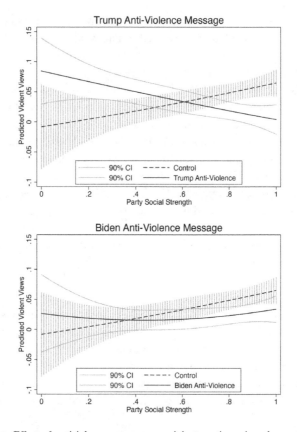

FIGURE 10.3. Effect of antiviolence messages on violent partisan views by partisan social strength—Republicans only. *Note*: Wave 2 panel. Predicted values for the partisan violence index drawn from a quadratic fit of partisan social identity for each treatment group. Regions around estimates indicate 90 percent confidence intervals.

line for the antiviolent message from Trump indicates a *reversal* of that relationship, though the rise among low-strength Republicans is not statistically distinct from the control. The Biden message effects look more like the others above, flattening the relationship among these Republicans by pacifying the views of the strongest ones.

Pacifying Violent Partisanship in 2020

For a result this important, replication is essential to show the finding isn't just a fluke. We repeated the antiviolence message experiment in our 2020 election survey in October—a time of far greater partisan stakes than September 2019, for the tests above. The results with the same Biden and Trump messages were even more promising: reading Trump's or Biden's antiviolence message significantly reduced support for violence if one's own party loses the 2020 election—by 6 points among *all partisans*, compared with no message. The control group average of 18 percent was cut to 12 percent by the antiviolence messages. (The net effect on this item replicates in our 2019 data, with a marginally significant drop of 3 points, from 10 to 7 percent.) Our 2020 data also show patterns for the strongest partisans similar to Wave 2, but they were not quite as statistically distinct in 2020 as they were in 2019.

In addition, the 2020 antiviolence messages significantly reduced a combined index of support for the three violent responses to election loss described in chapter 9—military coup, National Guard resistance, and citizens' stocking up on weapons—by 4 points. In contrast, we see no effects for our other three main violence questions—the two threat items and the "violence today" question. Although not definitive, the net effects of antiviolence messages seem to be particularly potent on pacifying violent reactions to election loss in particular in both experiments.

As in 2019, the antiviolence messages in October 2020 were similarly effective at reducing violent partisan views whether coming from Biden or Trump. Pacifying effects appeared for both Democratic and Republican respondents, Democrats responded similarly to Biden and Trump, and Republicans did too (though maybe a little more to Trump). Put simply, top party leaders have the power to regulate violent views in the public, with their followers who look to them for guidance, and in opposing partisan voters who look for signs of aggression or peace from the other party's leaders. As Joe Biden says in the chapter epigraph, "The words of a president matter."

* * *

Overall, we find that top party leaders can significantly reduce partisan vilification and approval of violence among partisans with their pacifying messages, even with a single message. This is especially effective among partisans who strongly identify socially with their party. Leaders have a unique opportunity—and sometimes a responsibility—to speak to their most loyal (and usually most radical) followers to help turn down the partisan fire they might otherwise be stoking.

In light of the violent 2020 election, our results suggest loud and clear that antiviolence messages from Donald Trump could have made a difference in reducing violent partisan views among Republicans in the public—and perhaps in pacifying some of his followers bent on violence. Instead, Trump's lies about the election incited that violence. Biden's antiviolence messages probably helped pacify Democrats, though they had fewer violent grievances as election winners.

Trump wasn't the only problem for radical partisanship, however. Pundits have long bemoaned the role of partisan news in polarizing the public, and Republican media seem to be playing a key role in radicalizing Republican viewers (O'Neil 2019). What evidence can we find that speaks to the broader role of partisan media in radical views? We explore that next.

Partisan News and Radical Views

In 2019, Ebony Williams, a former Fox News host, participated in a radio interview in which she stated that "Fox has a reputation for being bigoted and racist—all for a very good reason."[7] She described how Roger Ailes, the founder of Fox News, wanted the network to be focused on "the demonizing of the other," and to speak to "the fear of intrinsic devaluation of whiteness in this country." As we described earlier in the book, partisan moral disengagement is powerfully driven among Republicans by racial resentment and hostile sexism. Fox News is well known for peddling in vilifying and dehumanizing rhetoric, particularly directed at marginalized social groups (Mills 2017). Fox News functions as the propaganda arm of the Republican Party, but it also has direct effects on the behavior of the party's leaders (Arceneaux et al. 2016; Clinton and Enamorado 2014), including, famously, Donald Trump while he was president.[8]

How extensive is public exposure to Fox News? Forty percent of Trump supporters in 2016 relied on Fox News as their "main source" of political information (Gottfried, Barthel, and Mitchell 2020). The supporters of Trump rival Hillary Clinton relied on a far wider variety of news sources. As Alvin Chang at Vox reported in 2018, "Fox News immunizes its viewers from evidence that contradicts their reality. That reality shows that they were right to choose Trump because he's creating jobs, lowering unemployment, and securing our borders—and everyone who says otherwise is just trying to undermine a great president."[9]

Partisan websites are another source for political hand-wringing. Social media is too, even though most people use social media for nonpolitical purposes (McClain 2021). The rise of broadband internet access and the proliferation of digital partisan content have also contributed to partisan hostility (Lelkes, Sood, and Iyengar 2017), though the largest increases in partisan hostility are among older Americans (Grinberg et al. 2019). Each of these media outlets is a site of substantial partisan vitriol, though we should not forget that traditional news coverage displays plenty of partisan animosity just by quoting partisan leaders and activists. How, then, does consuming partisan media relate to partisan radicalism?

Scholars debate the extent to which partisan media are a cause of partisan hostility or a manifestation of it. Matthew Levendusky (2013) argues that partisan media are polarizing, not just in policy views but also in decreasing tolerance and increasing disdain for political opponents. But Arceneaux and Johnson (2013) find that the potential polarizing effects of partisan media are often limited to the people who don't actually consume it very much. In other words, patterns of self-selection mean that the people who opt into consuming these programs often have very concrete partisan views already that are unlikely to change and may only be reinforced by this content.

Our efforts here are aimed at providing a look at patterns of media use and radical partisan views rather than a definitive causal analysis, which we leave for the future. For example, party social identification may be a common cause for both partisan news consumption and radical partisanship, or its relationship in motivating partisan news choice may expose partisans to more radicalizing media content.

Partisan Media Use

One of our surveys included questions about partisan news consumption, focused on cable news outlets Fox News and MSNBC. The University of Maryland Critical Issues Survey was conducted in May 2018 by Nielsen in collaboration with scholars at the University of Maryland. This representative telephone survey of 1,200 American adults included three of our partisan moral-disengagement items and the two threat items from our usual four-item partisan violence index.[10]

We compare partisan-animosity levels among people who say their "primary source for political information" is Fox News, MSNBC, CNN, or broadcast television news. We focus our comparisons among TV news viewers, and especially on the three cable news options, though we also present averages from other sources. In the Nielsen survey, 23 percent of partisan respondents indicated Fox News was their primary source,

TABLE 10.3 **Extreme partisan animosity by political news source**

	Moral disengagement (0-1)	Violent threats (0-1)
CNN	.43	.03
Fox News	.60	.08
MSNBC	.43	.10
Network news	.47	.04
Public broadcasting	.51	.07
Print news	.44	.06
Internet / social media	.45	.07

Note: 2018 Maryland Critical Issues Survey. Values are weighted means.

21 percent said network news, 19 percent internet or social media, 14 percent print news, 9 percent CNN, 7 percent MSNBC, and 6 percent public broadcasting. These numbers are already instructive. Though pundits and some scholars often equate Fox News and MSNBC as the most prominent examples of ideological extremes, their reach is far different. Even if their content was equally radical (it isn't),[11] partisan content from Fox News has far more potential impact. This is helpful to keep in mind when interpreting the findings that follow.

Table 10.3 shows the average levels of radical partisanship among news consumers for each primary source. When it comes to partisan moral disengagement, the news sources are relatively similar, except for Fox News, which shows dramatically higher partisan moral disengagement than the rest. While the average moral disengagement score for the other news sources range from 0.43 (CNN) to 0.51 (public broadcasting), Fox News viewers score 0.60 on average—a significantly higher score. This means that Fox News viewers are generally more likely to vilify and dehumanize their partisan opponents than viewers of any other news source.

Viewers of both partisan news networks (Fox and MSNBC) endorsed violent partisan threats against leaders and ordinary citizens at levels significantly higher than CNN viewers, who are the least approving of partisan threats. In sum, Fox News viewers (compared with CNN viewers) are significantly more extreme across both dimensions of partisan radicalism that we measure here. MSNBC viewers are more extreme only in their acceptance of threats against out-party leaders and regular out-party partisans in the public. Digital news sources did not stand out from the rest.

Next, we test whether these relationships persist after accounting for other factors that contribute to consuming these news sources and other correlates of extreme views. Specifically, we add statistical controls to our weighted regression models, including sex, age, college graduate status, and partisan strength from the folded 7-point measure (see online appendix for full models). Even with these added control variables, Fox News viewers score significantly higher on moral disengagement (about 17 points higher than CNN viewers) and marginally higher on violent partisan threats (about 3 points higher than CNN viewers). MSNBC viewers remain similar to CNN viewers on moral disengagement, but they score significantly higher on partisan threats (about 6 points higher than CNN viewers). It is also interesting to note here that CNN—a network that was regularly attacked by Donald Trump for being "fake news" and "liberal media"[12]—enjoys the least radical viewership.

Overall, we find a significant relationship between partisan cable news and radical views, most of all for Fox News—the most broadly watched cable news channel and a bastion of Republican Party rhetoric. Fox News exposure is associated with the highest levels of partisan moral disengagement compared with all other media outlets, and it was essentially tied for the audience that endorsed violent partisan threats the most. We did find some relationship between a Democratic-leaning channel, MSNBC, and violent attitudes, but no relationship between MSNBC and moral disengagement and, notably, a far smaller cultural footprint.

Conclusions

Words matter, especially from top party leaders. Their words have power to ratchet up partisan radicalism in the public or, even more powerfully, to tone it down. We presented several experimental tests using enflaming and pacifying messages from Donald Trump and Joe Biden.

By far, our most important finding is that when Trump and Biden denounce violence, they significantly reduce support for partisan violence in the public, especially among partisans with strong social identification with the party. Both candidates' words were similarly effective, and their impact was similar on their own followers and their opponents (though Trump may have been slightly more effective among Republicans). We replicated these crucial pacifying effects in two large representative nations surveys, so we are confident in our conclusions. Appeals to national unity were not effective at reducing support for violence, but they did significantly reduce partisan moral disengagement—again, with similar effects for each leader on both sets of partisans.

We began the chapter with a finding that surprised us: exposure to any of the enflaming messages seemed to reduce partisan moral disengagement compared with no message. This might be a sign that even many partisans find the more extreme partisan rhetoric to be distasteful. Our clearest finding for specific enflaming messages showed that Joe Biden's message accusing Republicans of election rigging by disenfranchising Black voters increased support for partisan violence among Democrats. That finding reminds us again of the importance of race in partisan conflict past and present, including the radicalizing effects of accurately and justly naming the Republican Party's very real and racialized threats to democracy.

More broadly, we interpret our relatively meager findings for enflaming rhetoric as a limitation in our methods rather than a limitation in the power of enflaming rhetoric. A single exposure of relatively mild text attributed to a leader is a very minimal intervention compared with the repeated extreme audiovisual vitriol some partisans see daily. Finally, in our last section, we presented observational evidence that long-term exposure to partisan cable news—and especially Fox News—has enflaming effects on partisan radicalism. This was a first snapshot relating political news exposure and radical partisanship, and we look forward to more studies ahead.

This chapter concludes our investigation into how political context shapes radical partisanship and ends our broader empirical investigation into these extreme views and behaviors among ordinary Americans. In our next and final chapter, we consider the lessons of radical American partisanship, including both its dangers and its opportunities for democracy.

CHAPTER ELEVEN

The Future of Radical Partisanship: Risks and Opportunities

In a democratic republic, freedom and diversity lead inexorably to conflict. Yet they need not lead to inexorable conflict. For among a people guided, even in their conflicts, by a talent for conciliation and a commitment to the principles and institutions of a democratic republic, both freedom and diversity might flourish. — Robert Dahl, *Pluralist Democracy in the United States: Conflict and Consent* (1967)

There has never been an anti-racist majority in American history; there may be one today in the racially and socioeconomically diverse coalition of voters radicalized by the abrupt transition from the hope of the Obama era to the cruelty of the Trump age. All political coalitions are eventually torn apart by their contradictions, but America has never seen a coalition quite like this. — Adam Serwer, "The New Reconstruction," *The Atlantic* (October 2020)

We've come a long way, and we have so much further to go. What holds for American democracy applies to our work here as well: we've only scratched the surface, even as we close this book. From a hunch informed by history, psychology, and contemporary warning signs, we set out to measure the extremes of American partisan opinion that previous researchers had overlooked.

Political violence that seemed unthinkable to many when we began this project is much more thinkable today after four years of growing turmoil during the Trump presidency. Those trends culminated in Republican efforts to illegitimately overturn the 2020 election through official channels and through violence in the January 2021 Capitol attack and other threatening episodes—dramatically embodying the partisan threats we found in our first 2017 survey, which went far beyond what the classic texts on mass political behavior and parties had taught us.

In our surveys and experiments, we found a small but growing number of partisans supporting political violence, and that a much larger fraction of partisans endorses several extreme forms of moral disengagement. Political and personal traits predispose some people to be more radical than others—especially partisan-social-identity strength and trait aggression—and these orientations manifest in aggressive political behaviors as well as attitudes. These radical attitudes respond to political circumstances including election losses and violence, undemocratic scenarios, and opinion leadership. Our findings inform what we know about partisan extremes in democracies and the very particular threats we face today. This book achieves our main goal to trace the outlines of radical American partisanship, but much more remains to be discovered.

In this chapter, we briefly review our findings: what they mean for American politics and democracy more broadly and what might lie ahead for the country—the future of radical American partisanship. We argue that grave risks for violence and authoritarianism persist and continue to grow (especially given Republican unwillingness to hold people to account for their violent Capitol insurrection), but we also see unprecedented opportunities for democratizing the United States. That essential work to defeat authoritarianism may lead to *more* conflict, but we know from history that the costs of surrender are too great—and advancing democracy is worth the fight.

What We Found

We sought to learn the degree of radical American partisanship and its causes. What did we find? Chapter 2 briefly reviewed the long history of political violence in the US. Conflict between advocates of white supremacy and advocates of democratization frequently grew violent, especially when those conflicts coincided with partisan competition. We also noted similar trends in other countries, where social-political alignments feed conflict, election times produce strategic and spontaneous violence, and violent acts risk sparking spirals of retaliatory violence. Chapter 3 described the social-psychological and political foundations for intense intergroup animosity in politics and noted how partisan concepts in political science missed the dangers that psychology scholars recognized. Those chapters set our expectations for radical partisanship in the rest of the book.

In chapter 4, we found large portions of American partisans—even majorities—view their opponents as national threats and evil. Substantial minorities of partisans saw their opponents as less than fully human and endorsed partisan violence today. That animus goes far beyond what other US public opinion scholarship has documented before. Chapter 5 traced a worrisome rise in all dimensions of radical partisanship between 2017 and 2021, including support for partisan threats, violence, and moral disengagement. Although Republicans and Democrats generally held similar levels of radical views over this time—empirical equivalence, not moral equivalence—our February 2021 survey held the largest partisan gap. Republicans were far more likely to endorse violence than Democrats, and more so than Republicans in all our prior surveys.

Chapter 6 showed that radical partisanship is fueled by aggressive personality traits, strong partisan attachments, and most of all the alignment of partisanship with the party's social identities and group attitudes. The roles of racism and sexism in moral disengagement views among Republicans starkly clarify the centrality of social hierarchy in radical partisanship. Chapter 7 identified some aggressive behavioral implications of radical partisan views. Many Americans have been the target of aggressive political behavior. Substantial numbers of American partisans admit insulting others over politics, but very few admit threatening people over politics or getting into physical altercations. Still, those who have are far more likely to endorse partisan violence, establishing a connection between attitudes and behaviors. We also find evidence of aggressive partisan behavior involving physically uncomfortable noise blasts with opposing partisans. In sum, radical partisan views correspond closely with physically harmful political behavior.

Chapter 8 found that Americans aren't pacifists in politics, despite four-fifths rejecting partisan violence today. Large majorities endorse political violence by citizens when thinking about the American Revolution (but not in other historical episodes), and, in the abstract, they see threats to individual rights as greater justification for violence than violations of free and fair elections. Chapter 9 established that election losses fuel radical partisan reactions—in anticipation and in actuality—and election-cheating views correspond with more violent partisan views. We also found evidence that hypothetical violence, actual violent attacks, and reminders of past violence against partisans briefly increase support for violence, increasing the risk for spirals of violence.

Finally, chapter 10 experimentally tested whether hostile political rhetoric fuels the fire and whether pacifying rhetoric can douse the flames of radical partisan attitudes. Real-world evidence in 2020 and 2021 leaves no doubt that leaders can mobilize violent partisan action: Democratic and

Republican leaders agreed that the Capitol attack was caused by Trump's rhetoric. In contrast, even Democrats who thought violence was appropriate remained peaceful, perhaps partly owing to Biden's consistent disavowal of violence. What about the effects of individual messages from party leaders?

The most important practical finding in the book is that antiviolence messages from Biden and Trump significantly reduced support for partisan electoral violence, especially among the strong partisans who are most inclined to support violence. We found minimal effects from individual *enflaming* messages from Trump and Biden in an already radicalized environment but with one telling exception. Biden's accusation that Republicans try to steal elections by disenfranchising Black voters—much like during Jim Crow—led to more support for violence among Democrats. That truth-telling is normatively essential, so the practical response should focus on mitigating any undue reactions rather than suppressing that kind of speech. The most effective strategy may be for Democrats to highlight Republican threats to democracy while also disavowing violence (when other means are available), as Biden and other Democrats have done. Chapter 10 also showed some correspondence between partisan media consumption and radical partisanship, most consistently so for Fox News, the media arm of the Republican Party.

Why Now?

Putting all our findings together raises some interesting questions, including why we saw violence from Republicans in 2020–21 and not, for instance, from Democrats in 2000, when Vice President Al Gore won the national vote but lost the Electoral College after apparent meddling and obstruction from prominent Republicans. In both cases, the losing party perceived the outcome as illegitimate. Bear in mind that a Pew Research Center survey from 1997 found some latent support for political violence then too, so violence was a real possibility. The most important answer is that Al Gore, unlike Trump, accepted his defeat and didn't call on his followers to revolt against that outcome, even though Gore had more reason to feel aggrieved, and Gore's supporters were certainly disgruntled (Imai and King 2004). "What remains of partisan rancor must now be put aside," Gore said in his concession speech (Ritter and Howell 2001). Long after the election, majorities of Republicans still believed Biden did not legitimately win the 2020 election.[1]

In addition, the partisan social-sorting process that is increasingly settled today—aligning social and political identities—was still in flux in 2000, producing higher levels of partisan animosity now than then (Mason 2018). Republicans now represent historically dominant groups on race and religion (and class too), all seeing relative decline in numbers and power. As we have argued throughout, Republican and right-wing violence in recent years reflects leadership and social-political conditions, not inherently greater tendencies for violence by Republicans compared with Democrats.

Trump's 2016 campaign and his presidency certainly added fuel to the fire by stoking Republican animus against Democrats and against minority groups, but he only accelerated and intensified growing tendencies among Republicans that other leaders had stoked for decades. Even so, Trump's rhetoric was the principal cause of the January 2021 attack on the Capitol—Republican Senate minority leader Mitch McConnell said as much. Trump's efforts to overturn his legitimate election loss were unprecedented in modern times, but the partisan and social animosity Trump channeled into violence has been encouraged by Republican leaders for a long time—weaponizing racial grievance politics for political gain (Maxwell and Shields 2019).

Implications for Studying Mass Politics and Parties

In this project, we aimed to raise an alarm about the dangers we saw mounting, which our public opinion field seemed to be neglecting. Toward that end, we extended measures of partisan affective polarization to include what were previously considered to be outrageous questions (even we thought they were outrageous at first). Had we not found any evidence for the existence of these extreme attitudes, we would have been relieved. Instead, we were moved to write a book-length treatment about the extent of partisan radicalism. Our evidence shows a far more contentious American partisan electorate than had been recognized, though many of our colleagues studying political history and race and ethnic politics have recognized the holes in conventional wisdom about parties, violence, and democracy for quite some time now (e.g., Du Bois [1935] 1997; Eckhouse 2020; Mickey 2015; Weaver and Prowse 2020).

In addition to new measures, we proposed and tested a political-psychological framework for understanding the extremes of individual and collective American partisanship, including correlates with individual traits, responsiveness to situations—events, contexts, and messages—and attitudes about equality. So much more is left to learn in those directions.

We expect to continue working in these directions along with many of our readers. Collaborations across fields and professions are essential here, to link violent-attitudes research with violent political acts in the US and abroad—present and past—across scholars and practitioners, all working on different angles of similar questions. Although methods focused on causal inference are important and useful, we believe more fulsome descriptions of radical partisan concepts and processes with diverse measures and methods will provide rich new opportunities too.

More broadly, bringing together the many threads in this book helps to reshape how we understand American parties, partisanship, and mass politics empirically and normatively, especially when we consider our results in historical and cross-national perspective. In particular, we have come to some uncommon conclusions:

1. Parties are essential for a well-functioning democracy, but they may also threaten to destroy democracy, especially when aligned with identity-based nationalism.

2. Violence generally undermines democracy, but democratizing violence—democratic revolution, suppressing autocratic rebellions, and physically enforcing civic equality—was historically essential for countering authoritarian violence. Sustaining and advancing democracy against its domestic foes sometimes demands bearing those severe costs.

3. Antidemocratic violence is a danger, but it may not be the gravest: legal efforts to thwart popular sovereignty—including voter disenfranchisement, refusal to accept the results of legitimate elections, and undemocratic legal institutions like the Senate and the Electoral College—are all threats to a people's government and civic equality.

4. Unlike many political observers, we recognize that "party polarization" isn't inherently bad—in fact, maintaining and exacerbating polarization is *essential* for a democratic party when it faces an authoritarian party. Thus, the valueless canard of "polarization" doesn't diagnose the problem—it hides the problem. Democracies need responsible parties that share a rock-solid commitment to fundamental democratic principles and norms, including elections that fully represent the people and civic equality for all. When a party deviates from that commitment, we need to recognize it as a radical departure and not just a sign of dreaded "polarization," and the more democratic party should *never* moderate for the sake of reducing that conflict.

In the epigraph that began the chapter, the political scientist Robert Dahl touted Americans' "talent for conciliation" and commitment to democracy as traits that allow the country to withstand its competing pressures of freedom and diversity. Conciliation is unlikely in the face of deep social divisions rooted in inequality and injustice: peace in that context requires systemic change. More important, peace that comes by sacrificing fair elections and the rights of oppressed people is morally indefensible, as with similar calls for compromise before, during, and after the Civil War and Reconstruction. In those far-gone cases, force—not compromise—was necessary to maintain and advance democracy. White Northerners initially maintained the will to do so, but their will ultimately failed—and the promise of multiracial democracy died for a century with that surrender. Our current position on that recurring historical arc emphasizes the failures to avoid and the essential reconstructive paths forward.

A Radical Partisan Future

Recent partisan violence is unsurprising considering America's violent political history and the Republican Party's decades-long reorientation around white-Christian nationalism. Yet, with a Biden administration in office, we sense that many Americans have once again let down their guard to continuing threats—including legal attacks on voting rights and fair elections that may pose graver risks to democracy than the violence we have focused on here.

The Republican Party could have responded to Trump's rhetorical and legal assault on the 2020 election and the violent Capitol attack that followed as a moment of truth, recommitting to democracy. Instead, most elected Republican leaders doubled down on disenfranchising voters and enabling Republican interference with future election administration and certification. They perpetuated the "Big Lie" that the election was stolen from them and purged the few Republican leaders who dared criticize the insurrection in its violent and legal forms.

In the near term, we warily approach the next two federal election cycles—first the congressional midterms in 2022 and then the presidential election in 2024. As we have seen, elections are regularly scheduled times of maximum contention, and so the threat of violence will be highest around those upcoming votes. The risk of violence is especially high from the losing side—most of all in presidential elections where many

Americans perceive higher stakes. Whichever party loses in 2024, we expect more violent views and perhaps more violent acts from losing-party members, especially if party leaders encourage them to reject the official election result—with good reason, or not.

Winning control of government isn't the only factor in political violence, however. Right-wing violence during Trump's presidency exceeded left-wing attacks, building on a decade of increasing radicalism among whites incensed by a Black Democratic president and the growing sense that white men and Christians were losing their unearned hegemony over US political and cultural life. Democratic efforts to move the country closer to a full democracy may prompt violent backlash from Republicans who see democracy as a violation of their assumed right to rule—especially if Democrats embrace the need to revise outdated and undemocratic political institutions. Right-wing grievances have also been correlated with gun ownership and opposition to gun control. Frankly, one party is much more heavily armed. Even with Republican wins, we might expect (and others have already observed) asymmetries in real-world violence.

However, a countertrend may emerge as Republican leaders work to undermine free and fair elections and defend undemocratic abuses against marginalized groups. Although nonviolent resistance to these moves is likeliest, some Democrats may turn to violence if they feel all alternatives for preserving fair elections and advancing civic equality have been exhausted. Our evidence linking election-cheating views to support for violence speaks clearly to that danger, and our hypothetical questions in chapter 8 showed violations of minority rights as another area that could prompt more violence from the Left.

Social, Demographic, and Partisan Change

> Throughout history, when a state has taken an exclusive and intolerant idea such as religion or ethnicity as its cornerstone, this idea has more often than not been the mainspring of violence and war. In days gone by, religion had to be displaced as the basis of the state before frightful religious wars came to an end. And there will be little hope of putting an end to wars . . . until, in some similar fashion the "nation" in ethnic terms ceases to be the basis of a state. — Former Canadian prime minister Pierre Trudeau, *Los Angeles Times*, June 21, 1990.

Taking a longer view predicts more conflict as well. Activists of color and their allies have moved persistent white supremacy and attacks on fair elections to the center of the national agenda and the core of the Democratic Party's platform. The staunchest defenders of systemic racism, patriarchy, and Christian nationalism are consolidated among Republicans. The result is a nation starkly divided once again along racial, religious, and partisan lines similar to the situation in the mid-1800s. Historically and today, transferring ethnic intergroup conflict onto the scaffolding of the American two-party system fuels an increasingly radical form of American partisanship characterized by vilification and dehumanization of political opponents and overt approval of violence for partisan ends (Kalmoe 2020; Mason 2018). This recurring radicalism is deeply engrained in partisanship today.

Beyond party-group realignments, the social groups themselves are changing in unprecedented ways that are stoking more violent threats from groups that have traditionally monopolized social, economic, and political power in the United States. The US Census projects that white non-Hispanic Americans will lose their majority status by the year 2045, and the percentage of US residents who are immigrants is approaching record levels set in the late 1800s (US Census Bureau 2019). The startling *Atlantic* article by the journalist Yoni Appelbaum (2019) entitled "How America Ends" argues that "the United States is undergoing a transition perhaps no rich and stable democracy has ever experienced: Its historically dominant group is on its way to becoming a political minority." That diversification upends the social order that has governed America since its founding, promising the potential for establishing a true multiracial democracy for the first time. The Republican Party's increasingly nativist and white identity means it will soon represent an ethnic minority seeking to maintain political power over a diverse multi-ethnic majority. That loss of social, economic, and political status is sure to drive more partisan conflict, including ethno-partisan violence and authoritarian efforts to retain power against the will of the people.

As scholars of comparative politics have long known, a fully representative and peaceful democracy cannot survive intact under the rule of an ethnic minority. Minority rule is a definitional violation of democracy: it means no equal representation nor equal rights, and coercive violence is required to maintain that power. Overturning the rule of ethnic minorities has often required massive and sometimes violent uprisings by the majority.

As we saw in chapter 6, radicalism in the parties is differently motivated by racism and sexism. In the Republican Party's backlash, we see the kind of radicalism that is required to maintain illegitimate rule that it has pre-viously held in government without much resistance from the public. In the Democratic Party, we *may* see an emerging type of radicalism that is required to overturn minority rule in a movement to realize the ideals of a fully representative democracy—a social and historical reckoning with the forces of power—though that effort does not seem fully manifested in the party leadership and throughout the base just yet.

Democracy has long been seen as a reliable way to accomplish self-government and the peaceful transfer of power, but a democracy riven by violent ethno-partisan conflict is dangerously unstable. The same social and political changes that feel threatening to Republicans today induce hope for Democrats, and vice versa. Understood through this lens, the prevalence of radical partisanship in the American electorate should not be surprising among those who seek to maintain undemocratic control and those seeking the civic equality of real democracy.

"Good Trouble": Democratic Opportunities from Contentious Politics

> Do not get lost in a sea of despair. Be hopeful, be optimistic. Our struggle is not the struggle of a day, a week, a month, or a year, it is the struggle of a lifetime. Never, ever be afraid to make some noise and get in good trouble, necessary trouble. — Tweet, John Lewis, civil rights leader and Congressman, June 2018

Despite all the risks, the present also holds great opportunities for demo-cratic growth. The consolidation of a multiracial democratic coalition in the Democratic Party provides hope that the United States may move closer than ever to realizing the democratic promises made 250 years ago in the country's founding documents—though in a multiracial form the founders could never imagine. (Even so, the Democratic Party generally has much further to go in embracing and achieving those aims.) Strides toward universal enfranchisement, equal protection under the law, and a guarantee that every citizen is equally represented in government are sure to cause more partisan conflict—including violence—but nothing is more politically necessary than that democratizing project.

Before the Civil War, Abraham Lincoln famously prophesied that Amer-ica's "house divided" between slavery and freedom would not—and could not—permanently stand. "It will become all one thing, or all the other," he said. The costly Civil War that followed initially established a new birth of freedom with a national democratic re-founding before it was abruptly abandoned a decade later (Foner 1988; 2019). We stand at a similar (but not identical) inflection point today—half multiracial democracy and half ethno-authoritarian rule, divided by party. We face similar opportunities for democratization and dangers of violence and backsliding, though violence on a Civil War scale is highly unlikely.

We know better than Lincoln that resolution of the tension is not inevitable—America could remain semidemocratic, backslide into autocracy, or slip into a hybrid model of federalized authoritarianism in some places like in the Jim Crow era. But "becoming all one thing"—a multiracial democracy—*must* be the central goal of our politics today, more so than any short-term policy aims. Envisioning and coordinating that massive democratizing effort against intense and even violent resistance will require willpower just as immense as in past eras of US democratization. While we should not *seek* partisan violence, neither should we retreat when faced with violent threats from present-day authoritarians, whose vision of racial, gender, and theological supremacy is ultimately indistinguishable in its aims from the views that misguided their ancestors. Suppressing violent resistance by authoritarians is essential to democratization, and it is costly.

Although our position aligns with one party today, it is ultimately nonpartisan. We emphasize the importance of representative and egalitarian democracy, which is rejected by most of today's Republican Party. A few Republican legislators have publicly endorsed democracy,[2] despite threats to themselves, their families, and their political futures,[3] but most of the party seems to be moving the wrong way, even after the 2021 Capitol attack.

Toward Civic Equality

We may finally be seeing the emergence of an antiracist majority, as the essayist Adam Serwer (2020) notes in the chapter epigraph. The Trump presidency shifted people with democratic racial attitudes toward Democrats, but opinion leadership against Trump also changed the attitudes of white Democrats. According to Pew, 64 percent of white Democrats in 2019 believed that "when it comes to giving black people equal rights with whites, our country has not gone far enough." Eighty percent of white Democrats believed that "the legacy of slavery affects the position of black people in American society today" (Horowitz, Brown, and Cox

2019). These are significantly more progressive attitudes than those held by white Democrats even ten years prior (Pew Research Center 2017).

In the summer of 2020, amid a global pandemic and a dire economic crisis, in response to the brutal police killing of a Black man named George Floyd, cities and towns across the nation erupted in mass protests against police brutality targeting Black Americans. These protests were unprecedented not only in scale but also in their racial diversity. While not explicitly partisan, this mass uprising to demand civic equality in its absence for Black Americans was an example of radical action toward democratic goals broadly shared by Democrats and largely rejected by Republicans.

Among nearly eight thousand protests associated with the Black Lives Matter movement between May and August 2020, over 93 percent were peaceful (Jones 2020). However, Republicans and Democrats perceived these protests very differently. President Trump vilified peaceful protests, calling them "acts of domestic terror,"[4] while Fox News Channel showed old footage of violence when reporting on peaceful protests, creating a false narrative of violence.[5] Attempts by white nationalists to discredit racial justice movements resemble the same playbook they used in the 1960s to fight the civil rights movement ("outside agitators"), in the 1920s to justify the violent resurgence of the Ku Klux Klan nationwide, in the 1870s to violently defeat federal Reconstruction of rebel states, in 1861 to justify the enslavers' rebellion, and in the 1830s to violently suppress antislavery speech.

In the 2020 election, Democratic candidate Joe Biden campaigned on a racial policy plan more progressive than any the Democratic Party had ever put forward, and the advocates of multiracial democracy found more committed allies among elected Democrats than ever before.[6] Not only do white Democrats exhibit less racial resentment than Republicans, but they also score higher on measures of "racial sympathy" developed by Jennifer Chudy (2021): empathetic responses that some white people feel when they hear about anti-Black racism. These changes suggest white Democrats in the public are growing more racially democratic—and may support significant political efforts aimed at remedying systemic racism in the future, though their level of commitment beyond survey responses remains to be seen. In parallel, though in different ways, the politics around women's equal role in society are also reshaping the parties—particularly through partisan sorting on sexism (Cassese and Holman 2019) and through the #MeToo movement's aims to end sexual harassment and violence against women (Holman and Kalmoe, 2021).

At no other time in American history has there been a major political party recognizing that racism, religious bigotry, *and* sexism are systemic problems requiring government intervention to ensure equal protection. The historic lack of political will to address these foundational problems is the reason those problems have not been resolved. A partisan divide defined mainly by matters of identity-based equality and justice creates an unprecedented opportunity to advance those causes, even when the other party defines itself against those rights.

Concluding Thoughts

The findings we presented here show growing radicalism in American politics, among reactionary Republicans, yes, but also among Democrats increasingly true to their party's name. Radical partisanship is a sign of serious political trouble in most of the forms we analyzed here—save for viewing Republican authoritarianism as a national threat, which is actually part of the solution. But trouble is inevitable as the nation convulses between democratizing and autocratizing parties in conflict with each other. And while that trouble can and should be managed, avoiding it by shirking our moral duty to advance American democracy isn't an option. That work is overdue because of our past moral failures, when avoiding conflict was valued over justice.

The best-case scenario is that today's radical partisanship is the necessary bumpy part of the road on the way to a more representative democracy with true civic equality. We would be naive to expect this social change to occur without a powerful and violent backlash from the many whites whose superior status is under threat—a backlash that has happened in every prior move toward multiracial democracy in the United States. With great commitment, the democratic side can eventually prevail, but we'll see more radical partisanship in the process.

Our hope is that America can withstand and grow through the upheaval of traditional social hierarchy—powerfully embodied by a diversifying nation and a Democratic Party that embraces and defends that diversity. The only just way to move *beyond* our current precarious situation is for Americans who support democracy to publicly and unapologetically advance the goal of democratizing the US, no matter the costs from intensifying conflicts that will inevitably follow.

Acknowledgments

The world our book enters *isn't* fundamentally different from when we first began this project on American partisan violence. But it certainly feels different for many people following the January 6, 2021, attack on the Capitol by Republicans who aimed to prevent Joe Biden's official recognition as the next president of the United States—the worst incident yet in that party's long radicalization.

Our work on modern-day violent American partisanship started in a coffee shop on the grounds of the Royal College of Surgeons in Edinburgh, Scotland. It was early July 2017, and we were meeting for the first time, at the annual research conference for the International Society of Political Psychology. We talked about our not-yet-published books on hostility in socially sorted parties and Civil War partisan violence, respectively, then moved to what comes next. We were both struck by the chasm between how researchers talked about intense partisan animosity—hatred, righteous fury, violence—and how our surveys measured it with milquetoast warm/cold ratings of each party.

True, the most recent published research had just begun to consider more contentious alternatives. Pew Research Center surveys found many partisans viewed their opponents as a national threat, and the scholars Shanto Iyengar and Sean Westwood had shown that partisan dislike could lead to material discrimination in social settings. But we knew from history that partisan hostility could go much further, and we recognized frightening trends in American politics that others seemed to underestimate or miss entirely, trends largely concentrated in an increasingly authoritarian Republican Party.

Rather than wait another decade or two for incremental tests of slightly more extreme partisanship in *reaction* to democratic deterioration, we wanted to get ahead of the dangers by measuring how close the public was to the partisan extremes we knew were possible—and that we saw occurring anecdotally. We acutely felt the country was headed into dangerous waters without knowing what lay ahead, because no one was measuring the latent potential for partisan violence in the public.

With a compelling research idea burning and the urgent need to document where the country stood, we rapidly designed one set of new questions on extreme partisan hostility following the psychological model of "moral disengagement" and another set on support for partisan violence and threats. Luckily, we had some research money available, and we pooled resources with several other scholars—LaFleur Stephens-Dougan, Ashley Jardina, and Spencer Piston—in hopes of buying a module on the 2017 Congressional Cooperative Election Survey. The July deadline for reserving space on the fall survey had just passed, but the study organizers graciously allowed us access.

The initial results were sobering. Most partisans rejected violence, but a substantial minority did not. We presented our first findings at the 2018 annual meeting of the American Political Science Association (APSA), held in Boston that year. The scholarly reception there and at subsequent presentations was generally encouraging, but we heard from several people that our working title—"Lethal Mass Partisanship"—seemed overblown, despite our direct questions on violence. Others said extreme hostility may just be partisans blowing off steam—they don't *really* mean it. (We've heard less of that after recent episodes of partisan violence.) We persisted, adjusting our framing and designing subsequent studies to answer doubters.

We were blessed with extraordinarily generous external funders and substantial research support from our universities, which supported a series of over a dozen national surveys across four years mapping the scope, trends, and conditions for violent partisan attitudes and aggressive behaviors. That yielded a trove of invaluable data measuring a huge range of views, correlates, and several experimental interventions testing what drives them and how to reduce them. This book presents key findings, but we have much more to say on important questions about social media, emotions, race, gendered violence, election legitimacy, geographic and ecological tests, and much else—some of which briefly appears here but which deserves fuller treatment.

Lily's work was supported by the University of Maryland political science department, and Nathan's work was supported by research professorships from donors to the Manship School of Mass Communication at Louisiana State University (LSU): Tom Jarreau Hardin and Howard and Nantelle Mitchiner Gittinger. Martin Johnson, Josh Grimm, Hyojung Park, and Mike Bosworth were especially helpful with funding and administrative support at LSU. Democracy Fund massively accelerated our writing timetable with grants increasing our writing capacity during the academic year. These grants were overseen by Chris Crawford, Anne Gleich, and Laura Maristany.

Facebook's Integrity Research Grant provided our largest sum of support, funding our three-wave 2019–20 panel and the final February 2021 survey in this book's collection. We initially proposed a cross-national comparison to supplement US surveys, but democratic deterioration in the US prompted us to refocus just on American data. We were glad to work with Alex Leavitt and Devra Moehler at Facebook. Although we take issue with Facebook's insufficient responses to its many corrosive enabling effects on society and politics in the US and abroad, we appreciate the company's support for basic social science research without substantial obligations or strings attached.

Nearly all our surveys in the book are nationally representative, administered online by YouGov. The research team at YouGov was especially helpful in managing our complicated survey design instructions— Marissa Shih, Ashley Grosse, Sam Luks, and Caitlin Collins—and we are grateful to Steve Ansolabehere and Brian Schaffner for coordinating the Cooperative Congressional Election Studies (CES) where we had 2017, 2018, and 2020 modules, with costs defrayed by National Science Foundation grants. Thanks to Rob Griffin with Voter Study Group and Brendan Nyhan with the team at Bright Line Watch for fielding some of our items and making the data available.

Thanks to research assistants Jared McDonald and Jennifer St. Sume at University of Maryland, along with Cole Catherine Dunnam, Brianna Jones-Williams, and Trey Poche at LSU for assistance with content coding, design, and references.

We were glad to have many public forums to sound the alarm during our book-writing process, including essays in *Politico*, the *Washington Post*'s *Monkey Cage* political science blog, and the Voter Study Group's blog hosted by Democracy Fund. Some of our basic findings were also reported in popular outlets like the *New York Times*, FiveThirtyEight, Vox, the *New Yorker*, and the *National Review*, among others. We also participated in a 2019 workshop at the Carnegie Institute for International

Peace organized by Rachel Kleinfeld, who assembled a diverse group of politicos, donors, foundations, antiviolence and democracy groups, journalists, and researchers to plan ways to avert violence around the 2020 election.

Our book project benefited from great feedback from start to finish at presentations in various venues, including APSA 2018 and 2019; the National Capital Area Political Science Association 2018 meeting; a 2019 Cornell workshop on democratic resilience; the Cooperative Congressional Election Studies 2019 conference; a 2019 Brigham Young University partisanship conference honoring David Magleby; and in 2021, the Center for the Study of Democratic Politics at Princeton University; Hakeem Jefferson's American politics class at Stanford; and Stanford's Center on Democracy, Development, and the Rule of Law. We also benefited from comments at a presentation for Mike Podhorzer's (AFL-CIO) Open Mic series.

Our most important input came from a brilliant set of interlocutors whose comments on the whole manuscript in a fall 2020 book conference really brought the work into focus. Erin Cassese, Michael Tesler, Marc Hetherington, and Josh Gubler helped us develop themes and through lines, rethink our framing, fill theoretical gaps, and cut through the thicket of analysis pared down to essential findings here. Alexandra Filindra also provided helpful feedback on our introduction. The book would surely be better if we had taken more of their advice.

Thanks to our editor Chuck Myers, the series editor Adam Berinsky, three anonymous reviewers, and the production team at University of Chicago Press for enthusiastically encouraging and ably supporting the book from inception to publication. We're thrilled this work joins Chicago's unrivaled catalog in American political behavior, and we're honored to be among the last book projects Chuck shepherds into print. We especially appreciate his insistence that the book await updates with 2020–21 election surveys and context, which we all felt was essential despite the delay in publication.

Of course, the views we express here are our own and do not necessarily represent the views of our employers, funders, or any other organizations or individuals. We both contributed equally to producing this book, with our names listed alphabetically.

We'd also like to thank our families and the many friends and colleagues whose inspiration and support guide and sustain us. This book couldn't have come together at a more challenging time for us as we sprinted to the finish amid a pandemic, political and social unrest, and extreme personal highs and lows. There are too many wonderful people to mention, but we'll name a few whom we worked especially closely with lately—Mirya Holman, Ashley Jardina, Alex Theodoridis, and Julie Wronski. And a shout-out to our extended network on Twitter.

Nathan is forever grateful to Katie Will for her sustaining love and support, and for the essential care work she provided for their beloved baby daughter, all of which made this book possible. He's also remembering his dad, David Kalmoe, and mentor and friend Martin Johnson, both of whom passed away in the last year of writing, amid everything else.

Lily wishes to thank all her colleagues at the University of Maryland, College Park, who offered such warm support and friendship in her six years there. She also thanks her parents, David Anthony and Dory Brown, for all of the phone calls of commiseration, celebration, and small talk that kept the three of them close when they couldn't be together. She thanks her two daughters for being the types of kids that she actually wants to be locked in a house with for over a year while writing a book. And most of all, she thanks Dave Mason for taking on the lion's share of keeping the family fed and alive while they weathered a global pandemic.

Fittingly for our book's subject, we write these acknowledgments on Memorial Day 2021—a holiday first commemorated 156 years ago by formerly enslaved Black South Carolinians immediately after the American Civil War. Their purpose: honor the sacrifices made by hundreds of thousands of Black and white US soldiers who died suppressing the racial-partisan rebellion that white enslavers led against Lincoln's 1860 election.

We hope our work advances the scientific understanding of mass political behavior, and that it serves the moral imperative of democratizing the United States—so that every citizen's voice will one day count equally in government, and that government will ensure equal protection for all.

Notes

Chapter One

1. Alexandra Jaffe, Steve Peoples, and Will Weissert. "'Hate Just Hides': Biden Vows to Take on Systematic Racism." *AP NEWS*, June 2, 2020, https://apnews.com/article/virus-outbreak-joe-biden-ap-top-news-wilmington-delaware-bf2d8 2afc6ae2d0e8b22a5d2b48491ff.

2. Andrea Shalal, "Biden, Harris Condemn US Racism, Sexism in Blunt Language," *Reuters*, March 21, 2021, https://www.reuters.com/article/us-usa-biden-racism /biden-harris-condemn-u-s-racism-sexism-in-blunt-language-idUSKBN2BE019.

3. Paul D. Shinkman, "Prosecutors: Capitol Rioters Intended to 'Capture and Assassinate' Elected Officials." *US News and World Report*, January 15, 2021, https://www.usnews.com/news/national-news/articles/2021-01-15/prosecutors-capitol -rioters-intended-to-capture-and-assassinate-elected-officials.

4. Associated Press, "'Clear the Capitol,' Pence Pleaded on Jan. 6: New Details of Riot Response Are Revealed," *Associated Press*, April 10, 2021, https://www .mprnews.org/story/2021/04/10/clear-the-capitol-pence-pleaded-on-jan-6-new -details-of-riot-response-are-revealed.

5. We do not mean to imply that all mid-nineteenth-century Republicans were committed to democracy or abolition—far from it—only that the party's overarching goals and their actions in practice served to unambiguously advance democracy in stark contrast with the Democratic Party. With party realignments on race, people like Lincoln are Democrats today, and the Confederates (and their Democratic allies) are now Republicans, though on religion, Republicans have always favored the dominant Protestant group, often with substantial animus toward religious minorities.

6. Trump notably said of a protestor during one of his 2016 rallies, "I'd like to punch him in the face," and "In the old days [protesters would] be carried out on stretchers." When asked about a Black Lives Matter protestor who was punched and kicked by rally-goers at a different event, Trump replied, "Maybe he should have been roughed up." See Diamond (2016) for all three quotes.

7. Kendall Karson, "Michigan Gov. Whitmer: Protests 'Undermine' State's Response to COVID-19 Crisis," *ABC News*, May 13, 2020, https://abcnews.go.com/Politics/michigan-gov-whitmer-protests-undermine-states-response-covid/story?id=70645516.

8. Michael Krafcik, "Whitmer Kidnap Ringleader Wanted to Televise Executions, Attorney General Says," *WWMT*, November 13, 2020, https://wwmt.com/news/local/whitmer-kidnap-ringleader-wanted-to-televise-executions-attorney-general-says.

9. Ben Collins and Brandy Zadrozny, "In Trump's 'LIBERATE' Tweets, Extremists See a Call to Arms," *NBCNews.com*, April 18, 2020. https://www.nbcnews.com/tech/security/trump-s-liberate-tweets-extremists-see-call-arms-n118656.1.

10. Matthew S. Schwartz, "Trump Speaks Fondly of Supporters Surrounding Biden Bus in Texas." *NPR*, November 1, 2020, https://www.npr.org/2020/11/01/930083915/trump-speaks-fondly-of-supporters-protecting-biden-bus-in-texas.

11. Aaron Blake, "On Election Eve, Trump Dances around a Powder Keg with a Lit Match," *Washington Post*, November 2, 2020, https://www.washingtonpost.com/politics/2020/11/02/election-eve-trump-dances-around-powder-keg-with-lit-match/.

12. Blake, "On Election Eve."

13. Andrea Mazzarino, "The Far-Right Militias Supporting Trump," *Nation*, October 29, 2020, https://www.thenation.com/article/society/trump-militia-election/.

14. Paul P. Murphy, "Trump's Debate Callout Bolsters Far-Right Proud Boys," *CNN*, October 1, 2020, https://www.cnn.com/2020/09/30/politics/proud-boys-trump-debate-trnd/index.html.

15. Marissa Lang et al., "After Thousands of Trump Supporters Rally in D.C., Violence Erupts When Night Falls," *Washington Post*, November 15, 2020, https://www.washingtonpost.com/dc-md-va/2020/11/14/million-maga-march-dc-protests/.

16. Ryan Lucas, "4 Proud Boys Charged with Conspiracy Over Jan. 6 Capitol Riot," *NPR*, March 19, 2021, https://www.npr.org/2021/03/19/979304432/4-proud-boys-charged-with-conspiracy-over-jan-6-capitol-riot.

17. Julia Ainsley, "Internal Document Shows Trump Officials Were Told to Make Comments Sympathetic to Kyle Rittenhouse," *NBCNews.com*, October 1, 2020, https://www.nbcnews.com/politics/national-security/internal-document-shows-trump-officials-were-told-make-comments-sympathetic-n1241581.

18. Our approach also focuses on violence carried out by civilians rather than agents of the state, but partisan violence does not end there. We recognize that partisan violence can be laundered through the legitimizing veneer of state authority, and that the organized process of institutionalized violence is often more lethal.

Chapter Two

1. Republicans also opposed Latter Day Saints (Mormons), with stated objections to polygamy. In fact, antislavery and antipolygamy were the two foundational tenets of the 1856 founding Republican platform. Mormons were the only US group

to have an extermination order put out against them, by the Missouri governor in 1838. They were then driven out of Illinois with violence in 1846, and the US government sent federal troops out west to suppress them in the late 1850s (Smith 2015).

2. The Republicans advancing democracy in the South were called Radical Republicans. Radicalism can be good.

3. Low-level political violence (e.g., riots) may function somewhat differently from the maximal violence of civil wars, however (Gubler, Selway, and Varshney 2016).

Chapter Three

1. Religion was a substantial partisan cleavage, with Republican Protestants against Democratic Catholics. Eisenhower was elected as a Republican in 1952 and reelected in 1956. The latter election provided the context for the Michigan Election Study survey that informed the classic work *The American Voter*. Outside the South, whites and Protestants were more evenly distributed between the two major parties, owing in large part to white Democrats in the South who effectively functioned as a third party in national politics.

2. The authors were relatively sympathetic toward Black citizens, at least for that time, and they explicitly discussed and even analyzed Black disenfranchisement in the South over a few pages, but race plays a far smaller role in their account of political behavior than it should. Likewise, their comments about women's votes following their husbands' votes—rather than their voting the same way because of shared circumstances and local political culture—reflect a patronizing view common at the time.

3. They wrote: "Popular election combined with representation . . . has offered a creative solution to the age-old problem of transferring authority without violence" (Campbell et al. 1960, 5).

4. Tajfel provides essential psychological foundations for understanding group conflict. He was also a serial sexual harasser of women he encountered in academia. We regret that the centrality of his work in the field makes citing a terrible person unavoidable.

5. In some cases, the "own the libs" phenomenon—saying or doing something simply to make liberals mad, regardless of its depravity—may be an example of this tradeoff between status and well-being.

6. *The American Voter* does engage with Adorno and colleagues' F scale (authoritarianism measure) but only for predicting conventional votes and views.

Chapter Four

1. Emma Nolan, "Jon Voight Compares Joe Biden to Satan, Says Democrat Win Is 'Greatest Fight since Civil War.'" *Newsweek*, November 11, 2020, https://www.newsweek.com/jon-voight-donald-trump-joe-biden-twitter-satan-civil-war-1546654.

2. Robert O'Harrow Jr., Andrew Ba Tran, and Derek Hawkins, "The Rise of Domestic Extremism in America," *Washington Post*, April 12, 2021. https://www.washingtonpost.com/investigations/interactive/2021/domestic-terrorism-data/?itid=hp-top-table-main.

3. These items are a subset of more than twenty items that we first deployed in the 2017 election survey, including more dimensions of moral disengagement and a third conceptual category of partisan schadenfreude that we set aside for concision. See the chapter 4 online appendix for those additional items. We evaluated items by examining internal consistency with conceptually related items along with convergent, discriminant, and predictive validity. YouGov is widely considered to be the "gold standard" for online survey research. They maintain a panel of two million respondents in the United States, and they approximate a nationally representative probability sample using matching and weighting techniques.

4. For analysis of radicalism among pure independents and independent leaners compared with avowed partisans, see our chapter in an edited volume (Kalmoe and Mason, forthcoming).

5. We also tested the stability of these items and indices over months and years in our YouGov panel (Wave 1: June 2019, Wave 2: September 2019, Wave 3: February 2020). Here, we report Pearson's correlations of stability, which showed the kind of strong overall stability indicative of real attitudes. These results are only for people who reported the same partisan category in both paired waves, since different responses yield different question wording. This excludes about 5 percent of the sample and only slightly strengthens the results. For the three-item moral disengagement index, W1-W2 is 0.75, and it is 0.70 for W1-W3. For the four-item partisan violence index, W1-W2 is 0.66, and it is 0.68 for W1-W3. The violence stability test excludes people randomly selected to answer the future election question if their party *won*. For comparison, the difference between Republican and Democratic Party feeling thermometer ratings is stable at 0.93 for W1-W2 and 0.93 for W1-W3.

6. From the short form of the Buss-Perry aggression questionnaire: Bryant and Smith 2001; see Kalmoe 2015 for additional validation. In subsequent surveys, we used four-item and twelve-item trait-aggression scales.

7. Here, we use the "interflex" STATA tool (Hainmueller, Mummolo, and Xu 2019) to account for a nonlinear interaction effect. This plots the marginal effects based on a kernel smoothing estimator. It produces marginal effect estimates of moral disengagement on partisan violence at a series of values of trait aggression using kernel-weighted locally linear regressions. The results indicate there is a slightly nonlinear marginal effect of moral disengagement on partisan violence across levels of aggression. As aggression rises from zero to about the midpoint of the scale, there is only a weak marginal effect of moral disengagement on partisan violence. However, above the midpoint of the scale the slope increases, indicating larger effects of moral disengagement on partisan violence at the higher levels of

aggression, and that this marginal effect increases more rapidly at higher levels of aggression.

8. Laurel Wamsley, "'They Just Started Waling on Me': Violence in Portland as U.S. Agents Clamp Down." *NPR*, July 20, 2020, https://www.npr.org/sections/live-updates-protests-for-racial-justice/2020/07/20/893082598/they-just-started-whaling-violence-tension-as-u-s-agents-clamp-down-in-portland.

Chapter Five

1. Paul Waldman, "Trump's Attack on 'Democrat Cities' Is Right out of the GOP Playbook," *Washington Post*, September 2, 2020, https://www.washingtonpost.com/opinions/2020/09/02/trumps-attack-democrat-cities-is-right-out-gop-playbook/.

2. Mike Levine, "'No Blame?' ABC News Finds 54 Cases Invoking 'Trump' in Connection with Violence, Threats, Alleged Assaults." *ABC News*, May 30, 2020, https://abcnews.go.com/Politics/blame-abc-news-finds-17-cases-invoking-trump/story?id=58912889.

3. Some of our surveys differed substantially in content preceding the radical partisanship questions, so we cannot totally rule out methodological influences on trends in that form. However, most of our surveys followed the same general order of question types and wordings. The most important design factor that we do not analyze directly here is the net impact of experimental messaging tests of one sort or another in most of our surveys. We analyze many of those experiments in chapters 9 and 10. Generally, we do not find net effects among all partisans, and so the impact of those treatments is probably minimal for the trends. Another potential confound is attrition. Most of our studies had a panel component, whether short (pre-/postelection) or multiyear (our YouGov panel, Voter Study Group's December study). The rising trends we find in this chapter apply even if we only look at the first wave of each panel. Those dates are November 2017, October 2018, June 2019, October 2020, and February 2021. Additionally, all YouGov's samples are from a pool of panelists, though that pool is continually refreshed as people leave. We did not measure moral disengagement in our 2018 election survey nor did it appear in Voter Study Group's December 2019 survey.

4. Jason Wilson, "US Police and Public Officials Donated to Kyle Rittenhouse, Data Breach Reveals," *Guardian*, April 16, 2021, https://www.theguardian.com/us-news/2021/apr/16/us-police-officers-public-officials-crowdfunding-website-data-breach.

5. We asked: "On January 6th, supporters of President Trump stormed the US Capitol to protest lawmakers certifying Joe Biden's election victory. Based on what you have read or heard about this, do you support or oppose these actions?" "How much do you feel it is justified for [Own party: Democrats/Republicans] to use violence to take over state government buildings to advance their political goals these days?"

Chapter Six

1. Quoted in Craig, Tim. "U.S. Political Divide Becomes Increasingly Violent, Rattling Activists and Police," *Washington Post*, August 27, 2020, https://www.washingtonpost.com/national/protests-violence/2020/08/27/3f232e66-e578-11ea-970a-64c73a1c2392_story.html?hpid=hp_hp-top-table-high_protestviolence-630am%3Ahomepage%2Fstory-ans.

2. Seth Masket, "Op-Ed: What Broke the Republican Party?" *Los Angeles Times*, November 16, 2020, https://www.latimes.com/opinion/story/2020-11-16/op-ed-what-broke-the-republican-party.

3. Transition Integrity Project, *Preventing a Disrupted Presidential Election and Transition*, August 3, 2020, https://assets.documentcloud.org/documents/7013152/Preventing-a-Disrupted-Presidential-Election-and.pdf.

4. The names in this section are pseudonyms based on popular names by sex and age appropriate for the person.

5. Our account here may make radical partisans seem milder than they are. In response to an open-ended question, one of our most extreme respondents wrote, "Demoncraps are all commie scum and should be either deported or executed."

6. We measure ideological identification strength with a folded version of a standard 5-point scale: "Very liberal," "Liberal," "Moderate," "Conservative," and "Very conservative." This determines how strongly people associate with their ideological label. However, caution should be taken in interpreting these answers as indications of a consistent policy-based belief system (Kinder and Kalmoe 2017). Mason (2018) found a disconnect between what people call themselves and what issue positions they hold. In this study, identification with the liberal or conservative label was more strongly connected to out-group animosity than were issue positions.

7. First, each dot indicates a coefficient (the size of which can be determined by looking at the number directly below the dot on the horizontal axis). The coefficient represents the substantive size of the relationship between each element on the left and moral disengagement, independent of the influence of all the other elements (variables). If the dot is to the left of the zero line, that variable has a negative relationship with moral disengagement. In other words, as the values of that variable increase, moral disengagement decreases. If the dot is to the right of the zero line, that indicates a positive relationship between the variable and moral disengagement. As the level of that variable increases, moral disengagement increases. The larger the coefficient, the bigger the relationship between the variable and moral disengagement. The lines around each dot represent 90 percent (thick line) and 95 percent (thin line) confidence intervals. These provide information about the certainty we have in these estimates based on the size of the sample and the strength of the relationship between the two variables. If the confidence interval lines cross the vertical zero line, we cannot reject the possibility that this coefficient is equal to zero. That relationship is not "statistically significant." If the confidence interval lines do not cross the zero line, we have some certainty that

the relationship between these variables really exists. These guides apply to every model we present in this way for the remainder of the book.

8. Among people of color, the scale could indicate a different kind of racial conservatism (Kam and Burge 2018) rather than racial animus.

9. Work by Kane, Mason, and Wronski (2021) suggests that at least some of this relationship is explained by racist and sexist attitudes predicting partisan identity, which also fits macro-partisan histories involving social realignment between the parties.

Chapter Seven

1. Josh Bazan, "Man to Serve 4 Months for Punching Anti-Trump Protester outside Downtown Rally," *WCPO*, January 9, 2020, https://www.wcpo.com/news/crime /man-convicted-of-assault-for-punching-anti-trump-protester-outside-presidents -cincinnati-rally.

2. Jeremy Roebuck, "A Pittsburgh-Area QAnon Supporter Who Told Followers He Was 'Going to Fight' Is Charged in the Capitol Attack," *Philadelphia Inquirer*, January 26, 2021, https://www.inquirer.com/crime/kenneth-grayson-capi tol-riot-arrest-qanon-pittsburgh-facebook-livestream-20210126.html.

3. "Because of your political views, has anyone ever . . . Insulted you? . . . Threatened you? . . . Physically attacked you?"

4. Over two-thirds of US adults have a Facebook account, and so a focus on social media users is not as exclusive as it may seem (Perrin and Anderson 2019).

5. CES 2020: "Do you ever insult people because of their politics? . . . Do you ever threaten people because of their politics? . . . Do you ever grab, push, hit, or throw things at people because of their politics?" Responses: no, never; yes, once or twice; yes, occasionally; yes, often. Panel Study Wave 3: "Have you ever insulted someone because of their politics? . . . Have you ever threatened someone because of their politics? . . . Have you ever grabbed, pushed, hit, or thrown something at someone because of their politics?" Responses: never; yes, one time; yes, a few times; yes, several times; yes, quite often; yes, almost every day.

6. We asked about online and in-person behaviors separately in the second wave (September 2019, N=1903). Combining each pair of items in Wave 2, 38 percent said they had insulted someone online or off, 7 percent had threatened someone over politics, and 5 percent of our respondents reported getting physically aggressive. The stability correlation for these dichotomized, slightly different items across waves was good: r=.54 for insults, r=.42 for threats, and r=.56 for physical aggression.

7. We should note, however, that the nature of a physical fight might make it harder to distinguish these two questions.

8. The demographic traits are interesting too but not directly relevant to our story here. In particular, older people are significantly less likely to report making threats and getting into physical altercations over politics, even after accounting for trait aggression, which is lower among older people (Kalmoe 2015). Beyond

personality, the physical capacity for aggressive behavior diminishes with age, and threats of physical force seem to follow that trend. Women are also less likely to insult others, all else equal, but their rates of threats and physical aggression are no different from those of men after accounting for the other factors. College graduates are marginally more likely to insult others over politics—perhaps leveraging some of their added verbal acuity—but are no different for the other two behaviors.

9. In the panel study data, the correlation with our partisan violence index is weak for insults ($r=.19$), strong for threats ($r=.51$), and strong for self-reported physical altercations over politics ($r=.55$). Thus, the attitude-behavior links are strongest for items specifically linking threats and physical harm and weaker for verbal aggression, which lacks that matching specificity (Ajzen and Fishbein 1977). We find a weak correlation with our partisan moral disengagement index for insults ($r=.16$) and nonexistent tie for political threats ($r=.04$) and physical aggression ($r=.03$). All the action runs through violent views.

10. We also conducted two similar experiments with student participants that generally show similar results, but which were grossly underpowered with small samples owing to unanticipated recruiting limits in each semester.

11. We informed participants in the debrief that their responses would be aggregated after all, rather than assigned to individual participants. We ultimately decided to present these national responses in a subsequent student study.

12. See the online appendix for the full experiment prompt (nathankalmoe.com /radical-american-partisanship/).

13. We recognize that Pape is a somewhat controversial figure among violence researchers, but we turn to his analysis here since it appears sound for our purposes, and we found few similar studies by others soon after the attack.

14. Jaclyn Diaz and Rachel Treisman, "Members of Right-Wing Militias, Extremist Groups Are Latest Charged in Capitol Siege," *NPR*, January 19, 2021, https://www.npr.org/sections/insurrection-at-the-capitol/2021/01/19/958240531 /members-of-right-wing-militias-extremist-groups-are-latest-charged-in-capitol-si.

15. "Live Exit Polls 2020: Election Day Exit Polls for Trump vs. Biden." *NBCNews .com*, August 5, 2020, https://www.nbcnews.com/politics/2020-elections/exit-polls.

16. More than one hundred additional individuals have been arrested since the Pape study, with 495 arrests as of May 26, 2021.

Chapter Eight

1. Transcription from the Stone Engraving in the National Archives, accessed July 30, 2021, https://www.archives.gov/founding-docs/declaration-transcript.

2. The short-lived Corsican Republic in the 1750s and 1760s guaranteed universal adult suffrage, including women, so the US was an early adopter of some democratic forms but far from the forefront of democratic institutions.

3. For example, we have recently seen the emergence of the Republican "Tea Party" movement, which took its name from Revolutionary property destruction, and even an antigovernment militia named the "Three Percenters," derived from the mistaken belief that only 3 percent of American colonists took up arms against the Crown.

4. This survey, run by Lucid, also included the Revolution and Confederate violence questions above. Those results are similar to the election survey results, adding confidence for these last two historical tests.

5. However, we caution that a similar pattern for Lucid data in the Confederate case moved in the opposite direction in the 2020 YouGov election survey data.

6. Responses for these four scenarios fit surprisingly well together, despite varying levels of opposition. Naturally, the odd one is the American Revolution. Dropping that item produces a Cronbach's alpha reliability score of .69 compared to .62 with the Revolution included, with all measured as an indicator for "no" responses. The two 20th century items fit best together, yielding a .80 alpha.

7. The data suggest all "conditions for violence" items reflect the same underlying violent/nonviolent factor despite variations in percentages across items (Cronbach's $\alpha = .91$).

8. Also, only 20 percent chose "never" for all nine questions, so half or more of the opposition on each individual question is from people who do not reject violence in other scenarios.

9. For more systematic comparisons of violence rationales, we coded responses into several categories. Comments received more than one category if they were multidimensional. Nine percent were blank or said something like "don't know," and we exclude those from the denominators here. The first category rejected violence, declared by 51 percent. Twenty percent mentioned "rights" or the Constitution in a vague way, while 3 percent mentioned some specific right, like guns or speech. Eight percent referenced citizens individually or personally threatened with physical harm.

The remaining categories of interest to us had only a smattering of mentions. Two percent referenced presidential acts, 3% mentioned undemocratic elections, 4% indicated unlawful government violence against civilians, and less than 1% mentioned imprisoning political opponents. One percent mentioned violence as a response to violence by opponents, 2% said in response to targeting specific groups with discrimination or other harm, and 1% made reference to historical or cross-national comparison case. Ten percent fell into some category not coded above. Less than one percent said (unprompted) that the conditions justifying violence exist now.

Chapter Nine

1. In each of this chapter's tests, we average responses across experimental treatment conditions. Since those are randomized, they should not inhibit tests for contextual change, unless those changes also interact with the treatments.

2. We find inconsistent differences between Republicans and Democrats in the size of the win/loss experimental effect. Republicans responded differently in February 2020 while Democrats did not. The reverse held true in October 2020. And both parties showed equally sized effects in September 2019. We did not anticipate these variations, and we do not have a good explanation for them, and so we focus on the average effect across both parties in each test.

3. This corresponds with 781 respondents from Waves 2 and 3. Only 3 percent chose more legitimate violence with an in-party win, perhaps owing to changing circumstances or measurement error. The average from all that change is +.03 mean out-in difference on the response scale ($p<.01$), identical to the between-subjects experimental test in the third wave. Interestingly, a simple OLS model predicting this difference with trait aggression and party social identity strength continues to show trait aggression is the more powerful predictor. This is notable since trait aggression predicts more support for violence regardless of target ($b=.08$, $p<.001$), whereas party strength changes valence depending on the target ($b=-.01$, $p>.10$). Thus, trait aggression motivates greater out-group harm relative to in-group, and not just out-group harm.

4. Bright Line Watch (2021) found no real change in views about partisan threats and slight declines in support for partisan violence after the 2020 election using similar items to ours, and they found slightly greater support for violence among Trump approvers than among Trump disapprovers both before and after the election. Some of the difference may be due to its using presidential approval rather than party ID, or perhaps slight differences in its response options may matter. Sampling variations are always a potential culprit.

5. The numbers were somewhat different when we asked who appeared to have won the Electoral College and the popular vote. Among Republicans, 28 percent said Trump won the Electoral College, and 40 percent said he won the popular vote.

6. Rob Kuznia et al., "Stop the Steal's Massive Disinformation Campaign Connected to Roger Stone," *CNN*, November 14, 2020, https://www.cnn.com/2020/11/13/business/stop-the-steal-disinformation-campaign-invs/index.html.

7. The survey software automatically inserted the name of the respondent's party's candidate—either Joe Biden or Donald Trump.

8. We combine the three items into a reliable index (Cronbach's alpha=.79). The specific loss violence index is robustly related to our 3-item general partisan violence index (Pearson's $r=.33$), and it relates even more strongly to our general partisan violence item about 2020 election-related violence conditional on a loss (Pearson's $r=.44$), as we would expect with loss-focused items.

9. Olga Khazan, "5 Ways White Supremacists Use Victimhood to Their Advantage," *Atlantic*, August 15, 2017, https://amp.theatlantic.com/amp/article/536850/.

10. We preregistered these analytical cut-points after the attacks but before we had access to our survey data. We also do not rule out the possibility that the later respondents happened to be more pro-violence than the late respondents by

nature. However, our analyses suggest that a general sample imbalance is not the reason for the difference.

11. Five of the six most violent days of responses occur immediately after the week of bombs and the synagogue attack, and the one exception occurs during the week of bombs.

12. Sam Stein, "Sharron Angle Floated '2nd Amendment Remedies' as 'Cure' for 'The Harry Reid Problems.'" *HuffPost*, December 7, 2017, https://www.huff post.com/entry/sharron-angle-floated-2nd_n_614003.

13. Giffords wording: "In January 2011, Democratic Congresswoman Gabby Giffords was shot and seriously wounded, along with several other people." Scalise wording: "In June 2017, Republican Congressman Steve Scalise was shot and seriously wounded, along with several other people."

14. $b=.03$, $p=.04$.

Chapter Ten

1. Kirit Radia and Allie Yang, "World Leaders Condemn Pro-Trump Protesters Overrunning US Capitol," *ABC News*, accessed May 28, 2021, https://abcnews .go.com/Politics/world-leaders-condemn-pro-trump-protesters-overrunning-us /story?id=75093385.

2. BBC, "US Election: Trump Won't Commit to Peaceful Transfer of Power," *BBC News*, September 24, 2020, https://www.bbc.com/news/election-us-2020–54274115; Melissa Quinn, "'Stand Back and Stand By': Trump Declines to Condemn White Supremacists at Debate," *CBS News*, September 30, 2020, https://www.cbsnews.com /news/proud-boys-stand-back-and-stand-by-trump-refuses-to-condemn-white -supremacists/.

3. We do not consider these pairings to be morally equivalent, though we aimed for some level of functional equivalence within the limits of what each leader actually said.

4. We also included a manipulation check—whether they remembered who the message was from, with six response options. Eighty-one percent got the question right. Generally, results are similar whether or not we filter results on the basis of this check.

5. We debriefed all participants with links that either showed the original context of the quote or explained the editing and provided links to the original sources. We also included a third message that was over-the-top in its extremity, just from Trump. Counterintuitively, some scholars have found that extreme messages from in-group members can actually reduce out-group animus. The results are basically null, and we decided to exclude them from the narrative to keep the chapter concise. The authors are happy to discuss those results and may publish them elsewhere.

6. While the antiviolence messages were effective at reducing approval of violence among strong partisans, the appeals to national identity had little effect across levels of partisan identity.

7. Erin Durkin, "Ex-Fox News Host Says Its Reputation for Racism Is 'for Very Good Reason.'" *Guardian*, April 19, 2019, https://www.theguardian.com/media/2019 /apr/19/fox-news-racism-whites-host-eboni-williams.

8. According to Media Matters, Trump live-tweeted Fox programs 1,146 times from September 2018 through August 2020. See Matt Gertz, "Study: Two years of Trump's Fox Live-Tweeting Obsession, by the Numbers," *Media Matters*, October 9, 2020, https://www.mediamatters.org/donald-trump/study-two-years-trumps -live-tweeting-obsession-numbers; Jane Mayer, "The Making of the Fox News White House," *New Yorker*, March 11, 2019, https://www.newyorker.com/magazine /2019/03/11/the-making-of-the-fox-news-white-house.

9. Alvin Chang, "The Stories Fox News Covers Obsessively—and Those It Ignores—in Charts," *Vox*, May 30, 2018, https://www.vox.com/2018/5/30/17380096 /fox-news-alternate-reality-charts.

10. Because of space considerations and practitioner preferences, we were not able to include the two measures that assessed the acceptability of political violence. For the moral disengagement items, scored 0–1, the mean was 0.49, and standard deviation was 0.27. Cronbach's α=0.57. For the two threat items, scored 0–1, the mean was 0.06, and standard deviation was 0.14. Cronbach's α=.062.

11. A 2020 study found that Fox News viewers are significantly less informed about American society-oriented knowledge than consumers of other news media (Licari 2020).

12. Axios, "Trump Attacks CNN as 'Dumb b*stards' for Continuing to Cover Pandemic," *Axios*, October 19, 2020, https://www.axios.com/trump-attacks-cnn-covid -9342befa-8790-42e6-b6e5-d8472d19ecec.html.

Chapter Eleven

1. Kathy Frankovic, "Republicans Who Share Trump's 2020 Doubts Say They Are Very Likely to Vote in 2022," *YouGov*, November 1, 2021, https://today.you gov.com/topics/politics/articles-reports/2021/11/01/republicans-distrust-election -results-still-voting.

2. John Eligon and Thomas Kaplan, "These Are the Republicans Who Supported Impeaching Trump," *New York Times*, January 13, 2021, https://www.nytimes .com/article/republicans-impeaching-donald-trump.html.

3. Juliegrace Brufke, "House Republicans Say Threats of Violence Could Be a Factor in Impeachment Decision," *Hill*, January 13, 2021, https://thehill.com/home news/house/534113-house-republicans-say-threats-of-violence-could-be-a-factor -in-impeachment.

4. David Jackson and Michael Collins, "Calling Violent Protests 'Acts of Domestic Terror,' Trump Says He'll Send in Military If They Aren't Controlled," *USA Today*, June 2, 2020, https://www.usatoday.com/story/news/politics/2020/06/01/george-floyd-donald-trump-order-additional-help-cities-amid-protests/5312338002/.

5. Jake Lahut, "Protests This Past Week Have Been Largely Peaceful, but Fox News Continues to Show Old Footage to Rile up Viewers," *Business Insider*, June 11, 2020, https://www.businessinsider.com/fox-news-replays-violent-old-protest-footage-actual-protests-calm-2020–6.

6. Fabiola Cineas, "How Biden Has—and Hasn't—Harnessed the National Reckoning on Race," *Vox*, August 19, 2020, https://www.vox.com/2020/8/19/21372408/joe-biden-racial-justice-policy.

References

Abramowitz, Alan I., and Steven W. Webster. 2018. "Negative Partisanship: Why Americans Dislike Parties but Behave like Rabid Partisans." *Political Psychology* 39:119–35. https://doi.org/10.1111/pops.12479.

Ahler, Douglas J., and Guarav Sood. 2018. "The Parties in Our Heads: Misperceptions about Party Composition and Their Consequences." *Journal of Politics* 80 (3): 964–81.

Ajzen, Icek, and Martin Fishbein. 1977. "Attitude-Behavior Relations: A Theoretical Analysis and Review of Empirical Research." *Psychological Bulletin* 84 (5): 888–918. https://doi.org/10.1037/0033-2909.84.5.888.

Anderson, Christopher J., André Blais, Shaun Bowler, Todd Donovan, and Ola Listhaug. 2005. *Loser's Consent: Elections and Democratic Legitimacy.* New York: Oxford University Press.

Anderson, Craig A., and Brad J. Bushman. 2002. "Human Aggression." *Annual Review of Psychology* 53:27–51.

Ansolabehere, Stephen, Samantha Luks, and Brian F. Schaffner. 2015. "The Perils of Cherry Picking Low Frequency Events in Large Sample Surveys." *Electoral Studies* 40:409–10. https://doi.org/10.1016/j.electstud.2015.07.002.

APIA Vote. 2020. "2020 Asian American Voter Survey." APIAVote. https://www.apiavote.org/research/2020-asian-american-voter-survey.

Appelbaum, Yoni. 2019. "How America Ends." *Atlantic*, November 17, 2019. https://www.theatlantic.com/magazine/archive/2019/12/how-america-ends/600757/.

Arceneaux, Kevin, and Martin Johnson. 2013. *Changing Minds or Changing Channels?* Chicago: University of Chicago Press.

Arceneaux, Kevin, Martin Johnson, René Lindstädt, and Ryan J. Vander Wielen. 2016. "The Influence of News Media on Political Elites: Investigating Strategic Responsiveness in Congress." *American Journal of Political Science* 60 (1): 5–29. https://doi.org/10.1111/ajps.12171.

Arendt, Hannah. 1994. *Eichmann in Jerusalem: A Report on the Banality of Evil.* New York: Penguin Books.

Bai, Hui, and Christopher Federico. 2020. "White and Minority Demographic Shifts, Intergroup Threat, and Right-Wing Extremism." PsyArXiv, October 20, 2020. https://doi:10.31234/osf.io/vzgah.

Bakker, Bert N., Yphtach Lelkes, and Ariel Malka. 2020. "Understanding Partisan Cue Receptivity: Tests of Predictions from the Bounded Rationality and Expressive Utility Models." *Journal of Politics* 82 (3). https://doi.org/10.1086/707616.

Bandura, Albert, Claudio Barbaranelli, Gian Vittorio Caprara, and Concetta Pastorelli. 1996. "Mechanisms of Moral Disengagement in the Exercise of Moral Agency." *Journal of Personality and Social Psychology* 71:364–74.

Barber, Michael, and Jeremy C. Pope. 2019. "Does Party Trump Ideology? Disentangling Party and Ideology in America." *American Political Science Review* 113 (1): 38–54.

Bar-Tal, Daniel, Lily Chrnyak-Hai, Noa Schori, and Ayelet Gundar. 2009. "A Sense of Self-Perceived Collective Victimhood in Intractable Conflicts." *International Review of the Red Cross* 91 (874): 229–58.

Bartels, Larry M. 2002. "Beyond the Running Tally: Partisan Bias in Political Perceptions." *Political Behavior* 24 (2): 117–50.

———. 2020. "Ethnic Antagonism Erodes Republicans' Commitment to Democracy." *Proceedings of the National Academy of Sciences* 117 (37): 22752–59.

Berinsky, Adam J. 2009. *In Time of War: Understanding American Public Opinion from World War II to Iraq*. Chicago: University of Chicago Press.

Berlin, Ira. 2003. *Generations of Captivity: A History of African-American Slaves*. Cambridge, MA: Belknap Press of Harvard University Press.

Blackmon, Douglas A. 2008. *Slavery by Another Name*. New York: Doubleday.

Blattman, Christopher. 2009. "Comparative Violence." *American Political Science Review*, 103 (2): 231–47.

Bliuc, Ana-Maria, John Betts, Matteo Vergani, Muhammad Iqbal, and Kevin Dunn. 2019. "Collective Identity Changes in Far-Right Online Communities: The Role of Offline Intergroup Conflict." *New Media and Society* 21 (8): 1770–86.

Bond, Alyson, and Malcolm Lader. 1986. "A Method to Elicit Aggressive Feelings and Behaviour via Provocation." *Biological Psychology* 22 (1): 69–79.

Brady, Henry E., Sidney Verba, and Kay Lehman Schlozman. 1995. "Beyond SES: A Resource Model of Political Participation." *American Political Science Review* 89 (2): 271.

Bratton, Michael. 2008. "Vote Buying and Violence in Nigerian Election Campaigns." *Electoral Studies* 27 (4): 621–32.

Bright Line Watch. 2021. *American Democracy at the Start of the Biden Presidency*. Report, Bright Line Watch website. http://brightlinewatch.org/american-democracy-at-the-start-of-the-biden-presidency/.

Brown, Anna, Kiana Cox, and Juliana Menasce Horowitz. 2019. "Views on Race in America 2019." Pew Research Center, April 9, 2019. https://www.pewsocialtrends.org/2019/04/09/race-in-america-2019/.

Brown, Jacob R., and Ryan D. Enos. 2021. "The Measurement of Partisan Sorting for 180 Million Voters." *Nature Human Behaviour* (March): 1–11.

Bryant, Fred B., and Bruce D. Smith. 2001. "Refining the Architecture of Aggression: A Measurement Model for the Buss-Perry Aggression Questionnaire." *Journal of Research in Personality* 35:138–67.

Burger, Jerry M. 2014. "Situational Features in Milgram's Experiment That Kept His Participants Shocking." *Journal of Social Issues* 70:489–500.

Bushman, Brad J. 1995. "Moderating Role of Trait Aggressiveness in the Effects of Violent Media on Aggression." *Journal of Personality and Social Psychology* 69 (5): 950–60.

Buss, Arnold H., and Mark Perry. 1992. "The Aggression Questionnaire." *Journal of Personality and Social Psychology* 63 (3): 452–59.

Calhoon, Robert M. 1973. *The Loyalists in Revolutionary America, 1760–1781.* New York: Harcourt Brace Jovanovich.

———. 1980. "Loyalism and Neutrality." In *A Companion to the American Revolution*, edited by Jack P. Greene and J. R. Pole, 235–47. Malden, MA: Blackwell Publishers.

Campbell, Angus, Philip E. Converse, Warren Miller, and Donald Stokes. 1960. *The American Voter.* Chicago: University of Chicago Press.

Caprara, Gian Vittorio, Roberta Fida, Michele Vecchione, Carlo Tramontano, and Claudio Barbaranelli. 2009. "Assessing Civic Moral Disengagement: Dimensionality and Construct Validity." *Personality and Individual Differences* 47 (5): 504–9.

Caprara, Gian Vittorio, Shalom Schwartz, Cristina Capanna, Michele Vecchione, and Claudio Barbaranelli. 2006. "Personality and Politics: Values, Traits, and Political Choice." *Political Psychology* 27 (1): 1–28.

Carmines, Edward G., and James A. Stimson. 1989. *Issue Evolution: Race and the Transformation of American Politics.* Princeton, NJ: Princeton University Press.

Cassese, Erin C., and Mirya R. Holman. 2019. "Playing the Woman Card: Ambivalent Sexism in the 2016 U.S. Presidential Race." *Political Psychology* 40 (1): 55–74.

Chappell, Bill. 2020. "'He Did Not Pray': Fallout Grows from Trump's Photo-Op at St. John's Church." NPR.org, June 2, 2020. https://www.npr.org/2020/06/02/867705160/he-did-not-pray-fallout-grows-from-trump-s-photo-op-at-st-john-s-church.

Chudy, Jennifer. 2021. Racial Sympathy and Its Political Consequences. *Journal of Politics* 83 (1). https://doi.org/10.1086/708953.

Clayton, Katherine, Nicholas T. Davis, Brendan Nyhan, Ethan Porter, Timothy J. Ryan, and Thomas J. Wood. 2021. "Elite Rhetoric Can Undermine Democratic Norms." *Proceedings of the National Academy of Sciences* 118 (23): e2024125118.

Clinton, Joshua D., and Ted Enamorado. 2014. "The National News Media's Effect on Congress: How Fox News Affected Elites in Congress." *Journal of Politics* 76 (4): 928–43.

Collier, Paul, and Anke Hoeffler. 2004. "Greed and Grievance Civil Wars." *Oxford Economic Papers* 56:563–95.

Collier, Paul, and Pedro C. Vicente. 2014. "Votes and Violence: Evidence from a Field Experiment in Nigeria." *Economic Journal* 124:F327–55.

Corder, J. Kevin, and Christina Wolbrecht. 2016. *Counting Women's Ballots*. Cambridge: Cambridge University Press.

Craig, Maureen A., and Jennifer A. Richeson. 2014a. "More Diverse yet Less Tolerant? How the Increasingly Diverse Racial Landscape Affects White Americans' Racial Attitudes." *Personality and Social Psychology Bulletin* 40 (6): 750–61.

———. 2014b. "On the Precipice of a 'Majority-Minority' America: Perceived Status Threat from the Racial Demographic Shift Affects White Americans' Political Ideology." *Psychological Science* 25 (6): 1189–97.

CSIS (Center for Strategic and International Studies). 2021. *The Escalating Terrorism Problem in the United States*. Report, CSIS website, May 16, 2021. https://www.csis.org/analysis/escalating-terrorism-problem-united-states.

Dahl, Robert. 1967. *Pluralist Democracy in the United States: Conflict and Constant*. Rand McNally Political Science Series. Chicago: Rand McNally.

Davis, Nicholas T., Kirby Goidel, and Keith Gaddie. Forthcoming. *The Meanings of Democracy: How Americans Think about Democracy and Why It Matters*. Ann Arbor: University of Michigan Press.

DeSante, Christopher D., and Candis Watts Smith. 2020. "Fear, Institutionalized Racism, and Empathy: The Underlying Dimensions of Whites' Racial Attitudes." *PS: Political Science and Politics* 53 (4): 639–45.

Diamond, Jeremy. 2016. "Donald Trump on Protester: 'I'd Like to Punch Him in the Face.'" *CNN*, February 23, 2016. https://www.cnn.com/2016/02/23/politics/donald-trump-nevada-rally-punch/index.html.

Druckman, James N., and Matthew S. Levendusky. 2019. "What Do We Measure When We Measure Affective Polarization?" *Public Opinion Quarterly* 83 (1): 114–22.

Druckman, James N., Matthew S. Levendusky, and Audrey McLain. 2018. "No Need to Watch: How the Effects of Partisan Media Can Spread via Interpersonal Discussions." *American Journal of Political Science* 62 (1): 99–112.

Du Bois, W. E. B. (1935) 1997. *Black Reconstruction*. New York: Free Press.

Dunaway, Johanna. 2008. "Markets, Ownership, and the Quality of Campaign News Coverage." *Journal of Politics* 70 (4): 1193–1202.

Dunning, Thad. 2011. "Fighting and Voting: Violent Conflict and Electoral Politics." *Journal of Conflict Resolution* 55 (3): 327–39.

Dyrstad, Karin, and Solveig Hillesund. 2020. "Explaining Support for Political Violence: Grievance and Perceived Opportunity." *Journal of Conflict Resolution* 64 (9): 1724–53.

Earle, Jonathan H. 2004. *Jacksonian Antislavery and the Politics of Free Soil, 1824–1854*. Chapel Hill: University of North Carolina Press.

Eckhouse, Laurel. 2020. "White Riot: Race, Institutions, and the 2016 U.S. Election." *Politics, Groups, and Identities* 8 (2): 216–27.

Edwards, Griffin S., and Stephen Rushin. 2018. "The Effect of President Trump's Election on Hate Crimes." SSRN paper. https://papers.ssrn.com/sol3/papers.cfm?abstract_id=3102652.

Edwards, Rebecca. 1997. *Angels in the Machinery: Gender in American Party Politics from the Civil War to the Progressive Era*. New York: Oxford University Press.

Ellis, Joseph J. 2015. *The Quartet: Orchestrating the Second American Revolution*. New York: Penguin Random House.

EJI (Equal Justice Initiative). 2017. *Lynching in America: Confronting the Legacy of Racial Terror*. Montgomery, AL: Equal Justice Initiative.

Fair, C. Christine, Neil Malhotra, and Jacob N. Shapiro. 2014. "Democratic Values and Support for Militant Politics: Evidence from a National Survey of Pakistan." *Journal of Conflict Resolution* 58 (5): 743–70.

FBI (Federal Bureau of Investigation). 2013. "Crime in the United States 2012 Arrests by Sex." https://ucr.fbi.gov/crime-in-the-u.s/2012/crime-in-the-u.s.-2012/tables/42tabledatadecoverviewpdf/table_42_arrests_by_sex_2012.xls.

———. 2019. "FBI Releases 2019 Hate Crime Statistics." Press Release, Federal Bureau of Investigation. https://www.fbi.gov/news/pressrel/press-releases/fbi-releases-2019-hate-crime-statistics.

Fearon, James D., and David D. Laitin. 2003. "Ethnicity, Insurgency, and Civil War." *American Political Science Review* 97 (1): 75–90.

Fessenden, Marissa. 2016. "How a Nearly Successful Slave Revolt Was Intentionally Lost to History." Smithsonian Institution, January 8, 2016. https://www.smithsonianmag.com/smart-news/its-anniversary-1811-louisiana-slave-revolt-180957760/.

Fisher, Noel C. 2001. *War at Every Door: Partisan Politics and Guerrilla Violence in East Tennessee, 1860–1869*. Chapel Hill: University of North Carolina Press.

Foner, Eric. 1988. *Reconstruction: America's Unfinished Revolution, 1863–1877*. New York: HarperCollins.

———. 2019. *The Second Founding: How the Civil War and Reconstruction Remade the Constitution*. New York: W. W. Norton.

Forbes, Gordon B., Leah E. Adams-Curtis, and Kay B. White. 2004. "First- and Second-Generation Measures of Sexism, Rape Myths and Related Beliefs, and Hostility toward Women: Their Interrelationships and Association with College Students' Experiences with Dating Aggression and Sexual Coercion." *Violence against Women* 10 (3): 236–61.

Francis, Megan Ming. 2014. *Civil Rights and the Making of the Modern American State*. Cambridge: Cambridge University Press.

———. 2020. "The White Press Has a History of Endangering Black Lives Going Back a Century." *Washington Post*, June 15, 2020. https://www.washington

post.com/politics/2020/06/15/white-press-has-history-endangering-black-lives
-going-back-century/.

Freeman, Joanne. 2018. *Field of Blood*. New York: Macmillan.

Gates, Henry Louis, Jr. 2013. "The Five Greatest Slave Rebellions in the United
States." *Public Broadcasting Service*, September 18, 2013. https://www.pbs.org
/wnet/african-americans-many-rivers-to-cross/history/did-african-american
-slaves-rebel/.

———. 2019. *Stony the Road: Reconstruction, White Supremacy, and the Rise of
Jim Crow*. New York: Penguin Press.

Gerber, Alan S., Gregory A. Huber, David Doherty, Conor M. Dowling, and Shang E.
Ha. 2010. "Personality and Political Attitudes: Relationships across Issue Do-
mains and Political Contexts." *American Political Science Review* 104 (1): 111–33.

Getmansky, Anna, and Thomas Zeitzoff. 2014. "Terrorism and Voting: The Effect
of Rocket Threat on Voting in Israeli Elections." *American Political Science
Review* 108 (3): 588–604.

Ginges, Jeremy, Scott Atran, Douglas Medin, and Khalil Shikaki. 2007. "Sacred
Bounds on Rational Resolution of Violent Political Conflict." *Proceedings of
the National Academy* 104 (18): 7357–60.

Gottfried, Jeffrey, Michael Barthel, and Amy Mitchell. 2020. "Trump, Clinton Voters Divided in Their Main Source for Election News." Pew Research Center,
August 28, 2020. https://www.journalism.org/2017/01/18/trump-clinton-voters
-divided-in-their-main-source-for-election-news/.

Grant, Keneshia Nicole. 2020. *The Great Migration and the Democratic Party: Black
Voters and the Realignment of American Politics in the 20th Century*. Philadelphia: Temple University Press.

Grimsted, David. 1998. *American Mobbing, 1828–1861: Toward Civil War*. New
York: Oxford University Press.

Grinberg, Nir, Kenneth Joseph, Lisa Friedland, Briony Swire-Thompson, and David Lazer. 2019. "Fake News on Twitter during the 2016 U.S. Presidential Election." *Science* 363 (6425): 374–78.

Grondahl, Paul. 2020. "Powerful Black Lives Memorial at Abolitionist John
Brown's Farm." *Times Union*, September 23, 2020. https://johnbrownlives.org
/powerful-black-lives-memorial-at-abolitionist-john-browns-farm.

Gubler, Joshua R., Joshua R., and Joel Sawat Selway. 2012. "Horizontal Inequality, Crosscutting Cleavages, and Civil War." *Journal of Conflict Resolution* 56
(2): 206–32.

Gubler, Joshua R., Joel Sawat Selway, and Ashutush Varshney. 2016. *Crosscutting
Cleavages and Ethno-communal Violence: Evidence from Indonesia in the Post-
Suharto Era*. United Nations report. https://www.wider.unu.edu/sites/default
/files/wp2016–129.pdf.

Guyer, Joshua, and Leandre Fabrigar. 2015. "The Attitude-Behavior Link: A Review of the History." *International Encyclopedia of Social and Behavioral Sciences*. New York: Elsevier.

Hacker, J. David. 2011. "A Census-Based Count of the Civil War Dead." *Civil War History* 57 (4): 307–48.

Hafner-Burton, Emilie M., Susan D. Hyde, and Ryan S. Jablonski. 2014. "When Do Governments Resort to Election Violence?" *British Journal of Political Science* 44 (1): 149–79.

Hainmueller, Jens, Jonathan Mummolo, and Yiqing Xu. 2019. "How Much Should We Trust Estimates from Multiplicative Interaction Models? Simple Tools to Improve Empirical Practice." *Political Analysis* 27 (2): 163–92.

Halperin, Eran, Alexandra G. Russell, Kali H. Trzesniewski, James J. Gross, and Carol S. Dweck. 2011. "Promoting the Middle East Peace Process by Changing Beliefs about Group Malleability." *Science* 333 (6050): 1767–69.

Harish, S. P., and Andrew T. Little. 2017. "The Political Violence Cycle." *American Political Science Review* 111 (2): 237–255.

Herrero, Juan, Francisco J. Rodríguez, and Andrea Torres. 2017. "Acceptability of Partner Violence in 51 Societies: The Role of Sexism and Attitudes Toward Violence in Social Relationships." *Violence against Women* 23 (3): 351–67.

Hewitt, Christopher. 2000. "The Political Context of Terrorism in America: Ignoring Extremists or Pandering to Them?" *Terrorism and Political Violence* 12 (3–4): 325–44.

Hitt, Matthew P., and Kathleen Searles. 2018. "Media Coverage and Public Approval of the U.S. Supreme Court." *Political Communication* 35 (4): 566–86.

Höglund, Kristine. 2009. "Electoral Violence in Conflict-Ridden Societies: Concepts, Causes, and Consequences." *Terrorism and Political Violence* 21 (3): 412–27.

Holman, Mirya, and Nathan P. Kalmoe. 2021. "Partisanship in the #MeToo Era." *Perspectives on Politics.*

Holzer, Harold. 2014. *Lincoln and the Press.* New York: Simon and Schuster.

Horowitz, Donald L. 1985. *Ethnic Groups in Conflict.* Berkeley: University of California Press.

Horowitz, Juliana Menasce, Anna Brown, and Kiana Cox. 2019. "Views on Race in America 2019." Pew Research Center, April 6, 2019. https://www.pewresearch.org/social-trends/2019/04/09/race-in-america-2019/.

Horwitz, Tony. 2012. *Midnight Rising: John Brown and the Raid That Sparked the Civil War.* New York: Gale / Cengage.

Huddy, Leonie. 2001. "From Social to Political Identity: A Critical Examination of Social Identity Theory." *Political Psychology* 22:127–56.

Huddy, Leonie, Lilliana Mason, and Lene Aarøe. 2015. "Expressive Partisanship: Campaign Involvement, Political Emotion, and Partisan Identity." *American Political Science Review* 109 (1): 1–17.

Humphreys, Macartan, and Jeremy M. Weinstein. 2008. "Who Fights? The Determinants of Participation in Civil War." *American Journal of Political Science* 52 (2): 436–55.

Imai, Kosuke, and Gary King. 2004. "Did Illegal Overseas Absentee Ballots Decide the 2000 U.S. Presidential Election?" *Perspectives on Politics* 2 (3): 537–49.

Iyengar, Shanto, Yphtach Lelkes, Matthew Levendusky, Neil Malhotra, and Sean J. Westwood. 2019. "The Origins and Consequences of Affective Polarization in the United States." *Annual Review of Political Science* 22 (1): 129–46.

Iyengar, Shanto, Guarav Sood, and Yphtach Lelkes. 2012. "Affect, Not Ideology: A Social Identity Perspective on Polarization." *Public Opinion Quarterly* 76: 405–31.

Iyengar, Shanto, and Sean J. Westwood. 2015. "Fear and Loathing across Party Lines: New Evidence on Group Polarization." *American Journal of Political Science* 59 (3): 690–707.

Jardina, Ashley. 2019. *White Identity Politics*. Cambridge: Cambridge University Press.

Jones, Sam. 2020. "US Crisis Monitor Releases Full Data for Summer 2020." ACLED, September 25, 2020. https://acleddata.com/2020/08/31/us-crisis-monitor-releases-full-data-for-summer-2020/.

Kaakinen, Markus, Atte Oksanen, and Pekka Räsänen. 2018. "Did the Risk of Exposure to Online Hate Increase after the November 2015 Paris Attacks? A Group Relations Approach." *Computers in Human Behavior* 78:90–97.

Kahn, Matthew E., and Doral L. Costa. 2008. *Heroes and Cowards: The Social Face of War*. Princeton, NJ: Princeton University Press.

Kalmoe, Nathan P. 2013. "From Fistfights to Firefights: Trait Aggression and Support for State Violence." *Political Behavior* 35 (2): 311–30.

———. 2014. "Fueling the Fire: Violent Metaphors, Trait Aggression, and Support for Political Violence." *Political Communication* 31:545–63.

———. 2015. "Trait Aggression in Two Representative U.S. Surveys: Testing the Generalizability of College Samples." *Aggressive Behavior* 41 (2): 171–88.

———. 2020. *With Ballots and Bullets: Partisanship and Violence in the American Civil War*. New York: Cambridge University Press.

Kalmoe, Nathan P., and Lilliana Mason. 2018. "Lethal Mass Partisanship." APSA conference paper. Boston, MA.

———. Forthcoming. "Stealth Fighters: Extreme Partisanship in Independent Partisans." In *Reconsidering Parties and Partisanship*, edited by Chris Karpowitz and Jeremy Pope. Ann Arbor: University of Michigan Press.

Kalyvas, Stathis. 2006. *The Logic of Violence in Civil Wars*. New York: Cambridge University.

Kam, Cindy D., and Camille D. Burge. 2018. "Uncovering Reactions to the Racial Resentment Scale across the Racial Divide." *Journal of Politics* 80 (1): 314–20.

Kane, John V., Lilliana Mason, and Julie Wronski. 2021. "Who's at the Party? Group Sentiments, Knowledge, and Partisan Identity." *Journal of Politics* 83 (3).

Kaplan, Jeffrey. 1993. "America's Last Prophetic Witness: The Literature of the Rescue Movement." *Terrorism and Political Violence* 5 (3): 58–77.

Karpowitz, Christopher F., J. Quin Monson, and Jessica Preece. 2017. "How to Elect More Women: Gender and Candidate Success in a Field Experiment." *American Journal of Political Science* 61 (4): 927–43.

Keele, Luke, William Cubbison, and Ismail White. 2021. "Suppressing Black Votes: A Historical Case Study of Voting Restrictions in Louisiana." *American Political Science Review* 115 (2): 694–700.

Kinder, Donald R., and Nathan P. Kalmoe. 2017. *Neither Liberal nor Conservative: Ideological Innocence in the American Public*. Chicago: University of Chicago Press.

Kinder, Donald R., and Cindy D. Kam. 2010. *Us against Them*. Chicago: University of Chicago Press.

Kinder, Donald R., and Lynn M. Sanders. 1996. *Divided by Color*. Chicago: University of Chicago Press.

King, Martin Luther, Jr. 1964. *Why We Can't Wait*. New York: New American Library.

Klar, Samara, Yanna Krupnikov, and John Barry Ryan. 2018. "Affective Polarization or Partisan Disdain? Untangling a Dislike for the Opposing Party from a Dislike of Partisanship." *Public Opinion Quarterly* 82 (2): 379–90.

Kleinfeld, Rachel, Nealin Parker, Shannon Hiller, Ashley Quarcoo, and Sadia Hameed. 2019. *Should America Be Worried about Political Violence? And What Can We Do to Prevent It?* Report, Carnegie Endowment for International Peace, September 16, 2019. https://carnegieendowment.org/2019/09/16/should-america-be-worried-about-political-violence-and-what-can-we-do-to-prevent-it-pub-80401.

Klinkner, Philip A., and Roberts M. Smith. 1999. *The Unsteady March: The Rise and Decline of Racial Equality in America*. Chicago: University of Chicago Press.

Kohut, Andrew, Kimberly Parker, Gregory Flemming, Molly Sonner, and Beth Donovan. 1998. "Deconstructing Distrust: How Americans View Government." March 10, 1998. https://www.pewresearch.org/wp-content/uploads/sites/4/legacy-pdf/Trust-in-Gov-Report-REV.pdf.

Kuran, Timur. 1989. "Sparks and Prairie Fires: A Theory of Unanticipated Political Revolution." *Public Choice* 61 (1): 41–74.

Kuziemko, Ilyana, and Ebonya Washington. 2018. "Why Did the Democrats Lose the South? Bringing New Data to an Old Debate." *American Economic Review* 108 (10): 2830–67.

Lawrence, Regina G. 2000. "Game-Framing the Issues: Tracking the Strategy Frame in Public Policy News." *Political Communication* 17 (2): 93–114.

Lazarsfeld, Paul, Bernard Berelson, and Hazel Gaudet. 1944. *The People's Choice*. New York: Duell, Sloan, and Pearce.

LeBas, Adrienne. 2006. "Polarization as Craft: Party Formation and State Violence in Zimbabwe." *Comparative Politics* 38 (4): 419–38.

Lee, Taeku. 2002. *Mobilizing Public Opinion: Black Insurgency and Racial Attitudes in the Civil Rights Era*. Chicago: University of Chicago Press.

Lelkes, Yphtach, Gaurav Sood, and Shanto Iyengar. 2017. "The Hostile Audience: The Effect of Access to Broadband Internet on Partisan Affect." *American Journal of Political Science* 61 (1): 5–20.

Lenz, Gabriel S. 2012. *Follow the Leader? How Voters Respond to Politicians' Policies and Performance*. Chicago: University of Chicago Press.

Levendusky, Matthew. 2013. *How Partisan Media Polarize America*. Chicago: University of Chicago Press.

———. 2018. "Americans, Not Partisans: Can Priming American National Identity Reduce Affective Polarization?" *Journal of Politics* 80 (1). https://doi.org /10.1086/693987.

Levine, Mike. 2020. " 'No Blame?' ABC News Finds 54 Cases Invoking 'Trump' in Connection with Violence, Threats, Alleged Assaults." ABC News. https://abc news.go.com/Politics/blame-abc-news-finds-17-cases-invoking-trump/story ?id=58912889.

Levitsky, Stephen, and Daniel Ziblatt. 2018. *How Democracies Die*. New York: Penguin.

Licari, Peter R. 2020. "Sharp as a Fox: Are Foxnews.com Visitors Less Politically Knowledgeable?" *American Politics Research* 48 (6): 792–806.

Lippmann, Walter. 1922. *Public Opinion*. New York: Macmillan.

Lipset, Seymour. 1960. *Political Man: The Social Bases of Politics*. New York: Doubleday.

Lopez, Jesse, and D. Sunshine Hillygus. 2018. "Why So Serious? Survey Trolls and Misinformation." *SSRN Electronic Journal*. https://doi.org/10.2139/ssrn.3131087.

Lowery, Wesley, Kimberly Kindy, and Andrew Ba Tran. 2018. "In the United States, Right-Wing Violence Is on the Rise." *Washington Post*. November 25, 2018. https:// www.washingtonpost.com/national/in-the-united-states-right-wing-violence-is -on-the-rise/2018/11/25/61f7f24a-deb4-11e8-85df-7a6b4d25cfbb_story.html.

Lyall, Jason, Graeme Blair, and Kosuke Imai. 2013. Explaining Support for Combatants during Wartime: A Survey Experiment in Afghanistan. *American Political Science Review* 107 (4): 679–705.

Margolis, Michele F. 2018. *From Politics to the Pews: How Partisanship and the Political Environment Shape Religious Identity*. Chicago: University of Chicago Press.

Marshall, M. A., and J. D. Brown. 2006. "Trait Aggressiveness and Situational Provocation: A Test of the Traits as Situational Sensitivities (TASS) Model." *Personality and Social Psychology Bulletin* 32:1100–13.

Mason, Lilliana. 2018. *Uncivil Agreement*. Chicago: University of Chicago Press.

Mason, Lilliana, and Nathan Kalmoe. 2018. "Surprised by the Anger toward McCain? Party Loyalists Can Hate Apostates as Much as Opponents." *Washington Post*, May 16, 2018. https://www.washingtonpost.com/news/monkey-cage

/wp/2018/05/16/surprised-by-the-anger-toward-mccain-party-loyalists-can
-hate-apostates-as-much-as-opponents/.

Maxwell, Angie, and Todd G. Shields. 2019. *The Long Southern Strategy: How Chasing White Voters in the South Changed American Politics*. Oxford: Oxford University Press.

McArdle, Terence. 2017. " 'Night of Terror': The Suffragists Who Were Beaten and Tortured for Seeking the Vote." *Washington Post*, November 10, 2017. https://www.washingtonpost.com/news/retropolis/wp/2017/11/10/night-of-terror-the-suffragists-who-were-beaten-and-tortured-for-seeking-the-vote/.

McClain, Colleen. 2021. "70% of U.S. Social Media Users Never or Rarely Post or Share about Political, Social Issues." Pew Research Center. https://www.pewresearch.org/fact-tank/2021/05/04/70-of-u-s-social-media-users-never-or-rarely-post-or-share-about-political-social-issues/.

McClosky, Herbert, and Alida Brill. 1983. *The Dimensions of Tolerance: What Americans Believe about Civil Liberties*. New York: Russell Sage Foundation.

McDermott, Monika L. 2016. *Masculinity, Femininity, and American Political Behavior*. New York: Oxford University Press.

Mettler, Suzanne, and Robert C. Lieberman. 2020. *Four Threats: The Recurring Crises of American Democracy*. New York: St. Martin's.

Mickey, Robert. 2015. *Paths out of Dixie: The Democratization of Authoritarian Enclaves in America's Deep South, 1944–1972*. Princeton, NJ: Princeton University Press.

Milgram, Stanley. 1965. "Some Conditions of Obedience and Disobedience to Authority." *Human Relations* 18 (1): 57–76.

Miller, Joanne M., Kyle L. Saunders, and Christina E. Farhart. 2016. "Conspiracy Endorsement as Motivated Reasoning: The Moderating Roles of Political Knowledge and Trust." *American Journal of Political Science* 60 (4): 824–44.

Mills, Colleen E. 2017. "Framing Ferguson: Fox News and the Construction of US Racism." *Race and Class* 58 (4): 39–56.

Mondak, Jeffery J., and Karen D. Halperin. 2008. "A Framework for the Study of Personality and Political Behaviour." *British Journal of Political Science* 38 (2): 335–62.

Moore, Celia. 2015. "Moral Disengagement." *Current Opinion in Psychology* 6:199–204.

Nash, Gary B. 2012. "The African Americans' Revolution." In *Oxford Handbook of the American Revolution*, edited by Jane Kamensky and Edward G. Gray, 250–72. New York: Oxford University Press.

Neely, Mark E. 2002. *The Union Divided*. Cambridge, MA: Harvard University Press.

Newkirk, Vann R. 2019. "The Great Land Robbery." *Atlantic*, September 29, 2019. https://www.theatlantic.com/magazine/archive/2019/09/this-land-was-our-land/594742/.

Nordlinger, Eric A. 1972. *Conflict Regulation in Divided Societies.* Cambridge, MA: Center for International Affairs, Harvard University.

O'Neil, Luke. 2019. "I Gathered Stories of People Transformed by Fox News." *New York Magazine*, April 9, 2019. https://nymag.com/intelligencer/2019/04/i-gathered-stories-of-people-transformed-by-fox-news.html.

Pape, Robert A. 2021. "What an Analysis of 377 Americans Arrested or Charged in the Capitol Insurrection Tells Us." *Washington Post*, April 7, 2021. https://www.washingtonpost.com/opinions/2021/04/06/capitol-insurrection-arrests-cpost-analysis/.

Pape, Robert A., and Keven Ruby. 2021. "The Capitol Rioters Aren't like Other Extremists." *Atlantic*, February 2, 2021. https://www.theatlantic.com/ideas/archive/2021/02/the-capitol-rioters-arent-like-other-extremists/617895/.

Parker, Kim. 2019. "The Growing Partisan Divide in Views of Higher Education." Pew Research Center, January 30, 2019. https://www.pewresearch.org/social-trends/2019/08/19/the-growing-partisan-divide-in-views-of-higher-education-2/.

Perrin, Andrew, and Monica Anderson. 2019. "Share of U.S. Adults Using Social Media, including Facebook, Is Mostly Unchanged since 2018." Pew Research Center, April 10, 2019. https://www.pewresearch.org/fact-tank/2019/04/10/share-of-u-s-adults-using-social-media-including-facebook-is-mostly-unchanged-since-2018/.

Pew Research Center. 2017. "Views on Race, Immigration and Discrimination." Pew Research Center, October 5, 2017. https://www.pewresearch.org/politics/2017/10/05/4-race-immigration-and-discrimination/.

Posner, Daniel N. 2004. "The Political Salience of Cultural Difference: Why Chewas and Tumbukas Are Allies in Zambia and Adversaries in Malawi." *American Political Science Review* 98 (4): 529–45.

Potter, David M. 1976. *The Impending Crisis: America before the Civil War, 1848–1861.* New York: HarperCollins.

Powell, G. Bingham. 1981. "Party Systems and Political System Performance: Voting Participation, Government Stability and Mass Violence in Contemporary Democracies." *American Political Science Review* 75 (4): 861–79.

Przeworski, Adam. 1991. *Democracy and the Market.* New York: Cambridge University Press.

Rakich, Nathaniel. 2019. "Most Americans Agree That WWII Was Justified: Recent Conflicts Are More Divisive." *FiveThirtyEight.* June 7, 2019. https://fivethirtyeight.com/features/most-americans-agree-that-wwii-was-justified-recent-conflicts-are-more-divisive/.

Reicher, S. D., S. A. Haslam, and A. G. Miller. 2014. "What Makes a Person a Perpetrator? The Intellectual, Moral, and Methodological Arguments for Revisiting Milgram's Research on the Influence of Authority." *Journal of Social Issues* 70:393–408.

Ritter, Kurt, and Buddy Howell. 2001. "Ending the 2000 Presidential Election: Gore's Concession Speech and Bush's Victory Speech." *American Behavioral Scientist* 44 (12): 2314–30.

Rosenstone, Steven J., and John Mark Hansen. 1993 *Mobilization, Participation, and Democracy in America*. New York: Macmillan.

Ross, Alex. 2018. "How American Racism Influenced Hitler." *New Yorker*, April 23, 2018. https://www.newyorker.com/magazine/2018/04/30/how-american-racism -influenced-hitler.

Saguy, Tamar, and John F. Dovidio. 2013. "Insecure Status Relations Shape Preferences for the Content of Intergroup Contact." *Personality and Social Psychology Bulletin* 39 (8): 1030–42.

Sanford, R. Nevitt, Else Frenkel-Brunswik, Theodor Adorno, and Daniel J. Levinson. 1950. *The Authoritarian Personality*. London: Verso.

Schaffner, Brian F., and Samantha Luks. 2018. "Misinformation or Expressive Responding?" *Public Opinion Quarterly* 82 (1): 135–47.

Schermerhorn, Calvin. 2017. "The Thibodaux Massacre Left 60 African-Americans Dead and Spelled the End of Unionized Farm Labor in the South for Decades." *Smithsonian Magazine*, November 21, 2017. https://www.smithsonianmag.com /history/thibodaux-massacre-left-60-african-americans-dead-and-spelled-end -unionized-farm-labor-south-decades-180967289/.

Schickler, Eric. 2016. *Racial Realignment*. Princeton, NJ: Princeton University Press.

Scrivens, Ryan. 2020. "Exploring Radical Right-Wing Posting Behaviors Online." *Deviant Behavior*, 1–15.

Sela, Shlomi, Tsvi Kuflik, and Gustavo S. Mesch. 2012. "Changes in the Discourse of Online Hate Blogs: The Effect of Barack Obama's Election in 2008." *First Monday* 17 (11). https://doi.org/10.5210/fm.v17i11.4154.

Serwer, Adam. 2020. "The New Reconstruction." *Atlantic*, September 9, 2020. https:// www.theatlantic.com/magazine/archive/2020/10/the-next-reconstruction /615475/.

Shafer, Ronald G. 2020. "The Ugliest Presidential Election in History: Fraud, Voter Intimidation and a Backroom Deal." *Washington Post*, November 24, 2020. https://www.washingtonpost.com/history/2020/11/24/rutherford-hayes-fraud -election-trump/.

Sherif, Muzafer. 1961. *Intergroup Conflict and Cooperation: The Robbers Cave Experiment*. Norman, OK: University Book Exchange.

Simi, Pete. 2010. "Why Study White Supremacist Terror? A Research Note." *Deviant Behavior* 31 (3): 251–73. https://doi.org/10.1080/01639620903004572.

Sinclair, Betsy, Steven S. Smith, and Patrick D. Tucker. 2018. " 'It's Largely a Rigged System': Voter Confidence and the Winner Effect in 2016." *Political Research Quarterly* 71 (4): 854–68.

Skocpol, Theda. 1979. *States and Social Revolutions*. New York: Cambridge University Press.

Smith, Candis Watts, and Christopher D. DeSante. 2020. *Racial Stasis: The Millennial Generation and the Stagnation of Racial Attitudes in American Politics*. Chicago: University of Chicago Press.

Smith, David T. 2015. *Religious Persecution and Political Order in the United States*. New York: Cambridge University Press.

Smith, Robert Michael. 2003. *From Blackjacks to Briefcases: A History of Commercialized Strikebreaking and Unionbusting in the United States*. Athens, OH: Ohio University Press.

Snyder, Jack L. 2000. *From Voting to Violence*. New York: W. W. Norton.

Tajfel, Henri, and John Turner. 1979. "An Integrative Theory of Intergroup Conflict." In *The Social Psychology of Intergroup Relations*, edited by Stephen Worchel and William G. Austin, 33-47. Monterey, CA: Brooks / Cole.

Tarrow, Sidney. 1998. *Power in Movement: Social Movements and Contentious Politics*. New York: Cambridge University Press.

Taylor, S. P. 1967. "Aggressive Behavior and Physiological Arousal as a Function of Provocation and the Tendency to Inhibit Aggression." *Journal of Personality* 35:297–310.

Tesler, Michael. 2016. *Post-racial or Most-Racial? Race and Politics in the Obama Era*. Chicago: University of Chicago Press.

Tilly, Charles. 2003. *The Politics of Collective Violence*. New York: Cambridge University Press.

Tulsa Historical Society and Museum. 2021. "1921 Tulsa Race Massacre." Tulsa Historical Society and Museum. Accessed June 1, 2021. https://www.tulsahistory.org/exhibit/1921-tulsa-race-massacre/.

Urdal, Henrik. 2008. "Population, Resources, and Political Violence: A Subnational Study of India, 1956–2002." *Journal of Conflict Resolution* 52 (4): 590–617.

US Census Bureau. 2019. "Older People Projected to Outnumber Children." United States Census Bureau, October 10, 2019. https://www.census.gov/newsroom/press-releases/2018/cb18–41-population-projections.html.

Uscinski, Joseph E., and Joseph M. Parent. 2014. *American Conspiracy Theories*. Oxford: Oxford University Press.

Valentino, Nicholas A., and David O. Sears. 2005. "Old Times There Are Not Forgotten: Race and Partisan Realignment in the Contemporary South." *American Journal of Political Science* 49 (3): 672–88.

Varshney, Ashutosh. 2003. *Ethnic Conflict and Civic Life: Hindus and Muslims in India*. New Haven, CT: Yale University Press.

Walker, James. 2021. "45 Percent of Republican Voters Support Storming of Capitol Building: Poll." *Newsweek*, January 7, 2021. https://www.newsweek.com/45-percent-republican-voters-support-storming-capitol-1559662.

Weaver, Vesla M., and Gwen Prowse. 2020. "Racial Authoritarianism in U.S. Democracy." *Science* 369 (6508): 1176–78.

Weber, Jennifer. 2006. *Copperheads*. New York: Oxford University Press.

Westwood, Sean J., and Erik Peterson. 2020. "The Inseparability of Race and Partisanship in the United States." *Political Behavior*. https://doi.org/10.1007/s11109-020-09648-9.

Wetts, Rachel, and Robb Willer. 2018. "Privilege on the Precipice: Perceived Racial Status Threats Lead White Americans to Oppose Welfare Programs." *Social Forces* 97 (2): 793–822.

Whitman, James Q. 2017. *Hitler's American Model: The United States and the Making of Nazi Race Law*. Princeton, NJ: Princeton University Press.

Wilkinson, Stephen I. 2004. *Votes and Violence*. New York: Cambridge University Press.

Zaller, John. 1992. *The Nature and Origins of Mass Opinion*. New York: Cambridge University Press.

Index

Chicago Studies in American Politics

A SERIES EDITED BY BENJAMIN I. PAGE, SUSAN HERBST, LAWRENCE R. JACOBS, AND
ADAM J. BERINSKY

Series titles, continued from frontmatter: